Productions in Print
Smith and Kraus Publishers, Inc.
177 Lyme Road, Hanover, NH 03755
www.SmithandKraus.com

Copyright © 2015 by David Ives. All rights reserved.

CAUTION: Professionals and amateurs are hereby warned that THE LIAR, THE HEIR APPARENT, and THE METROMANIACS are subject to a royalty. They are fully protected under the copyright laws of the United States of America and of all countries covered by the International Copyright Union (including the Dominion of Canada and the rest of the British Commonwealth), the Berne Convention, the Pan-American Copyright Convention, and the Universal Copyright Convention, as well as all countries with which the United States has reciprocal copyright relations. All rights, including professional, amateur stage rights, motion picture, recitation, lecturing, public reading, radio broadcasting, television, video or sound recording, all other forms of mechanical or electronic reproduction, such as CD-ROM, CD-I, information storage and retrieval systems and photocopying, and the rights of translation into foreign languages, are strictly reserved. Particular emphasis is laid upon the matter of readings, permission for which must be secured from the Author's agent in writing.

The English language stock and amateur stage performance rights in the United States, its territories, possessions and Canada for THE LIAR,
THE HEIR APPARENT, and THE METROMANIACS are controlled exclusively by DRAMATISTS PLAY SERVICE, INC., 440 Park Avenue South, New York, NY 10016. No professional or nonprofessional performance of these Plays may be given without obtaining in advance the written permission of DRAMATISTS PLAY SERVICE, INC., and paying the requisite fee. Inquiries concerning all other rights should be addressed to Abrams Artists Agency, 275 Seventh Avenue, 26th Floor, New York, NY 10001. Attn: Sarah Douglas.

ISBN-13: 978-1-57525-823-2

Cover Photos: Adam Green, David Sabin, and Christian Conn in *The Liar*; Floyd King in *The Heir Apparent*; Tony Roach and Amelia Pedlow in *The Metromaniacs*. Photos by Scott Suchman.
Cover Design: S. Christian Taylor-Low
Interior Layout: Elayna Speight
Editor: Heather C. Jackson
Manufactured in the United States of America

THE DAVID IVES TRILOGY

The Liar
adapted from *Le Menteur* by Pierre Corneille

The Heir Apparent
adapted from *Le Légataire universel*
by Jean-François Regnard

The Metromaniacs
adapted from *La Métromanie* by Alexis Piron

The Definitive Texts

Commissioned by:

 SHAKESPEARE THEATRE COMPANY
Recipient of the 2012 Regional Theatre Tony Award®
Artistic Director Michael Kahn
Managing Director Chris Jennings

as part of its ReDiscovery Series.

The commissioning and world premiere productions of these plays were made possible by the generous support of The Beech Street Foundation

About the Shakespeare Theatre Company

Recipient of the 2012 Regional Theatre Tony Award®, the Shakespeare Theatre Company (STC) has become one of the nation's leading theatre companies. Today, STC is synonymous with artistic excellence and making classical theatre more accessible.

Under the leadership of Artistic Director Michael Kahn and Managing Director Chris Jennings, STC's innovative approach to Shakespeare and other classic playwrights has earned it the reputation as the nation's premier classical theatre company. By focusing on works with profound themes, complex characters and poetic language written by Shakespeare, his contemporaries and the playwrights he influenced, the Company's artistic mission is unique among theatre companies: to present theatre of scope and size in an imaginative, skillful and accessible American style that honors the playwrights' language and intentions while viewing their work through a 21st-century lens.

A leader in arts education, STC has a stable of initiatives that teach and excite learners of all ages, from school programs and acting classes to discussion series as well as accessible programs like the annual Free For All, one of STC's most beloved annual traditions, allowing audiences to experience Shakespeare at no charge.

Located in our nation's capital, STC performs in two theatres, the Lansburgh Theatre and Sidney Harman Hall in downtown Washington, D.C., creating a dynamic, cultural hub of activity that showcases STC as well as outstanding local performing arts groups and nationally renowned organizations. STC moved into the 451-seat Lansburgh Theatre in March 1992, after six years in residency in the Folger Library's Elizabethan theatre. At that time the Penn Quarter neighborhood was not considered desirable by many; since then, STC has helped drive its revitalization. The 774-seat Sidney Harman Hall opened in October 2007.

SHAKESPEARE THEATRE COMPANY

Administrative Offices
516 8th Street SE
Washington, DC 20003

202.547.1122
ShakespeareTheatre.org

About the ReDiscovery Series

During my first season as Artistic Director of the Shakespeare Theatre Company, we presented four plays. Three came from our namesake playwright, whose works from the basis of our theatre's repertoire. But for our fourth production, we chose Niccolo Machiavelli's 1518 play *The Mandrake* in an available translation.

Over the years the company has seen many changes, including expanding into two theatres in downtown Washington, D.C., to accommodate a growing audience for classic theatre. But even as our repertory has expanded to six or seven productions in a season, we continue to program only three plays by William Shakespeare. The rest come from the vast range of world dramatic writing including many important but little-known works. Our efforts to find and produce these works escalated in 1994 with the launch of the ReDiscovery Series, in which we investigate relevant and neglected plays of the classic canon through readings that are presented free of charge. After 15 seasons, many plays featured in the series have made their way onto our stages, including Musset's *Lorenzaccio*, Euripides' *Ion*, Lope de Vega's *The Dog in the Manger*, and Johnson's *The Silent Woman*.

We believe that to ensure that theses plays remain resonant and accessible to contemporary audiences, they need to be translated and adapted by the best modern writers. In our 2009-2010 Season, thanks to a grant from The Beech Street Foundation, we made our first commission: to David Ives to translate and adapt Pierre Corneille's comedy, *The Liar*. Less than two years later, we renewed our collaboration with David's new version of *The Heir Apparent* by Jean-François Regnard. We are pleased to be able to complete this trilogy of rediscovered French comedies with the addition of Alexis Piron's *The Metromaniacs*.

I have always believed that re-introducing these works to modern audiences and the American theatre community is an essential part of our mission in preserving and reinvigorating the classical repertoire. After their premieres on our stages, we hope these plays take their rightful place on stages throughout this country.

Michael Kahn
Artistic Director
Shakespeare Theatre Company

Table of Contents

About David Ives 1

Corneille, Regnard, and Piron At a Glance 2

The Liar ***7***

The Whole Truth About *The Liar* 8

Powers of Invention 11

About Pierre Corneille 13

The Liar Script 16

The Heir Apparent ***129***

Comedy Tonight 130

Regnard Resurgent 132

About Jean-François Regnard 134

The Heir Apparent Script 138

The Metromaniacs. ***239***

Metromania Mania 240

Lost Inside a Dream. 242

About Alexis Piron. 244

The Metromaniacs Script 248

About David Ives

David Ives is the author of *All In The Timing*; *Venus In Fur* (both the play and the Roman Polanski film); *Time Flies*; *Lives Of The Saints*; *New Jerusalem*; *The School for Lies* (adapted from Molière's *The Misanthrope*); *Is He Dead?* (adapted from Mark Twain); *Ancient History*; and *Polish Joke*. He is a former Guggenheim Fellow in playwriting and lives in New York City.

Corneille, Regnard, and Piron At a Glance: A Century of French Comedy

1606   Pierre Corneille is born in Rouen.

1609   Johann Carolus of Germany publishes the *Relation*, the first newspaper.

1610   Upon the death of King Henry IV of France, his son Louis XIII becomes king at age nine.

1616   William Shakespeare dies in Stratford-upon-Avon.

1618   The Thirty Years' War begins, involving most of Europe in crippling conflict.

1624   Cardinal Richelieu becomes prime minister to King Louis XIII, centralizing the power of the state as never before.

1636   Pedro Calderón de la Barca – *Life is a Dream*

1636   Corneille – *The Theatrical Illusion*

1637   Corneille – *The Cid*

1641   René Descartes publishes *Meditations on First Philosophy*.

1642   A civil war breaks out in England as a result of a dispute between the parliament and King Charles.

1643   Upon the death of King Louis XIII, his son Louis XIV becomes king at age five.

       Corneille – *The Liar*

1648   The Peace of Westphalia ends the Thirty Years' War and the Eighty Years' War, marking the ends of Spain and the Holy Roman Empire as major European powers.

       In response to the raising of taxes, a civil war known as the Fronde breaks out in Paris.

1652   Corneille retires from the theatre after *Pertharite* receives poor reviews. He would unretire a few years later. Though his later plays met with little success, he remained a respected figure and his early plays were revived frequently.

1655   Jean-François Regnard is born in Paris, the eldest son in a well to-do family of merchants. Corneille is 49.

1661   Upon the death of his prime minister Cardinal Mazarin, Louis XIV takes on personal control of France.

1664	Molière – *Tartuffe*
1666	Molière – *The Misanthrope*
1670	French monk Dom Perignon creates champagne.
1673	Molière dies. Corneille is 67. Regnard is 18.
1677	Racine – *Phèdre*
1682	La Salle explores the length of the Mississippi River and claims Louisiana for France.
1683	Regnard returns from his travels to Italy, Scandinavia, and the Near East, where he had been captured by pirates and sold into slavery. The publication of his Voyages makes him famous.
1684	Corneille dies. Regnard is 29.
1689	Alexis Piron is born in Dijon. Regnard is 34.
1708	Regnard – *Le Légataire Universel*
1709	Regnard dies, after a bout of "indigestion" at his chateau in the French countryside. Piron is 20.
1712	Piron – *Ode à Priape*
1713	The War of the Spanish Succession ends, Louis XIV's unsuccessful attempt to place his grandson on the Spanish throne.
1715	Upon the death of King Louis XIV, his son Louis XV becomes king at age five.
1729	Isaac Newton's Principia translated from Latin into English.
1730	Marivaux – *The Game of Love and Chance*
1738	Piron – *La Métromanie*
1743	Goldoni – *The Servant of Two Masters*
1744	Louis XV bans all *opéras comiques* at Parisian fairground theatres, as part of an attempt to combat the increasing popularity of opera, pantomime, and *comédies-en-vaudevilles*, and preserve the Comedie Francaise's monopoly on "regular" comedy and tragedy.
1751	The first Encyclopédie is published, featuring contributions from Diderot, Voltaire, Rousseau, and d'Alembert.

1753	Piron is nominated for membership to the Academie Francaise, but Louis XV vetoes his candidacy, citing his obscene youthful writings (See 1712).
1759	Voltaire – *Candide*
1762	Mozart tours Europe as a six-year-old prodigy.
1763	The Treaty of Hubertusberg concludes the Seven Years' War, marking the end of France's reign as a major European power and the rise of Prussia.
	France and Spain lose their North American colonies to Britain.
1765	James Watt invents the steam engine.
1769	Lessing – *The Hamburg Dramaturgy*
1773	Piron dies.
1774	Louis XV dies, leaving the French monarchy at its political, financial, and moral nadir.
	Goethe – *The Sorrows of Young Werther*

DAVID IVES

The Liar

adapted from *Le Menteur* by Pierre Corneille

Commissioned by:

 SHAKESPEARE THEATRE COMPANY
Recipient of the 2012 Regional Theatre Tony Award®
Artistic Director Michael Kahn
Managing Director Chris Jennings

as part of its ReDiscovery Series.

The commissioning and world premiere production of *The Liar* was made possible by the generous support of The Beech Street Foundation

The Whole Truth About *The Liar*
by David Ives

When my agent called and asked if I'd be interested in translating Corneille's *The Liar* for the Shakespeare Theatre Company of Washington, I had never heard of the play. Nor had he. Not that I was all that up on French theatre, though I had recently found myself wading into the tricky waters of translation. Using the remains of my college French and memories of a romantic week in Paris, I had somehow managed translations of Feydeau's *A Flea In Her Ear* and Yasmina Reza's *A Spanish Play* to some success. As it turned out I needn't have been ashamed of my ignorance in the case of *The Liar*. I doubt there were 500 people in this republic of 300 million who knew the piece or even the title.

In any case: "Send the script along," I told my agent. "I'll take a look at it."

He sent, I looked, and several hours later, with the help of a fat French dictionary, I found myself astonished. Exhilarated. Giddy. For, lying on the desk before me, was one of the world's great comedies. I felt as if some lost Shakespeare festival comedy on the order of *Twelfth Night* or *Much Ado about Nothing* had been found. This particular Shakespeare comedy was unfortunately locked away in French (the French have a way of doing things like that), but I could remedy that. The prospect of Englishing this play made me feel like Ronald Colman distantly sighting Shangri-La.

Everything about it spoke to me. The rippling language. The rich simplicity of the premise. The gorgeousness of the set pieces. The seeming insouciance of the treatment alongside the classical rigor of the plotting. The way the play's wide understanding and humanity was nicely seasoned with several large pinches of social satire. *The Liar* is one of those plays that seem to be made out of almost nothing, yet end up being about so much. *The Importance of Being Earnest* comes to mind, and *Hay Fever*. It's one of those plays that are both a view on our world and their own separate world, one that we would happily inhabit.

Corneille (that's pronounced Cor-nay, by the way) wrote *Le Menteur* in the middle of his great career as a return to comedy, and it shows. The play has all the ease of a successful playwright completely in control of his powers. He seems to be improvising this *divertissement* before our eyes, riffing on the Spanish play he stole the basic plot from (and which he vastly improved). Though written in Corneille's middle age, *The Liar* sparkles with youth and put me in mind ever after of a poem by Robert Hillyer that Ned Rorem set to music: "Early in the morning / Of a lovely summer day, / As they lowered the bright awning / At the outdoor café, / I was breakfasting on croissants / And café au lait / Under greenery like scenery / Rue François Premier..."

All that being said, I have to add that what you hold in your hand is not... *exactly*...Corneille. For, having been bowled over by the play, I had to consider how to render this luminous world in English. There was one thing that I knew right away: it had to be in verse, just as it is in Corneille. *The Liar* is a portrait of a brilliant performer and, language being the wire Dorante dances upon, the language had to match his agile mind at every turn. Prose would have turned this into a "Seinfeld" episode and made it banal. Only rhyme would do.

Next question: translate the whole play, translate some of the play, or make another play "based on" Corneille (like Tony Kushner's version of Corneille's *The Illusion*)? Frankly, there were elements of the plot that did not satisfy me, and which I doubted would satisfy anybody else either: Lucrece was a cipher, indeed virtually a non-speaking role for most of the action; Cliton's relationship to Dorante and to the play's underlying themes wasn't clear; the two maids were thankless parts; and the wrap-up was cursory in the extreme. No offense intended, but the *dénouement* was very French: Dorante realizes he's gotten his lady love's name wrong and changes his mind, simply plopping for Lucrece and professing his love. Not good enough.

Samuel Johnson once said: "We must try its effect as an English poem; that is the way to judge the merit of a translation." I submit that the same principle applies to plays, especially old ones. In fact, for my money only playwrights should translate plays because the point is not to carry over sentences from one language to another but to produce a credible, speakable, playable, produceable play for today no matter what's in the original. "That's what he wrote in 1643," is no defense. If actors can't play every line, if every moment isn't comedic or dramatic or both—fuhgeddaboutit. Or as the French say, with a shrug: bfff!

What you hold in your hand is what I call a translaptation, i.e., a translation with a heavy dose of adaptation. For what I have realized in translating plays is that, in an odd way, the language of a play is of secondary concern. (Just look at the lumbering dialogue of O'Neill, which certainly doesn't obviate incomparable dramatic power.) In translating a play, I contend, one must think as a playwright, not as a translator. One must ask: what is the play underneath the words, what is going on beneath speeches rather than on their surface, who are these characters and what drives them, and finally what is this play actually all about? What was on Corneille's chest and how can I use what's on mine to create something with dramatic and comedic integrity? It seems to me that that's the only way a translated play can ever have what every good play has to have: a voice.

In other words, you have to write the play Corneille would have written today, in English.

If he were you. And vice versa.

In the end I did to *The Liar* what Corneille had done to his Spanish source. I ran with it. I trimmed some very long speeches (the French love them) and broke up others. I parceled out the action between interiors and exteriors rather than setting most of the action—as "classical" writers implausibly do—in a street. I let Cliton meet Dorante in scene one and gave him a problem with the truth that would complement his boss's problem. I beefed up Lucrece and tried to end her some personality, since the original part feels like it was written for some talent-free but gobsmackingly beautiful chorine that Corneille was sleeping with. I cut a useless manservant (save the producers some money!) and doubled the maids' parts, making them twins. (More saved money! Use it on costumes!) I added the queen, offstage, and cut some unimportant onstage remarks that many might find politically unacceptable today. Loving duels (who doesn't?) I wrote in the duel, which in the original happens offstage. I inserted a lying lesson—the equivalent of the specialty number at the top of virtually every musical's second act—and rejiggered the ending. I gave Philiste a love interest, tying him into the plot more than he was, and along the way I fell in love with Lucrece. (Who wouldn't?)

Of the three great 17th-century French playwrights—Corneille, Racine, Molière—I'm fondest of Corneille. He seems to me to have the largest heart and the most humanity, great as those other two are. He loves the world in a way those two don't, and this gives him, for me, a Shakespearean understanding and comprehensiveness. In that imaginary game of What Writers Would You Invite To Dinner, Corneille would be on my list rather than the others because Racine would pick at his food (after murmuring a pious grace over it) and suck up to the celebrities while Molière would hog Shakespeare all to himself to bitch about box office receipts and the loxes in his audience. I'd seat Corneille between the elfin essayist Charles Lamb, who would delight him, and Horace, who would hymn the waitress in deathless hexameters and keep all their glasses filled.

The truth, the whole truth and nothing but the truth, as refracted in a theatrical fun-house mirror. Welcome to *The Liar*.

Powers of Invention
by Akiva Fox

Paris in the 1600s was a city under construction. After nearly forty years of crippling civil war between Catholics and Protestants ended in 1598, King Henry IV set about changing the face of urban life in his capital. Assisted by his prime minister, the Duke of Sully, the architecture-obsessed king remodeled the Louvre palace, finished the Pont Neuf to bridge the Seine river, and built the great public squares called the Place Dauphine and the Place Royale. Personally supervising the design of the houses on those squares, Henry began to transform muddy, medieval Paris into a fashionable place to live.

Under Henry's son Louis XIII, the project progressed from constructing buildings to constructing a nation. Cardinal Richelieu, Louis' powerful prime minister, saw an opening for France to dominate war-weakened Europe. First, however, he needed to unite the country behind an absolute ruler. He set new rules to curtail the power of the nobles, and began to build up the iconography of the king. Funding a generation of architects, artists and craftsmen, Richelieu turned Paris into a creative center, revolving around Louis. In 1639, in fact, Richelieu placed a heroic statue of the king in the middle of the Place Royale, a social hub of the city.

Pierre Corneille wrote his first play set in Paris in 1629. As a native of Rouen, the outsider Corneille must have looked at the aspirations of his nation's capital as an ideal target for satire. He watched the lower-class worker strive to be like a middle-class merchant, who in turn strove to be like a gentleman, who in turn strove to be like a nobleman, who in turn strove to be like the king. This ambition to rise, no matter how futile, became the subject of Corneille's comedies.

Theatre proved the perfect medium for depicting the aspiring Parisians, who behaved in public as if on stage. In order to act like a person of a higher station, one had to carefully observe the latest mannerisms and social graces. No less necessary was buying the proper costumes and props, the fashionable "Paris articles" that marked out their wearer or bearer as a member of the elite. Any slip in performance could give away a person's true station, ruining his or her chance to pass in society. Corneille's early comedies, such as *The Palace Gallery* and *The Place Royale*, portray the young Parisians as show-offs, desperate to demonstrate their knowledge of every new cultural trend. The former play is even set in the 1630s equivalent of an upscale shopping mall.

With this aspiring city as his stage, Corneille finally created the perfect actor for it. Dorante, the title character of his 1643 comedy *The Liar*, arrives in Paris from the provinces with only a law degree and a copious imagination to his name. From the first moment, he constructs a more glorious identity than he really possesses: he passes himself off to a pretty girl as a war hero. His lies escalate from there, spinning Dorante a fantastical new likeness whenever he needs one (or when one might simply be fun). In a city constantly building fresh facades, Dorante's reinventions of himself hardly stand out; he is an unusually skilled player of a game everyone plays, and so they are all too willing to believe his lies.

By this description, Dorante is perhaps less actor than playwright. In order for his lies to succeed, he embellishes them with creative detail. He revels in the power of his imagination, taking as much (or more) delight in the implausibility of his scenarios and the narrowness of his escapes as he does in their success. Like his author, another provincial lawyer whose words took Paris by storm, Dorante realizes the value of virtuosity. Just as the playwright constructs elaborate worlds, elevating the degree of difficulty as he proceeds, so the liar constantly skirts danger with his inventive flair.

Dorante's creator Pierre Corneille used his work to become a master not only of creation, but of self-creation. Barely a decade after his first play appeared in Paris, Corneille and several members of his family received a noble title from King Louis XIII; this allowed Corneille entry into exclusive circles, and he would go on to marry a woman of a higher class. He owed his astonishing transformation, from minor lawyer and office-holder in Rouen to Parisian nobleman, to his facility with language alone. He never let his rivals forget this fact: in a poem written near the time of his ennobling, Corneille boasted that "I owe my fame to myself, and to no one else."

About Pierre Corneille

When Pierre Corneille unleashed his comic masterpiece *The Liar* on Paris in 1643, audiences must have been shocked. The comedy featured a cheerfully amoral hero, and its author was famous for his tragedies. Then again, Corneille had been flouting the rules for years.

Corneille, in fact, started out as neither a playwright nor a Parisian. Born in 1606 in the French city of Rouen, he worked there first as a tongue-tied lawyer and later a civil servant, suffering through a job his father had secured for him with the Department of Forests and Rivers. He wrote plays in his spare time, and managed to slip his first comedy, *Mélite*, to a touring company on its way back to Paris. The comedy was a success, and Corneille soon followed it to the capital. Corneille's early comedies were a sensation, dramatizing contemporary characters rather than stock characters, dealing with the problems of daily life in a big city.

Cardinal Richelieu, Chief Minister to King Louis XIII, was impressed by Corneille's success, and appointed him to "The Society of Five Authors." Feeling stifled, however, by the Cardinal's doctrinaire ideas about art, Corneille returned to Rouen in 1635. Away from Paris, Corneille wrote his masterpiece, the genre-defying history play *The Cid*. Borrowing a plot from Spain, *The Cid* was a swashbuckling romance and a colossal success with audiences in Paris (including Louis XIII). The play, however, drew the ire of Richelieu's newly-formed French Academy, who attacked the play under a hailstorm of criticism for breaking the so-called "classical unities."

In 1643, with the deaths of Louis XIII and Richelieu and a five-year-old Louis XIV on the throne, Corneille produced another surprise. Zigging away from the neoclassical vogue for tragedy, Corneille produced his comic masterpiece, *The Liar*. Looking once again to the Spanish, and to the cosmopolitan comedies of his youth, Corneille integrated the dexterous language and strong emotions that had marked his tragedies. The result was a high style of language and plotting, along with a contemporary relevance that brought comedy into a parallel, rather than inferior, relationship to tragedy.

Perhaps Corneille's greatest creation in *The Liar* is Dorante, the title character. Lying his way through the city with reckless abandon, Dorante nevertheless gains the trust of nearly everyone he meets; he even finds love. Like his author, Dorante is a lawyer from the provinces who comes to Paris and makes his name through his astonishing linguistic imagination. Comedy, Corneille seems to be saying, is the best of all possible worlds, a place where the rules are allowed to be broken. For a playwright who had seen his greatest success plagued by vehement controversy over "the rules," there is an unmistakable autobiographical subtext.

Corneille died in 1684, but his influence on French comedy cannot be ignored. The same year Corneille wrote *The Liar*, a 21-year-old Parisian named Jean-Baptiste Poquelin founded his first theatre. When he wrote his own plays (under the name Molière), he absorbed many of Corneille's techniques to craft hilarious and cutting satires on French society. As the writer and philosopher Voltaire once wrote, "We owe Molière to *The Liar*."

This adaptation of *The Liar* was first performed by the Shakespeare Theatre Company at the Lansburgh theatre in Washington, D.C., where it opened on April 12, 2010, under the direction of Michael Kahn.

Original cast
(in order of speaking)

CLITON
Adam Green*

DORANTE
Christian Conn*

CLARICE
Erin Partin*

LUCRECE
Miriam Silverman*

ISABELLE
Colleen Delany*

ALCIPPE
Tony Roach*

PHILISTE
Aubrey Deeker*

GERONTE
David Sabin*

SABINE
Colleen Delany*

* Member of Actors' Equity Association,
the Union of Professional Actors and Stage Managers

Original production team:

Director
Michael Kahn

Set Designer
Alexander Dodge

Costume Designer
Murell Horton

Lighting Designer
Jeff Croiter

Sound Designer
Martin Desjardins

Voice and Dialect Coach
Ellen O'Brien

Assistant Director
Alan Paul

Literary Associate
Akiva Fox

Stage Manager
M. William Shiner*

Assistant Stage Manager
Elizabeth Clewley*

The Liar Characters

DORANTE, a young man just arrived in Paris
CLITON, a servant
GERONTE, Dorante's father
CLARICE, a young lady of Paris
LUCRECE, Clarice's best friend
ALCIPPE, Clarice's secret fiancé
PHILISTE, Alcippe's friend } both played by the
ISABELLE, vivacious servant to Lucrece } same actress
SABINE, puritanical servant to Clarice

The setting is Paris in 1643.

PRONUNCIATIONS:
Doronte:	Dor-*ahnt*
Geronte:	Zhur-*ahnt*
Cliton:	Klee-*tone*
Clarice:	Kluh-*reece*
Lucrece:	Loo-*kreece*
Alcippe:	Al-*seep*
Philiste:	Fuh-*leest*
Isabelle:	*Iz*-a-bell
Sabine:	Suh-*bean*
mesdames:	may-*dahm*
messieurs:	may-*syoor*
Les Tuilleries:	Lay Twee-leh-*ree*
Champs Elysées:	Shawnz El-ee-*zay*
Poitiers:	Pwah-*tyay*
crise:	kreez
Zum Beispiel:	tsoom *bye*-shpeel
Aix:	eks
Gstaad:	G'*shtahd*
trompe l'oeil:	tromp *loy*

Note: First, the actors can freeze (comically) during other characters' aside, if the director likes. Second, the slaps administered during the play can be administered without physical contact by being mimed with the slapper saying, "SLAP!" Third, dialogue in parentheses indicates asides, either to the audience or to another actor.

This play's for Jay

(Binder, of course,

Casting's lord)

Whom gay Corneille

Would have adored.

—*David Ives*

ACT ONE

Scene One

The actor playing CLITON ENTERS.

CLITON ACTOR
Ladies and gentlemen! Mesdames, messieurs!
All cell phones off? All cellophane secure?
No eating, please. You think you're incognito?
Yes, you. The lady with the bean burrito.
Put it away. I have a crucial message!
(Points to a man in the audience.)
This guy looks worried. "Whoa, what does *this* presage?
I shell out for the tickets *plus* a meal,
The waiter's late with her organic veal,
We had to chug-a-lug that nice Bordeaux,
I hoped I'd be asleep by now, but no,
The curtain should be up, some bird comes on,
Prob'ly to say, *Our star's locked in the john...*
Well, set your minds at ease, reduce the strain,
And with your gadgets, please—turn off your brain.
Leave complications to our evening's hero,
A lying genius, if a moral zero.
No, my announcement may be even worse:
Tonight our actors will be speaking verse!
In case you hadn't noticed that small fact.
We'll speak PENTAMETER, to be exact.
And what the blank's pentameter, you say?
It's what I'm speaking now! On with the play!
(He picks up a SIGN that says: "RENT ME! CLITON. SERVANT FOR HIRE." He raps the staff on the stage.)
The Paris gardens of Les Tuilleries—
A fine spring day in 1643.
Servant! Servant for hire! Servant!

(DORANTE LEAPS ON, with sword drawn, in an outfit whose cuffs and collar are trimmed with lots of lace.)

DORANTE
En garde!
(CLITON hits the dirt with a cry.)
          Arise, you knave! Come, stand and fight!

CLITON
Sweet Jesus, man. I almost soiled my tights!

DORANTE
(fencing positions)
First. Second. Third. And parry. Lunge. *Allez!*
Am I in first?

CLITON
That's fourth, sir—in ballet.

DORANTE
I like your honesty.

CLITON
It's all I've got.
D'ya need a man? 'm cheap. C'mon, take a shot.
I don't eat much. Check my diameter.
I cook, I clean, I speak pentameter...

DORANTE
(pointing off left)
I'll ponder it upon the Elysées.

CLITON
(points off right)
Champs Elysées, my friend, lies that-a-way,
Unless the Louvre has mouvred since yesterday.
Just got to town?

DORANTE
Two hours.

CLITON
No.

DORANTE
Yes! Poitiers—
That's where I come from. Near Poitiers, I mean.
A lovely spot...

CLITON
(The exposition scene.)

DORANTE
I studied law there, but I got so bored
I clamored for a scabbard and a sword.
At last my Dad reluctantly agreed
And we convergec on Paris with all speed—
He to procure me some prosaic wife,
I for the soldier's more voltaic life.
So now begone, dull briefs, you legal pillory!
For here I stand within the Twillery—
Where ladies buzz and fancy dandies dart
And high society comes by the cart.
The gleaming palaces. Air crisp as ice.
My dreams have not deceived me. It's paradise!
(CLITON sounds dubious.)
But tell me. Do I look like "army ace"?

CLITON
No, you look like a rube who's caked in lace.

DORANTE
One wants a style, a character, a code,
An up-to-date persona à la mode.

CLITON
What you need, if you don't object to me,
Is a), a valet, b) lace-ectomy.
(Rips off some of Dorante's lace.)
The key to living here with proper flash?
Same secret you'll find everyplace.

DORANTE
                                    Um....

CLITON
                                            Cash.
But hey. You're young, you're free, so have no fear.
Stupider guys than you have made it here.

DORANTE
You're very blunt. I thought you sought a place.

CLITON
You think I'm gabbing here to please Your Grace?
You wanted my opinion. What's the matter?

DORANTE
It's not a minion's job to fawn and flatter?

CLITON
Why don't I truckle? Huh? I'll tell you why.
My tragic flaw: *I cannot tell a lie*.
Come on and test me. Put me in duress.
Ask if I've ever stolen.

DORANTE
                    Have you...?

CLITON
                                Yes.
The same thing fifty times has come to pass:
I tell my boss the truth, he fires my ass!
You chuckle?

DORANTE
            Not at all.

CLITON
                        Well, you inquired.

DORANTE
You look like just the man I need. You're hired.
(Shaking hands.)
Dorante.

CLITON
 Cliton. You won't regret this, sir.
You want a dry martini? I can stir!
Now how about a petty cash advance?

DORANTE
"Put money in thy…" These are the wrong pants!

CLITON
No prob. Your mug's as trusty as the map of France.
(Truth is—he's lying, but I don't know it yet.
Will I find out in time? You wanna bet?)
So! Your first wish, amongst the joys of Hades?

DORANTE
Tell me about your celebrated ladies.
Do they succumb, or are they hard to please?

CLITON
You just arrived in town, you want a squeeze?

DORANTE
I wouldn't mind one. Where would I find one?

CLITON
It's only nine a.m. Boy, you work fast!
I gather you have women in your past?

DORANTE
I've had adventures with the tender sex.
There was my time with—let's say "Princess X."
That night at Cannes with her pet cockatoo…
But you don't want to hear.

CLITON
 Oh, yes, I do!
Just stay away from this town's hotter blends.
You'll only burn your handle at both ends.
What you want is a socialite with spice,
A vestal virgin not averse to vice.

(CLARICE and LUCRECE ENTER, followed by Lucrece's maid, ISABELLE.)

DORANTE
But soft! Who're these fair dames?

CLITON
                                                  They're not my class.
These two are sterling. I commune with brass.

DORANTE
(to CLARICE, taking her hand)
Watch out there, mademoiselle! The pavement's tipped.
What luck I caught your hand or you'd have tripped.
No, don't let go. Your stumble was a sign.
O sov'reign joy to hold your hand in mine!

CLARICE
However sweet your manual sensation,
This hand's not meant, monsieur, for your palpation.
(She tries to pull her hand away, but he holds on.)

DORANTE
It's true that fickle fortune made us meet—
And that's what makes these digits bittersweet.
This prize is won yet I'd more happily bear it
If I had gained this prize through my own merit.

CLARICE
But favors won are merely favors bought.
As happiness is happiest unsought.
(Again she tries to pull her hand away. He hangs on.)

DORANTE
Yet happiness can always use a push.
A bird in hand, you know. Two in the bush...
(Bends to kiss her hand.)

LUCRECE
Ah-hem!

DORANTE
                Your mute friend disagrees. Or does she scoff?

CLARICE
Oh, she means nothing, sir.

LUCRECE
    Ah-*hem*!

CLARICE
                                       It's whooping cough.
Where were we?

DORANTE
                      You had lent me this rich alm.
But let me touch your heart, not just your palm.

(DORANTE bends again to kiss her hand.)

LUCRECE

AH-*HEM*!
(LUCRECE pulls CLARICE away, to speak aside.)

CLARICE

Excuse me, please.

LUCRECE

(Clarice, you could be *seen*.)

CLARICE

(Oh, peace, Lucrece. Be seen by whom?)

LUCRECE

(Alcippe.)

CLARICE

(Alcippe's asleep. So why so dubious?)

LUCRECE

(*Clarice*. Your fiancé's *Vesuvius*.)

CLARICE

(So let him spew. My lover's lava's nothing new.
Two years now we've been secretly engaged—
And he's the one who's chronically enraged?
Oh, very well.) A pleasure, sir. Adieu.
(CLARICE starts out.)

DORANTE

O, shatter, tortured soul! O, break, my heart!
Endure these weeks of fire, to see us part?

CLARICE

These weeks, you say? My eyes must have been misted.
I didn't even know that you existed.

DORANTE

You mean you haven't seen me haunt your door
Since I returned from fighting in the war?

CLITON

(The war?)

CLARICE

The war...?

DORANTE
Six months ago.

CLITON
(Six *months?*)

DORANTE
Artillery captain on the German front.
Ja! Spilling crimson streams I fought the Hun
At Leberwurst, Heissfrankfurter, und zo on.
Four years of hell. But King and France required me.

CLITON
(Is this the self-same simpleton who hired me?)

DORANTE
The siege of Zinkendorf, up on the walls?
I took not one but ten Teutonic balls.
That's how I got this scar along my jaw...

CLITON
(What scar?)

DORANTE
(Shut up.)

CLITON
(I thought you studied law!)

DORANTE
You may have read my name in the Gazette.
I caused, if not some buzz, then a buzz-*ette*.
That little dust-up north of Waterloo—
But you don't want to hear...

CLARICE
Oh, yes, I do!

DORANTE
The wounds are almost healed, the pain's abating...

CLITON
(Monsieur, did you know you're hallucinating?)

DORANTE
But then last year while here on winter leave
By chance I glimpsed a corner of your sleeve
In a coach window passing on the Pont Neuf.
It was eneuf, that innocent lace ceuf.
I gave up arms—for leuf!

CLITON
(Is this a dream?)

DORANTE
Yes, I who coolly spilled those crimson streams,
Now wept! Forgive me, goddess, if I'm fervent.
For six long months I've lived to be...
(Kisses her hand.)
...your servant.

ISABELLE
(glancing offstage)
(Madame Lucrece! Alcippe is on the way!)

LUCRECE
(Clarice! Alcippe is coming!

CLARICE
(You don't say.
WHAT?!) Lovely meeting you, monsieur. Good day.

DORANTE
(hanging onto her hand)
You'd go so soon, my treasure? Just like that?

CLARICE
I have no leisure for a longer chat.
Let go, monsieur! You've had your conversation!

DORANTE
But give me leave.

CLARICE
For what?

DORANTE
For adoration,
To know you, love you, have you! I implore!

CLARICE
True lovers ask no leave. They just adore.
(CLARICE and LUCRECE EXIT. ISABELLE lingers, winking at CLITON.)

DORANTE
Go chase the maid, Cliton. Find out her name.

CLITON
The maid's?

DORANTE
The mistress, fool!

CLITON

(to ISABELLE)

A word, madayme.

ISABELLE
My name is Isabelle, I'm twenty-eight,
Okay, I'm twenty-nine, I'm single, straight,
Catholic, but please don't let that interfere.
I like Italian food and English beer,
Stuffed animals, long walks, Chanel perfume,
Here's my address and the key to my room.
(She holds out a key.)

CLITON
To tell the truth...

ISABELLE
What's wrong? Not feeling sinful?

CLITON
Me? All the time. But it's your *lady's* info
I wanted. Name, address, any old fact.
Her personal data.

ISABELLE
Hey, what is this? Tact?
I'm not attractive? Not a perfect ten?

CLITON
Maybe an eight?
(She slaps him.)
(That tragic flaw again!)

ISABELLE
My lady's name's Lucrece. She's filthy rich.

CLITON
Primo. But wait a sec. So there's no glitch,
Those two who just were here—Lucrece is which?

ISABELLE
The greater beauty.

CLITON
Yeah, but...

ISABELLE
(drops the key into her dress)
Fine. Your loss.

CLITON
Wait, wait. And they live where, those two, your boss?

ISABELLE
The ladies are both neighbors on the Ploss.

CLITON
The "Ploss"?

ISABELLE
Royale.

CLITON
I knew it was a clue.

LUCRECE (O.S)
Isabelle!

ISABELLE
Maybe next time, pal. Adieu.
(ISABELLE EXITS.)

DORANTE
Well, what's the word?

CLITON
Lucrece.

DORANTE
Lucrece is who?

CLITON
I quote: "The greater beauty of the two."
So which is which, I leave the choice to you.

DORANTE
No contest there. It must be my enchanter.
The cutie who subdued me with her banter.
For beauty, she's the one who won the Fleece.
I feel it in my sternum. She's Lucrece.

CLITON
No disrespect to master's magic throat.
The shy one with the cough would get my vote.

DORANTE
That *sphinx*? The statue with the delphic stare?
That nun? That lox? The prettier of the pair?

CLITON
Your chatterbox might be Bernice, Felice...
For pulchritude? The quiet one's Lucrece.

DORANTE
Quiet? She's catatonic! Off the slab!
No, my Lucrece would share the gift of gab.

CLITON
If you ask me...?

DORANTE
Cliton, not one more peep!
(Voices, off.)
But who's this here? My ancient friend Alcippe!

CLITON
Looks like your friend's in quite a state.

(ALCIPPE ENTERS in heated conversation with PHILISTE. DORANTE and CLITON do not hear the next exchange.)

ALCIPPE
I *saw* Clarice. She just went through that gate.

PHILISTE
Alcippe, dear boy, *control*. Why so irate?

ALCIPPE
Because last night my servant, very late,
Observed Clarice slip out her own back door
And jump into a waiting coach. What's more?
She wore her diamond gown and ermine coat.
He chased her to the river, where a boat
Awaited, fixed with music, food, divan,
And (let-me-get-my-hands-on-him) a man.

PHILISTE
Oh, Lord. It was another girl, disguised!

ALCIPPE
He saw her float away with his own eyes!
I'll find Clarice's rake and make him bleed.

DORANTE
(stepping forward)
Alcippe...?

ALCIPPE
Dorante? Ah, just the friend I need!

(They embrace and do a special handshake.)
You know Philiste? The beau monde's favorite beau?

DORANTE
The man they call the Baron Comme Il Faut?
We know each other from Poitiers.

PHILISTE
                     Monsieur,
A peerless and unparalleled *plaiseur*.

DORANTE
You two seemed deep in dish.

PHILISTE
                Don't start. He's bitter.

DORANTE
Well, well. Some juicy gossip? What's the twitter?

ALCIPPE
A girl and an anonymous gallánt.

DORANTE
Well, tell me more.

PHILISTE
             I tell you, *stop*, Dorante.

ALCIPPE
There was a moonlight picnic with the jade.

DORANTE
And let me guess about this escapade.
Maybe a boat, to further float their joy?

ALCIPPE
How did you...?

DORANTE
             Boat trips? They're an age-old ploy.
Water's like kerosene on Cupid's flame.
And no one knows the happy Don Juan's name?
The backer of this bacchanalian jaunt?

ALCIPPE
Don't tell me it was *you!?*

DORANTE
               'Twas I. Dorante.
I wouldn't let it out... What's with the frown?

ALCIPPE
It couldn't be you, you just got into town!

DORANTE
Oh, I've been here a year...

CLITON
(A year?)

DORANTE
...or less.
I'd certainly be lacking in finesse
If after all this time I lacked success
Locating and seducing succubi.

CLITON
(Monsieur...)

DORANTE
With hearts like harps to pluck you by...

ALCIPPE
Uh-huh. So what about this "bacchanale..."?

DORANTE
Since you're my friend, Alcippe, I'll tell you all.

CLITON
(Monsieur, if I were you right now? *Postpone.*)

DORANTE
The barge we lay in like a burnished throne
Burned on the water. Soft music stoked our fire—
Two boats before us with cathedral choir,
And two behind with woodwinds, strings and brass.
I felt that hiring more would be too crass.
But how their plaintive harmonies caressed
The balmy air, as melodies tumesced
And voices mixed in tender competition!
They played a suite of my own composition.
We two reclined meanwhile and sucked moist figs
Within a baldachin of willow twigs
Enlaced with jasmine, while, like circling planets,
Five blindfold virgins served us pomegranates
On alabaster plates. I won't repeat
The panoply of sweets that stained our sheets
(And us) as we lolled there. I won't recall
The dinner courses, no, you'd be appalled.
There were fifteen. A roast, a pig, a calf,
A tumid cock, Lafite in our carafe...
Enough! The list would render you inert.

But then milady offered as dessert
Whipped cream licked from her navel's humid valley.
Then—as a small postprandial finale—
A thousand skyrockets rise up and zoom
From every ark! They penetrate the gloom,
Then, moaning, spill their luminescent spume
Into the wombing dark, their falling embers
Gilding her bare, enthralling, sprawling members—
Like brilliant peelings of some cherub's tangerine...
As prudish night called "curtain" on the scene.
We danced and fondled till the jasmine drooped
And jealous Sun dispersed our happy troupe
Then parted at the call of Chanticleer
When mere reality deposited me here.

ALCIPPE
So you're the one.

DORANTE
'Fraid so.

ALCIPPE
The foul seducer.

DORANTE
You'd like the wench. Sometime I'll introduce her.

PHILISTE
That feast would cost the substance of a king!

DORANTE
Philiste, I had an hour to plan this fling.
A small flotilla, yes, but worth the prices.
The lady melted faster than the cherry ices.

ALCIPPE
(as PHILISTE holds him back)
(How could he be in town a full year's lease
And not know my connection to Clarice?)

PHILISTE
(Alcippe, control yourself. It's all a lie.)

ALCIPPE
(Don't come between us or you also die.)
(To DORANTE:)
You. I. But. Never. When I. Oh? *Goodbye!*

(ALCIPPE EXITS.)

PHILISTE

He had some business to be clarified.
Alcippe...!
(PHILISTE EXITS.)

DORANTE

He seemed upset.

CLITON

Upset! I'm *terrified*!
But sir, could I request a word or twain?

DORANTE

Ask anything you like.

CLITON

Are you insane?

DORANTE

I'm sorry, I don't see...

CLITON

The German front,
Zum Beispiel. Were you really once a grunt
At Schinkenhasenpfefferdinkendorm?

DORANTE

You know how ladies love a uniform.
Just reel off any military muddle,
The dame will deliquesce into a puddle.
In time you share these private lovers' codes.
You just say "Germany" and she explodes.

CLITON

And what about this blow-out on your yacht?
A regatta straight outta Camelot.
"Five Boats, One Woman, or: Don Juan's Thanksgiving."

DORANTE

Cliton, the unimagined life's not worth living.
When someone's got a juicy tale to dish,
I have to add some sauce, re-spice the fish.
A man starts spooning tales of sweet amour
I have to make that man my *dupe du jour*.

(GERONTE ENTERS.)

GERONTE

Dorante, what are you doing, standing idle?

DORANTE

(My Dad.)

GERONTE
You know my business here.

DORANTE
                    To bridle?

GERONTE
Exactly. No. Though *bridle* is well said.
You need a bride, my boy, a wife well-bred
With sense enough to damp your youthful fire.
And I've found just the girl whom you require.
The niece of an old friend—your perfect frau.
I'm on my way, in fact, to meet her now.

CLITON
(Tell him about the gal who you just met.)

DORANTE
(Oh, let him dance his harmless minuet.
I'll sidestep any charmless fiancée.)

GERONTE
What's this? A beggar?

DORANTE
                No, my new valet.

CLITON
"A *beggar?*"

GERONTE
            "A *valet?*"

DORANTE
            Years of experience.

GERONTE
With what?

DORANTE
      Some high-placed Presbyterians.
But didn't you say you're off to make my marriage?

GERONTE
Have you no plans?

DORANTE
            I do. The royal carriage
Just passed...

GERONTE

No!

DORANTE

Yes. The damn thing came this close.
The sleepy driver, nearly comatose
Happened to graze my boot. We heard a crunch.
No harm done, but the Queen's asked me to brunch.

GERONTE

The Queen?!

DORANTE

I had to say yes, to placate her.

GERONTE

(hugs him)
My boy, you're on your way!

DORANTE

Let's catch up later!

GERONTE

(exiting)
The Queen...! The Queen...!

CLITON

In this town, they will put you through a sieve.

DORANTE

My friend, the thing I'm not will make me live.
But all this chatter's kept me from Lucrece.
That girl is going to be my masterpiece,
My coup, and I won't rest till she's my wife.
Now come and learn the way to spin your life.

(THEY EXIT, and the SCENE CHANGES.)

Scene Two

(Clarice's drawing room. CLARICE and GERONTE confer while LUCRECE and ISABELLE attend in the background.)

GERONTE
You won't be disappointed, mademoiselle.
My son is handsome, clever, speaks quite well.
And just to show he's not a travesty—
He's brunching right now with Her Majesty!

CLARICE
Brunch? With the Queen?

GERONTE
    He cannot tell a lie.

CLARICE
She never brunches—and is in Versailles.

GERONTE
If you had met my son you wouldn't doubt him.
His love of fact's the foremost fact about him!
He's youthful but he's truthful, that's Dorante.

CLARICE
I'm sure your son's a gem, Monsieur Geronte,
He's of your family and shares your breed.
But...

GERONTE
    Not to fear. Your uncle has agreed.
The two of us were friends at school, you know.
We talked of you two marrying long ago.
For that to be, we only lack your voice.

CLARICE
I'm flattered endlessly to be your choice...

LUCRECE
(What of Alcippe?)

CLARICE
    And yet, Monsieur Geronte,
I fear I'd need to be a clairvoyante
To marry sight-unseen your son... [*Can't recall the name.*]

GERONTE
    Dorante.

CLARICE
It also shows a most unseemly lust
To have a husband. Tell me, is this just:
Could you devise a way for me to see him?
A covert glimpse someday at the museum?

GERONTE
"Someday," Madame Clarice?

CLARICE
         Next month, next year...

GERONTE
You can examine him today, right here!

CLARICE
All right.

LUCRECE
(And if Alcippe arrives?)

CLARICE
               Um—*no*.
Uncle's infirm upstairs, the to-and-fro...

GERONTE
How's this: today upon the stroke of three
I'll draw him to your street and you shall see
My son—though from afar—to your content.
I have no doubt you'll give your quick consent.
Madame Clarice, I tell you he's a prize.

CLARICE
I'll view him first, and then let's rhapsodize.
Till three, then.

GERONTE
        He's reliable, faithful, steady...

CLARICE
Fear not, monsieur. I love the man already.

GERONTE
Mamselle.
(To LUCRECE:)
    Mamselle.

(GERONTE EXITS.)

LUCRECE
    Please leave us, Isabelle.

(ISABELLE EXITS.)

LUCRECE (CONT'D)
Clarice, don't say you'd entertain the thought...!

CLARICE
Lucrece, at this point, sell me and I'm bought.
So heck, I'll vet some mystery candidate.

LUCRECE
You'd quit Alcippe?

CLARICE
Alcippe's two years too late.
Though this...oh, what's his name...

LUCRECE
Dorante.

CLARICE
Dorante
Sounds like an idiot. And I don't mean *savant*.
I wouldn't want, because of this palaver,
To honeymoon with some jejune cadaver.
Lucrece, oh, please don't look at me like that.
Of course I'd take Alcippe, just drop a hat.
Or get his gouty father here from Ghent
And wring from him the requisite consent.
I want a husband, cuz.

LUCRECE
You're telling *me?*

CLARICE
And *you're* the gem, you darling. *You* should be
The bride, not I.

LUCRECE
In truth, I've lost all hope.
For I can see without a microscope
I'm as deserving of a first-class mate
As other women. Yet I stand and wait.
Because I'm silent—all right, call it nervous—
Most men just never see beneath my surface.

CLARICE
Most men can't read you like a crystal ball
Because most men are surface—and that's all.
Though surfaces are nice, in their own way...

LUCRECE
The surface of that man that we met today?

CLARICE
The pretty soldier with the palmist's touch?

LUCRECE
Don't tell me you were interested...

CLARICE
      Not much.
Though if this son is half as gaily wrapped,
I'll scoop him up and sell Alcippe for scrap.

LUCRECE
Well, you'll find out at three o'clock today.

CLARICE
But find out *what* from fifty feet away?
How'll I know if he's a tower or a basement
By seeing his surface from my parlor casement?
We women know that looks are error-prone,
Having to please men's eyes but doubt our own.

LUCRECE
An epigram?

CLARICE
   No, verbal diarrhea.
But wait a moment. *I* have an idea!
You haven't a volcanic fiancé.
What if you wrote this son a note? You say
You've noticed him somehow and want to chat.
To "get to know him," with this caveat:
That for this powwow you require *discretion*.
Some way to meet without transgression.
(Calls:)
Sabine!—*I* know! Across your garden gate,
Shrouded by tactful night. So make it late.

LUCRECE
But how...?

CLARICE
   I speak as you. You hold your peace.
He'll think I'm you—some random girl, "Lucrece."
I find out what he is and what he's not.
Alcippe will never know.

LUCRECE
   I like this plot!

(Sitting to write.)
And I address this now?

CLARICE
"To My Adonis."

LUCRECE
He'll think I'm joking.

CLARICE
No, he'll think you're honest.

Sabine!

(SABINE ENTERS. She is played by the same actress who played ISABELLE but is a sterner, stricter presence.)

SABINE
Madame?

CLARICE
Sabine, there's going to be a letter.

LUCRECE
As courier, mightn't Isabelle be better?

CLARICE
Is there a difference, when Sabine's her twin?

SABINE
Madame, I hope this note's no cause for sin.
My sister Isabelle may feed your plots...

CLARICE
No need, Sabine, to tie yourself in knots.

SABINE
I'll brook no looseness or lubricity.

CLARICE
This note demands no dark duplicity.
Just, please, go easy on the rough detergent.

SABINE
Monsieur Alcippe is here. He says it's urgent.

CLARICE
Uh-oh. That means Mount Etna is emergent.

ALCIPPE (O.S.)
Clarice!

CLARICE
Sign, quick!

LUCRECE
(writing)
"Lucrece, your fond bacchante..."

CLARICE
Come back at three, we'll vet this—damn...

LUCRECE
Dorante.

CLARICE
Dorante!

("Mwah." "Mwah." LUCRECE and SABINE EXIT.)

ALCIPPE (O.S.)
Clarice! Clarice!
(ALCIPPE ENTERS.)

ALCIPPE
You Jezebel! Avaunt!

CLARICE
Now what's all this? Stop growling. Speak your piece.

ALCIPPE
O faithless, fickle, fraudulent Clarice!
Avaunt, I say! My once-prospective spouse!

CLARICE
I can't avaunt, Alcippe. This is my house.

ALCIPPE
Clarice, Clarice...!

CLARICE
Will you stop baying my name like some remonstrance?

ALCIPPE
I only hope that you've ransacked your conscience.

CLARICE
Now what's the matter, pug? Why all these sighs?

ALCIPPE
Oh, why these sighs, you say? Why all these *lies*?
This mask of guiltlessness, this fictive frown?

CLARICE
Speak lower, please. My uncle might come down.

ALCIPPE
Your uncle—last night fortunately ailing
While you were very publicly out *sailing*.

CLARICE
Sailing?

ALCIPPE
    While you were skulling on the Seine
And sucking figs. Did "uncle" come down then
Or interrupt you in the midst of sin
To rip you from your jasmine *baldachin*?

CLARICE
I'm sorry. What's a baldachin?

ALCIPPE
    Your nest?
Oh, do I need to catalogue the rest?
"*Baldachin*'s" not enough? All right. A test.
"Flotilla." Does "flot lla" ring a bell?

CLARICE
Not really.

ALCIPPE
    Maybe "*pomegranate*"?

CLARICE
    Well,
I do like pomegranates, truth to tell.

ALCIPPE
Ah-ha! I wonder you can say the word…

CLARICE
"Pomegranate"?

ALCIPPE
…and not turn into a curd
Of quivering, pasty shame! The word's mere sound…

CLARICE
"Pomegranate"?

ALCIPPE
…should fling you to the ground,
Onto your knees, and leave you there to squirm.

CLARICE
Why? Is there something lethal in the term
"Pome"...?

ALCIPPE
Will you stop saying "*pomegranate*"?

CLARICE
Could you explain...

ALCIPPE
You've taken me for granted
All too long. Who am I, your party clown?
Explain? What for? Your uncle might come down!

CLARICE
I swear...

ALCIPPE
The next time you take out your *barge*,
Could you not publicize the trip at large?

CLARICE
My barge?

ALCIPPE
Yes, next time you decide to cheat,
Could you please choose a lover more discreet?

CLARICE
A lover?

ALCIPPE
Oh, he's told me everything—
With orchestra and chorus there to sing
An oratorio about your jaunt!

CLARICE
And who's this lover, please?

ALCIPPE
Dorante.

CLARICE
Dorante?!

ALCIPPE
Oh, yes, that's good. That's very credible.

CLARICE
Dorante?

ALCIPPE
"Oh, *who?*" You found him beddable
Enough last night!

CLARICE
I've never met the man!

ALCIPPE
Then why'd I see the father of his clan
Leaving your house just now with my own eyes?

CLARICE
My uncle's an old friend of his.

ALCIPPE
Lies, lies!

CLARICE
He *is!*

ALCIPPE
Is this a stage? Are these just props?
Perhaps Dorante's for nighttime, day's for Pops!

CLARICE
Alcippe, I've never even seen his face!

ALCIPPE
Was it too dim inside your trysting place?
Inside your *baldachin?* You had a date
With cherry ices, alabaster plates,
Five boats with blindfold virgins, calf, cock, pig,
Chateau Lafite, God knows what else to swig,
You spend a whole night being jocular,
You didn't spot your interlocutor?
A thousand Roman candles shoot through space
Spilling their loads of luminescent spume,
Their artificial sun banishing gloom,
And yet you somehow never glimpsed his face?
You didn't peek, you didn't drop the screen
While posing as some naked tangerine?
You didn't spy between your sprawling members?

CLARICE
Well, if I did, I think that I'd remember.

ALCIPPE
You think that I could make this up?

CLARICE
No, no...

ALCIPPE
It's fine. Run off with your Dorante. Go. Go!
Forget Alcippe, the man who loved you once.

CLARICE
I might. Now will you hear me out, you dunce?
I spent last night right here on my rear end.

ALCIPPE
Don't raise your voice. Your uncle might descend.
If he's up there. If he exists at all.
Hello! Is anybody--?

CLARICE
Stop this brawl!
What will convince you this is some huge blunder?

ALCIPPE
The settling of our marriage, since you wonder.
Wed me tomorrow, all my doubts are spent.

CLARICE
But what about your Dad—Lord Gout of Ghent?

ALCIPPE
I'll handle him.

CLARICE
You think that he won't frown?

ALCIPPE
Clarice...

CLARICE
Stop. Wait. My uncle's coming down.
You're joking, right? Oh, pug. You're such a clown.
(CLARICE EXITS.)

ALCIPPE
Go. Giggle. Heap Alcippe with ridicule!
Each snigger only frees me from your rule,
Each snicker snaps another chain. Snap! Snap!
I loved Clarice. She gave me my first slap
Standing right here—no, here—on this parquet.
How many a fight did these planks underlay,
How many break-ups with make-up bouquets...

But now that nouveau fop would snap her up,
My pseudo-friend would taste her hungry kiss?
Would lick Clarice's minty dentifrice?
(Draws his sword.)
Let's see how well he likes the taste of this.
I'll spear that double-dealing troubadour!
Not here, though. I don't want to stain Our Floor.
I'll leave him nowhere to put on his cap,
I'll slice him into bits, I'll leave no scrap,
With snap! And snap! I must stop saying that.
Oh, what the hell. Snap, snap, snap, *snap!*

(ALCIPPE EXITS. SCENE CHANGE.)

Scene Three

(The Place Royale. Before Clarice's house. GERONTE ENTERS.)

GERONTE

(calls offstage)
Dorante! This lassitude is unbecoming!
(To us:)
My wedding plans are absolutely humming.
The Place Royale—and there's Clarice's house.
Once I display him to his future spouse
The lady will annex him on the instant.

(DORANTE and CLITON ENTER, DORANTE studying a map. GERONTE does not hear the following exchange.)

DORANTE

"The Place Royale. G-3..." It can't be distant.
Cliton, we're right in its vicinity.

CLITON

(pointing to a street sign)
Doesn't that say...

DORANTE

Sing out, divinity!
I sense your presence like some soft chorale!
Where are you, O my darling?

CLITON

..."Place Royale"?

DORANTE

If I don't find her, I shall go insane.

GERONTE

Well, well. Now isn't this a handsome lane!
What time is it, Dorante?

DORANTE

What? Nearly three.

GERONTE

Perfect. Why don't you step out of the lee
Into the sun. Just look at these fine buildings!
The ornaments, the pediments, the gildings!
These silvery trees—it's like some pastorale!

DORANTE

Yes, very nice...

(Just noticing a street sign;)
(Cliton—the Place Royale!)

GERONTE
(moving DORANTE forward to be better seen)
Don't hug the walk.

DORANTE
(Lucrece lives on this row!)

GERONTE
Chin up. Hands at your sides. Good. Shoulders low.

(A CHURCH CLOCK CHIMES THREE O'CLOCK.)

GERONTE (CONT'D)
There's three o'clock!

DORANTE
Um, Dad, are we expected?

GERONTE
My boy, you realize I've not neglected
Your welfare.

DORANTE
No, sir. I'd say, *au contraire*.

(Behind them, CLARICE and LUCRECE appear in a window of Clarice's house. GERONTE signals to say, "This is he.")

DORANTE (CONT'D)
Why are you waving?

GERONTE
Waving?

DORANTE
In the air.

(During the following, DORANTE keeps wandering away, GERONTE keeps pulling him back into position beneath the window.)

GERONTE
A cramp. Well, now you want to go to war.
And given the perils that might lie in store—
I know how thirst for glory tempts young blades
To risk their necks in reckless escapades—
I want to see you married, and with speed.
The only thing we lack 's the wedding deed.

DORANTE
But, sir...

GERONTE
She beautiful. She's rich...

DORANTE
Sublime.
But, sir, these things take thought, and talk, and time.

GERONTE
Her uncle's an old friend to say the least.

DORANTE
Right now I'm thinking I might be a priest.

GERONTE
She lives right on this street.

DORANTE
She what?

GERONTE
It's true.
Indeed, *the lady has her eye on you*.

DORANTE
It couldn't *be*...

GERONTE
Yes.

DORANTE
Sir, I know this niece!

GERONTE
You do?

DORANTE
We met today!

GERONTE
You know...?

DORANTE
Lucrece?

GERONTE
Clarice?

DORANTE
I do! What? *Who?*

GERONTE
Clarice.

DORANTE
Clarice?
No, no. It's some mistake. Clarice?

GERONTE
The same.

DORANTE
But, father, I know no one by that name.

GERONTE
Well, you will now. She'll carry on our line.

DORANTE
No, please.

GERONTE
I want a grandson.

DORANTE
Grandson? Fine. But not by some *Clarice*. Oh, please, sir. *Please*.

GERONTE
I say you will.

DORANTE
(clasping Geronte's legs)
I beg you! On my knees!

GERONTE
Get up!

DORANTE
And anyway, I can't. You see?

GERONTE
You can't?

DORANTE
Complete impossibility.

GERONTE
But why?

DORANTE
Well—inadmissibility.

GERONTE
Inadmiss... You don't mean virility?

DORANTE
No, no.

GERONTE
Sterility? Fertility?

DORANTE
I'm speaking, sir, of immorility.
Morality. And illegality.
Back in Poitiers, you see, for such is life...

GERONTE
Enough! Why can't you wed?

DORANTE
I have a wife.

GERONTE
WHAT?!

CLITON
WHAT?!

GERONTE
Without my knowledge, or consent?

DORANTE
They forced me, sir. O, curse the sad event!
If you but knew! Now I can't eat, or sleep... [*"Weeps."*]

GERONTE
I want the facts, you understand? *Don't weep.*
Tell all. But if you lie to me, or hide...

DORANTE
Who, I, sir?

GERONTE
Now then, who's this sudden bride?

DORANTE
Her family's noble, if downwardly mobile.
Her name's Orphise. Her father, Armidon.

GERONTE
I've never heard of either one. Go on.

(As DORANTE acts out the story, CLARICE and LUCRECE look on, baffled.)

DORANTE
There is a willow grows aslant a brook.
'Twas there I first beheld her, saw the look
Of gypsy in those eyes, those calves of cream
As she hised up her skirts to toe the spangled stream.
I didn't dawdle. In an hour I knew
Her name, within a day we'd met, in two
We two'd confessed our crush, within a week
I'd vault her wall and mount a bush to seek
Her in her room and whisper, lip to lobe.
But then one night Orphise lay in her robe—
O fateful date! The second of September!
It's more than I can bear to re-remember!—
We hear a sound. A footstep in the halls.
Her father's voice outside. "Daughter!" he calls,
And pounds our door, unwisely left unlocked.
"One minute, sir!" she stalls, while I, half-cocked,
Go scrambling for the window. There's no time!
He's coming in. But she—a genius—climbs
His neck, embracing him, while I secrete
Myself behind the bed. He takes a seat
This far away from me, and starts to talk,
Showing some ring, a diamond like a rock.
But suddenly my blood begins to freeze.
Some suitor wants to wed...
(He can't remember her name.)

GERONTE
Orphise...?

DORANTE
Orphise!
I stop my mouth to stifle a mad moan.
"Say, what was that?" her father says. "That groan..."
"A fart," she says. "*Pardón.*"

GERONTE
She's brilliant.

DORANTE
Right?
But now the blanket's fallen. I'm in sight!
So casually she covers me with bedding,
Placates her Dad about this cursèd wedding.
He's slinking out now with his vulgar ring
When suddenly... [*He's at a loss.*]

GERONTE
Well, what?

DORANTE
"*Ding ding ding ding!*"
My watch goes off!

GERONTE & CLITON
No!

DORANTE
Yes! "Now what's that noise?"
He cries. She says, "My watch"—with total poise.
Suspicion burns within his beady eyes.
"What watch? From where? Some cad? I'll have no lies!
I swear to God I'll scatter this man's brains!
Show me the thing!" "Yes, father." She maintains
Her cool, shoots me a wink, I grab the fob,
When suddenly the...

GERONTE
What?

DORANTE
The...thingmabob...

GERONTE
The watch?

DORANTE
No.

CLITON
Stem?

DORANTE
Oh, what d'you call it...?

GERONTE
Chain?

DORANTE
Yes! Catches on my pistol's trigger. *Bang!*
The girl falls headlong.

GERONTE
Dead?

DORANTE
Apparently.

I spring to view. Her Dad, transparently
Terrified, runs into the hall and yells
"*Assassin! Murder!*" Voices are heard. Bells
Outside. With Tarquin's ravishing stride I
Attempt the hall. There's no place to hide. I
See servants bounding up the stairs. I draw
My knife, but—*damn!*—it shatters in my claw,
Struck by a bullet! Flinging off the pieces
I back into the room. Meanwhile, Orphise's
Crise—nothing but a fainting spell—has passed.
We seize some furniture and, working fast,
Erect a barricade against the door.
The mattress, dresser, wardrobe, junk galore,
The chamber pot, the trunks—

GERONTE
All right, all right!

DORANTE
We seem to've sealed ourselves in nice and tight,
We've just embraced into a seamless ball...

GERONTE
Yes? Suddenly—?

DORANTE
A battering ram bursts through the wall.

GERONTE & CLITON
NO!

DORANTE
Yes! We're almost buried under plaster!
And then comes striding through the hole...The Master!

GERONTE
Her father.

DORANTE
Yes. Um...

GERONTE
Armid...

DORANTE
Armidon!
And so I did what any man had done.

GERONTE
You wed.

DORANTE
          I dead. I did. And so, dear father,
I won a prize with just a spot of bother
That Jupiter would give Olympus for.
Condemn me. Call me simple. I adore!
(CLARICE and LUCRECE leave the window.)

GERONTE
No, no. I won't play God. I'm not a stone.
Those love hath joined are soldered at the bone.

DORANTE
How true, how true.

GERONTE
          But why so mum, dear boy?
You wouldn't share your news with me? Your joy?

DORANTE
I only feared her dowry'd be too meager.

GERONTE
What need for dowry? You're on fire. She's eager.
True love's a pearl, mere property...

DORANTE
          A carbuncle.

GERONTE
I'm going to settle with Clarice's uncle
And call that wedding off.
(Embracing him.)
          Congratulations!

DORANTE
Thanks, Dad.

GERONTE
          This day's a day for jubilation!

(GERONTE EXITS.)

DORANTE
So how'd you like my latest fabulation?

CLITON
Your what?

DORANTE
          My shpiel.

CLITON
You mean your wedding wasn't *real?*

DORANTE
A stratagem to shed this foul Clarice
And gently substitute the fair Lucrece.
CLITON
Yeah, but...

DORANTE
Imagine if I hadn't lied!
I'd be engaged right now *to the wrong bride!*
You see, you need a lie with proper flavor...

CLITON
Monsieur...

DORANTE
Cliton?

CLITON
Could you do me a favor?
Next time you're lying, could you, like, shoot a wink?
A poke, a wave, a nod—whatever you think—
So while you're fictifying in full spectrum
I don't just stand there like some gaping rectum?

DORANTE
Fear not, my friend. To show I comprehend,
I hereby name you my sole confidante.
My second soul. The conscience of Dorante.
Depository of my inmost key,
And closest nursemaid of my bosom.

CLITON
Gee.
That's somewhat closer than I planned to be.

DORANTE
And no more lies. I swear. Today I cease.

(SABINE ENTERS with a LETTER, looking around.)

DORANTE
(Good *God!*)

CLITON
(What, what?)

DORANTE
(The servant of Lucrece!)
Speak to me, maiden! Ask me what you want!

SABINE
I'm looking for some rascal named "Dorante"?

DORANTE
That's me!

(DORANTE grabs the LETTER and steps aside to read it.)

CLITON
Hello there, you.

SABINE
I beg your pardon?

CLITON
We meet again.

SABINE
We do?

CLITON
The Twillery garden?
Today? The trees?

SABINE
I've never seen you in my life.

CLITON
The grass? The breeze? A conversation *rife*
With innuendo?

SABINE
Really.

CLITON
What's this? *Tact?*

SABINE
Please go away.

CLITON
Okay. Okay. React
Like that. I was an asshole.

SABINE
Were you.

CLITON
                                                  Wait!
All that I said about you being an eight?
It's just I have this problem with the truth.
I have to say it all the time!

SABINE
Forsooth.

CLITON
Just watch. I'll try to tell you you're a ten.
You're a t... You're a t... I'll try a pen.
("Writes" on his hand.)
You're a t... See my point?

SABINE
This is inane.

CLITON
Now where's your room key?
(She slaps him.)
                                  What are you, *insane?*

DORANTE
(to SABINE
Please tell the writer that I'd be delighted.
(SABINE EXITS.)

DORANTE (CONT'D)
                                                     God!
Doubt on, Cliton! You poor benighted sod.

CLITON
Who, me? Just now I was your bosom's nurse!

DORANTE
A tender invitation interspersed
With delicate endearments. Look. "*Adonis*."
That's me.

CLITON
            What is she, blind?

DORANTE
                        Perceptive. Honest.
"Might we two have a late night tête-a-tête?"
The girl I met this morning. Want to bet?
For here, an inch below the scented crease,
A telltale signature, to wit, "Lucrece."
But I'll need information, facts to go on.

Her background, family, history and so on.
I want it all up here [*points to his head*] as I require.
Memory! Keystone of the master liar!
So ask around. Go weasel out her data.

CLITON

Just keep that crazy maid away. Well—later!

(CLITON EXITS.)

DORANTE

Lucrezia! Italian might allure her...
"Che bella notte...! Che bella figura...!"

(PHILISTE ENTERS, bows formally.)

PHILISTE

Monsieur.
(Holds out a note.)
>Alcippe awaits you in the Bois.

DORANTE

What's this? Another note for poor old moi?
I certainly am popular today.
"Thou bastard. Meet me, bring a sword, and pray."
And what offense could force my childhood neighbor
To make me spit him on my trusty saber?

PHILISTE

The rules of honor, section 40, say
A challenge mayn't be questioned, come what may.

DORANTE

Ah, yes, old section 40, I'd forgot.
Well, tell him I'll be there. To die—or not.
(More bows. PHILISTE EXITS.)
O, Paris, how I love you! Geez, it's fast here.
At this rate I don't see how I can last here.
I just arrived, I haven't any pull,
And look—my calendar's already full!
Fess up. Are any of you as quick as I—
The master of the airtight alibi?
As sly, yet trusty on the witness stand?
A certain Senator just raised his hand.
I'm sorry, sir. No chance. I win the laurel.
First challenge? Right. Alcippe's mysterious quarrel.
Well, it's a chance for exercise, some sun.
Let's see how I finesse it. Might be fun.

(EXITS, whistling.)

Scene Four

(The Bois de Boulogne. ALCIPPE and PHILISTE ENTER.)

PHILISTE
(entering)
No, no, no no...

ALCIPPE
My pride and honor are at stake, Philiste.

PHILISTE
You lose both, fighting with this arriviste.
And all for what? I swear—a misperception!

ALCIPPE
Upon my oath, he'll die for this deception.
Enough!

(DORANTE ENTERS.)

DORANTE
Well, gentlemen.

ALCIPPE
You got my note?

DORANTE
I must have, since I'm here. So. Shall we smote?

PHILISTE
Gentlemen, might   make one last appeal?

ALCIPPE
Too late. The gauntlet's thrown, there's no repeal.

PHILISTE
Then take your marks. Who first draws blood is victor.

DORANTE
Who first draws blood...?

PHILISTE
Or kills.

DORANTE
Ah, good. Much stricter.

(ALCIPPE and DORANTE take their places with hands on their hilts.)

PHILISTE

En garde!

(DORANTE is instantly in motion, only miming drawing his sword, just as he mimes all the following. ALCIPPE and PHILISTE merely stare, boggled.)

DORANTE

And *ding!* They're off! Dorante is quick
Out of his corner, with an expert *flick*
He plunges in the fray! Left lunge! Right jab!
My God, this kid can play! *Another* stab!
And look at that, he nips his rival's sleeve!
(ALCIPPE grabs his sleeve as if hit.)
And now the other one!
(ALCIPPE grabs the other sleeve.)
He bobs, he weaves.
There's still no blood. Alcippe looks stunned! He's dazed
As Kid Dorante just leaves him in the haze!
Alcippe is backing off now, he's retreating...
Is this the end? Is Kid Alcippe conceding?
No, wait! Alcippe's in action now!
(ALCIPPE, too, mimes drawing his sword.)
Attack!
The gloves are off now and Alcippe is back!
And *one*, he shags out left! And left again!
Off right! Dorante ripostes...ripostes again...
And now they both go at it with a yen!
Their blades so quick they might as well be air!
And parry, lunge, and look! With savoir faire
Each snips a lock of his opponent's hair!
(Each grabs at his hair to check.)
Oh, what a duel, folks! Still no blood spilt!
What's this? They're chest to chest! They're hilt to hilt!
(The two press chests, eye to eye.)
My God, these kids are close enough to floss!
Who'll crack? Who'll flinch? Who'll give the *coop duh grace*?
Who'll still be standing when he leaves this ring?
Is this *ka-ching* for one of these fine—

PHILISTE

DING!

I mean, all hold!
(ALCIPPE and DORANTE part.)
You've honored Honor's law,
Therefore I deem this duel a noble draw.

DORANTE

Fine. Chalk this match love-love. But for the audit
I'd love to know the reason that we fought it.
Has someone slandered me?

(Pulling an imaginary pistol.)
I'll shoot the chough!

ALCIPPE
You ought to know the reason well enough.

PHILISTE
Tell him, Alicippe. You've fought now. Call his bluff.

ALCIPPE
I'll only say two words. *Pomegranate.*

DORANTE
Keep going.

ALCIPPE
Baldachin. You didn't plan it
As an affront, your intimate excursion
In five huge punts, then blurting this diversion
Down to a certain naked tangerine?
You didn't know, you stinking libertine,
That I've been secretly engaged, betrothed
To that same feral fruit whom you unclothed
With Roman candles spilling their hot sap?
Well, I say *snap*, my friend. Snap, snap, snap, snap!

DORANTE
Alcippe, you've snagged yourself in your own trap.
My sailing pal can't be your fiancée.

ALCIPPE
Why not?

DORANTE
She *has* a husband—in Calais.
Fifi's a well-fixed Florentine from Aix
Who visits me for nights of frenzied sex
Whenever she's in Paris on a "shopping trip."

ALCIPPE
Fifi...?

DORANTE
A purple birthmark on her hip,
Red hair to here. Your girlfriend has the same?

ALCIPPE
Fifi...?

DORANTE
So Fifi's not your girlfriend's name?

ALCIPPE
But my valet's report...

DORANTE
　　　　　Not to debunk it.
He must've mixed mine with some other junket,
Some other amatory marathon.

ALCIPPE
How could I doubt you? O, you paragon!

DORANTE
I'll say but this: beware of jealousy,
My friend. It is the green-eyed monster which
Doth mock the meat it feeds upon!

ALCIPPE
So young, and yet so wise?

DORANTE
　　　　　　So young, but true.

ALCIPPE
O why can't I be wise, Dorante, like you?

DORANTE
Perhaps with time and more experience.
Adieu.

(DORANTE EXITS. ALCIPPE lets out a cry of frustration.)

PHILISTE
　　Still growling? Why?

ALCIPPE
　　　　　　　Siberians
Don't live in deeper dark than I, Philiste!
If not Dorante, then who's the horny beast
Who took her sailing? Who did my man spy?

PHILISTE
You want to know? I'll tell you. It was I.
(ALCIPPE goes for his throat.)
But, but, but, *but!* The girl was not Clarice.
It was Sabine, in your girl's ermine piece.
You know Clarice's ermine cape?

ALCIPPE
　　　　　　　It's hooded.

PHILISTE
You know the lane at her back door?

ALCIPPE
It's wooded.

PHILISTE
The woman whom your man saw slip outside
Was not your own but my prospective bride.

ALCIPPE
You mean...?

PHILISTE
It was Sabine. So have no fear.

ALCIPPE
Sabine...?

PHILISTE
Whom I've been courting for a year.

ALCIPPE
You mean...?

PHILISTE
A servant, hence the need for stealth.

ALCIPPE
Sabine...?!

PHILISTE
Whom I, in spite of all my wealth,
My taste, my style, my elegant chateau
Am nuts for. And whom I, in my bateau,
Took for a quiet row along the river,
With one guitar—no band—and chicken liver.
I tried to set you straight about my outing.
You wouldn't hear.

ALCIPPE
No, I was busy shouting.
Sabine? No.

PHILISTE
Yes!

ALCIPPE
That scourge?

PHILISTE
                        So call it sickness.
I love the girl, Alcippe. I love her strictness.
She's adamant as truth, she's hard to rattle,
And on a picnic—expert with a paddle.

ALCIPPE
Then I shall love her, too! Platonically.
But wait. You mean this duel...?

PHILISTE
                        Ironically,
Was over nothing. Oh, and by the by?
All that about his mistress was a lie.

ALCIPPE
There's no libidinous creature from Aix?

PHILISTE
A feature of his inner multiplex.

ALCIPPE
No well-fixed Florentine?

PHILISTE
             He traded up.

ALCIPPE
No luminescent spume?

PHILISTE
             He made it up.

ALCIPPE
No calf? No cock?

PHILISTE
             Nor figs on the buffet.
How could there be? He just arrived today!

ALCIPPE
He minted all those lies? I stand in awe.

PHILISTE
Well, don't forget, Alcippe: he studied law.

ALCIPPE
What should we do?

PHILISTE
With him? I hereby prophesy:
He'll get his just desserts. Just let him lie.

(THEY EXIT. SCENE CHANGE.)

Scene Five

(Clarice's bedroom. Evening. CLARICE, LUCRECE and SABINE. CLARICE is getting dressed.)

CLARICE
I told you write this note and you first sneered.
Though as coincidence it's slightly weird.
Can you imagine? (Lace me up, Sabine.)
Dorante—on whom this father was so keen—
Turns out to be this morning's musketeer
Who dandled my poor hand and bent my ear.

LUCRECE
"Poor hand"? You almost made a gift of it.

CLARICE
Sometimes one does things for the lift of it.
But out there in the street this afternoon
What *was* that pantomime? Like Pantaloon
Relating some vast epic to the Dad.
I couldn't hear the words.

LUCRECE
    Perhaps he's mad.

CLARICE
So that's Dorante! Who knows? This might be fate.

LUCRECE
That's what girls often say—*before* the date.

(SABINE finishes fastening Clarice's dress, and EXITS.)

CLARICE
Oh, poor, untried Lucrece.

LUCRECE
    You think *I'm* green?
When *you* think he's a soldier?

CLARICE
    What—you mean...?

LUCRECE
Your so-called "musketeer"? Oh, poor Clarice.
This guy's so slippery he's a sea of grease.
Men cook up battles, conjure naval storms—
They know how maidens melt at uniforms,
And then to please some girl their brain begot,
Impersonate a person whom they're not.

This one's quite dear. A diamond in the raw.
He's probably a student. I'd say Law.
He'd lie to anyone, be it him, be it her...

CLARICE
How did you *learn* all this?

LUCRECE
   By going to theatre.

CLARICE
Well, as a trickster he out-tops the heap.
He duped not only me. He duped Alcippe.
Something about a baldachin, a boat --
Enough to make my sweetie bark and gloat.
"*Pomegranate! Pomegranate!*" he kept shouting,
Apparently the highlight of this outing—
Except the fireworks' pornographic spume
That found me sprawling naked, as the gloom
Was brightened by their artificial sun.
Now that I think of it, it sounds like fun.

LUCRECE
But this must mean Dorante's in love with you...!
Today when he was hand in glove with you
His heart, however slippery, must have seen
That you're predestined as his lifelong queen.
Wedding his native cleverness to Fate,
Undoubtedly aware Alcippe's your mate—
Intended mate, at any rate—and zealous
To win, he tricked Alcippe to make him jealous
With all those baldachins and blindfold virgins.
Then! Working brilliantly as any surgeon,
He sent his father here to intercede,
To claim your hand and frame a wedding deed,
Leaving Alcippe abandoned in the haze!

CLARICE
Lucrece, I think you've seen too many plays.
He's no Leander. I'm no Hellespont.

(SABINE ENTERS with a LETTER.)

SABINE
A message, madam, from Monsieur Geronte.

LUCRECE
You don't believe me? Skeptic! Why d'you scoff?

CLARICE
(reading the letter)
Well, this is interesting. The wedding's off.

LUCRECE
How could it be?

CLARICE
My theories are rife.

SABINE
I'll tell you why. The young man *has* a wife.

CLARICE & LUCRECE
NO!!

SABINE
Yes. I overheard his father say
Dorante has wed some gypsy from Poitiers.

LUCRECE
He *can't* be married! How could he have sought you?

CLARICE
I guess that's one thing theatre never taught you.
A wedded gander too will chase us geese.
Well, now it's time for me to play Lucrece.

LUCRECE
But if he's married, why still keep this tryst?

CLARICE
To watch him squirm and dodge, and make him twist.
Sabine, please post your sister at the gate.
We'll serve this trickster on an alabaster plate.

(ALL EXIT. SCENE CHANGE.)

Scene Six

(The garden gate at Lucrece's house. Night. DORANTE and CLITON ENTER.)

DORANTE
This must be it—and isn't this ironic?
We're off the Place Royale!

CLITON
Wow, man. *Harmonic.*
(Takes out paper.)
I got that private info on Lucrece.
Her Dad's a hotshot judge. Her Mom's deceased...

DORANTE
Her father's name?

CLITON
Perander. Rich as God.
A Tuscan villa. Ski place in Gstaad...

DORANTE
Perander. Tuscany. [*Points to head.*] It's there. Entire.
Memory! Keystone of the master liar!

CLITON
I wish she had your tricky disposition,
To even out this evening's competition.
If she was born to lie, I'd be elated.

DORANTE
Liars aren't born, Cliton. They're fabricated.

(Across the gate, ISABELLE, CLARICE and LUCRECE ENTER.)

ISABELLE
(It's he.)

CLARICE
(It's he.)

DORANTE
(It's she. Watch this.)

CLARICE
(The fool.)

DORANTE
Lucrece?

CLARICE

Dorante?

DORANTE

'Tis I. Your willing tool.
Lay down your law. Subject me to your rule!

LUCRECE

(You recognize the style? Torrid, but florid?)

CLARICE

(But has he recognized my voice? It's horrid.)

CLITON

(It's her, okay. I recognize the voice.)

DORANTE

(What did I say? And you still doubted me?)

CLARICE

(I hope to God I haven't outed me.)

DORANTE

Sweet Aphrodite!

CLITON

(Me?)

DORANTE

(Her.) Would I could efface
The years I've spent not living in your grace.
To live without you's fate's most cruel blow.
It's hardly life at all. It's death, it's woe.
Make me your slave, your pawn, your dog, your pet!

CLARICE

(Strong words for someone whom he's never met.
Lucrece, what did you put into that note?)

LUCRECE

(This speech is prerehearsed. It's one long quote.)

DORANTE

You are to me as thread is to the eyelet,
As the well-rounded rhyme is to the triolet,
As key to lock, as rain is to the—

CLITON

(Toilet.)

DORANTE

...violet.
You put to shame the paradise that's Dante's!
You are a peak atop the highest—

CLITON

(Panties.)

DORANTE

Andes!

(DORANTE silently remonstrates with Cliton, while...)

CLARICE

(You go to plays. What do I say to *that*?)

LUCRECE

(It might be best to lower the thermostat.
Express some cautious interest. Toy with him.)

CLARICE

(Just what does "cautious" mean?)

LUCRECE

(Be coy with him.
Be distant. Play the comic ingénue.)

CLARICE

(So, cautious.)

LUCRECE

(Echo me and I'll be you.
My God, you're sexy!)

CLARICE

God, you're sex... (That's *cautious*?)

LUCRECE

(You want to make him twist?)

CLARICE

(I want to make him nauseous.
I want his head turned back-to-front and spinning,
But not with compliments.)

LUCRECE

(Clarice, you're winning.
He's in your power.)

DORANTE
Did I hear you say "sexy,"
My dove?

LUCRECE
(*Indeed.*)

CLARICE
Indeed.

LUCRECE
(*Like apoplexy...*)

CLARICE
Like apoplexy...

LUCRECE
(*You make boil my blood.*)

CLARICE
You make... (No, really?) ...you make boil my blood?

LUCRECE
(*I am a torrent.*)

CLARICE
I am a torrent.

LUCRECE
(*A flood!*)

CLARICE
A flood!

LUCRECE
(*Come find me, god!*)

CLARICE
Come find me, god???

LUCRECE
(*I am a spring! Thou'rt my divining rod!*)

CLARICE
(I won't say that.)

LUCRECE
(*You must.*)

CLARICE
(*Divining rod?*)

DORANTE
(This girl is deep.)

CLITON
(So deep she's got two voices.)

DORANTE
Sweet lady, how my listening heart rejoices!
You cherish me. I'll serve you without cease.
I kneel to say it. Marry me, Lucrece!

CLARICE
You mean Clarice.

LUCRECE
You mean Lucrece!

CLARICE
Lucrece!

CLITON
(You didn't hear that? Christ, she's like a chorus!)

DORANTE
(It's *love*. They get that way, get more sonorous.)

CLARICE
My broken voice should help you to infer
The shock of your proposal. For, good sir,
Your suit is impish and impossible.

DORANTE
For you? The wildest river's crossible,
The vortex of Charybdis a mere eddy!

CLARICE
But can you wed me when you're wed already?

DORANTE
What? Who? I? Married? That's a slanderous libel!
A calumny! I'd swear it on a Bible!
May God erase me if I have a spouse!

CLITON
(Hey, watch your step.)

DORANTE
(It's true!)

CLARICE
(He's such a louse.)

DORANTE
Mademoiselle, teach me. How can I persuade you?

CLARICE
What need? Your gypsy marriage has unmade you.

DORANTE
I know: meet me at dawn at altarside.
All doubts will be undone when you're my bride.

CLARICE
Bigamist! You don't fear you'd be unmasked
By all those other women whom you've asked?

DORANTE
I only fear the jealousies I'd stir,
The thousand envious duels that I'd incur.

CLARICE
What? *You* fear duels? With all the wars you've won?

DORANTE
You know how many men I've killed?

CLARICE
Yes. *None.*

DORANTE
But crimson streams...

CLARICE
The only "crimson streams"
You've spilled were in your cups—or in your dreams.
You must have magic powers, though, I must say.
To be here six months—yet arrive *today?*

DORANTE
Uhhh...

CLARICE
What, no words? What is this sudden shyness?

DORANTE
Uhhh...

CLARICE
Tell me, how was breakfast with *Her Highness*?

DORANTE
Uhhh....

CLARICE
Well, well. Tongue-tied, sir? The facts must scare you.

CLITON
(Finiggle outa this one, sir. I dare you.)

CLARICE
As for your nuptials...

DORANTE
Darling, they were feigned!
Your admiration will be unrestrained
When you hear *why* I feigned them.

CLARICE
Mere caprice?

DORANTE
My goal was simple. To win you, Lucrece.
I had to fake that marriage to undo
A union that my father had in view.

CLARICE
(This should be good. Here comes some epic saga.)

DORANTE
Some dowager, "Clarice." I'm sure she's gaga.
I? Wed some shrew? Obscene, oblong, obese?
And not the fair, the fine, divine Lucrece?

CLARICE
I know Clarice quite well, just to be fair.
Indeed, Clarice goes with me everywhere.

CLITON
(She knows Clarice?)

DORANTE
(Well, isn't that ironic.
Must be her coughing friend, the catatonic.)

CLARICE
You have strong feelings.

DORANTE
One gets finical
When threatened with Clarice the Clinical.
O, be my bride!

CLARICE
Such ardor makes me wary.
Not knowing me, why would you want to marry?

DORANTE
Not knowing you? (The thing!)
(Motions hastily for the paper. CLITON digs for it.)

CLARICE
Not that I doubt you.

DORANTE
My dear Lucrece, why, I know all about you!
(Squints at the paper, trying to read.)
Your brother's dead.

CLITON
(Her *mother*.)

DORANTE
Mother's dead.
Your father's hot...fudge?

CLITON
(*Judge*.)

DORANTE
Just as I said,
A judge. His name is Derrr...

CLITON
(Peran...)

DORANTE
Deran...

CLITON
(*Pe*ran...)

DORANTE
Perander. The son of a kook.

CLITON
(A *duke*.)

DORANTE
Etruscan...

CLITON
(*Tuscan.*)

DORANTE
Shire, spire...

CLITON
(*Squire.*)

DORANTE
Squire.
A ski chalet. What more do you require?

CLITON
(Memory! Keystone of the master liar!)

DORANTE
And you say I don't know you? Ask away!

CLARICE
(I think he wants you, cuz.)

LUCRECE
(Or my chalet.)

CLARICE
But this Clarice of yours. Obese, obscene?
Some find her quite the glamorous gamine.

DORANTE
There's only one thing missing from the tart.
A personality. A ticking heart.

CLARICE
A friend of yours proposed to her this afternoon.

DORANTE
Good luck. I'd rather wed a dead baboon.

CLITON
(*Nice one.*)

CLARICE
Yet just this morning you were seen with her,
Fondling her paw, oblivious of her fur.

DORANTE

Another lie! The paw, the fur—well, both!

LUCRECE

(I don't believe it!)

CLARICE

(Watch—another oath.)

DORANTE

Lucrece, I swear!

CLARICE & LUCRECE

(Ten points.)

DORANTE

As God is true,
The only girl I've met today is you!

CLARICE

Well, that's enough! The impudence! The gall!
When I saw you two eyeball to eyeball?
How craven, how pathetic, how transparent!
Even when forced to face the facts you daren't!
You lie, you swear, and sully what you swore!
You breathe deceit, you skunk, from every pore.
Find an asbestos tux and button it well
Because I'll only marry you *in hell*,
You dog, you beast, you cad, you...son of a bitch!

(CLARICE and LUCRECE EXIT.)

CLITON

Well, I'd say that went off without a hitch.
Was all that "kiss me," in some private code?
Say "Germany" and watch—she will *explode*.

DORANTE

Cliton, I'm this close.

CLITON

Close to what?

DORANTE

To winning!

CLITON

What, her? This was the end of the last inning!
You lost! She called you *liar*!

DORANTE
I don't know why.

CLITON
Well, maybe 'cause you had your pants on fire!

DORANTE
But everything I said to her was true!

CLITON
Encyclopedias turn to lies with guys like you.

DORANTE
Did I say she was deep? This girl's an ocean!

CLITON
So that explains her weird bi-polar motion?

DORANTE
She's playing hard to get. Fine. What a day!

CLITON
What are you gonna do?

DORANTE
A soft duvet
And six hours' dreaming ought to show the way.
Let me submit my mind unto the moon—
Lucrece will be my wife by afternoon.
Good night, Cliton. Sweet dreams.

(DORANTE EXITS.)

CLITON
This guy's a loon!

(ISABELLE pokes her head through the gate.)

ISABELLE
Hello there.

CLITON
Ahhhh!

ISABELLE
Remember me? It's Izzy.

CLITON
You recognize me?

ISABELLE
Sure!

CLITON
I'm getting dizzy.
But what about the time we met before?

ISABELLE
Listen. I came to let you know the score.
Just tell your master he should keep on hoping.

CLITON
After all *that*? He's lucky he's still coping.

ISABELLE
Lucrece—I mean the *real* Lucrece?—let's say...
She finds him *very interesting*.

CLITON
Oh-kay...
What "real Lucrece"? She must be a duet.
Part One's the wacko harpy we just met.

LUCRECE (O.S.)
Isabelle!

ISABELLE
You're so cute.
(She kisses him.)
Au revoir, my swell.

(She kisses him, and EXITS.)

CLITON
I too submit me to the moon! Ah, Isabelle,
Sweet Isabelle, who really truly is a belle!
I'd find more rhymes if only she were visabelle.
Is it not risibelle how most invisabelle
The indivisibelle Isabelle...is?
And oh how miserabelle am I, bereft of peace,
But hey, what's this about "the real Lucrece"?
And after that he shouldn't give up hope?

(SABINE ENTERS from Clarice's house.)

SABINE
Hey! You!

CLITON
Ah, there you are, my canteloupe!
(She slaps him.)
Say, what was *that*?

SABINE
I'll give you both what-for.

CLITON
What *for*?

SABINE
For being here. Now clear the door!

(SABINE EXITS.)

CLITON
The maid is just as schizo as her matron.
Well, what a day, to quote my crazy patron.
So that's Act One. Think I'll go have a think.
(SABINE sticks her head out.)

SABINE
Hey! *Hey!*

CLITON
I'm going!
(To us:)
All you—go have a drink!

CURTAIN

END OF ACT ONE

ACT TWO

Scene One

(The Place Royale. Morning. DORANTE ENTERS. CLITON drags in behind him.)

DORANTE
Still barely dawn. She draws me like a lure.
And here's her street! My dreams in miniature!
Lucrece, my love! Lucrece!

CLITON
                Monsieur Dorante?
It isn't *dawn* yet for a debutante.
The rich live in their whole own later time zone,
So quit your shouting or we'll be a crime zone.

DORANTE
Let them arrest me, throw the book at me!
I must get her this note. [*Producing a LETTER.*]

CLITON
            Don't look at me.

DORANTE
My brain's on fire, Cliton, and she's the fuel.

CLITON
What's this I hear—Alcippe, he fought some duel?

DORANTE
Alcippe?

CLITON
      Your friend?

DORANTE
     A duel?

CLITON
             Uh-huh.

DORANTE
                  With whom?

CLITON
Well, oddly, someone very much like you'm.
And since I was away an hour or two'm
Yesterday afternoo'm,
Would you have any info on this rumor?

DORANTE
You want the truth?

CLITON
Like any wise consumer.

DORANTE
I swore I'd not make known the sad event.
But how can any earthly vow prevent
Divulging it to you, my confidante,
My second soul, the conscience of Dorante,
Depository of my inmost key,
The closest nursemaid of my bosom?

CLITON
Gee.
So you were saying...

DORANTE
This duel.

CLITON
And your own role?

DORANTE
It is the cause, it is the cause, my soul!
For ten long years he'd stalked and baited me.
I needn't tell you why he hated me.
It was a night at cards in Paraguay.
A girl named Peepa, too much bootleg rye...
We knew that one would die at our next meeting.
You saw him yesterday. His hearty greeting
Dissembling all the venom he showed later.
He sent a challenge through an arbitrator,
We met, we fought with pistol, sword and cape.
My rapier left a gaping hole, the shape
Of Peepa's head. He fell, cold to the touch.

CLITON
No!

DORANTE
Yes.

CLITON
He's dead?

DORANTE
I left him there for such,
Face down in gore.

CLITON
Poor guy.

DORANTE
So young.

CLITON
What's more?
A gentleman. With *character*.

DORANTE
Times ten.

CLITON
Hot-headed, yeah. But *genuine*?

DORANTE
Amen.

CLITON
I doubt this world will see his like again.

(ALCIPPE ENTERS, carrying a bottle of champagne.)

ALCIPPE
My friend! Let me embrace you! What a morning!
A miracle! Completely without warning!
I feel alive again! I could combust!

CLITON
(I gotta say, your victim looks robust.)

ALCIPPE
My father's come to Paris! That old sneak.
Who would've dreamed?

CLITON
I'm dreaming as you speak.

DORANTE
I'd love to share your glee—and to augment it...

ALCIPPE
But you don't know what's up! I seem demented.
A *wedding contract's* in my Dad's valise.
That means I can get married to Clarice!

DORANTE
Clarice?

CLITON
Clarice?

ALCIPPE
My fiancée!

DORANTE
You jest.

ALCIPPE
I swear to God.

DORANTE
I never would've guessed.
Well, what a turn.

ALCIPPE
That's why I'm off my head!

CLITON
(I thought it was because he wasn't dead.)

ALCIPPE
I'm off to her, to get her uncle's nod.
If he exists! At this point, nothing's odd!
Then she and I can pop this sparkling wine.
I wanted you to know, for auld lang syne.
(They do their special handshake.)

DORANTE
How wonderful to know our friendship's mended.
And please, pass on my best to your intended.

ALCIPPE
I will! But now...

DORANTE
Yes, go! Go see your bride.
And Jupiter be always at your side!

ALCIPPE
Au 'voir!

DORANTE
Your joy, an ever-gushing font!

(ALCIPPE EXITS.)

CLITON
What was I, now? Oh, yeah. Your *confidante?*
Your second soul? The conscience of Dorante?

Depository of your inmost key?
The closest nursemaid of your bosom?

DORANTE

                                                             Gee.
How good to see him stand there as he did.

CLITON

You mean the imaginary invalid?

DORANTE

What...? *What?* You think that I trumped up that duel?

CLITON

No disrespect. Is there a molecule
Of truth in anything that stems from there?
(Points to Dorante's mouth.)
'Cuz you lie anytime and anywhere
And prob'ly in your sleep! You can't speak truth
To Christians, Hindus, Musselmans, or Jewth!

DORANTE

I see. You were surprised to see Alcippe.

CLITON

Well, *yeah*.

DORANTE

        Surprised at his recovery.

CLITON

A *bit*.

DORANTE

        Well, there's this new discovery—
Perhaps you've heard of it—called "Powdered Health"?

CLITON

I've seen it on the shelf...

DORANTE

                        And what a wealth
Of healing herbs and rare ingredients.
Can't beat the stuff for sheer expedience.

CLITON

I never heard it raised you from *the dead!*
Or plugged up sword wounds shaped like some broad's head!
He woulda danced, if we'd'a had a band!

DORANTE
What you're referring to's the *regular* brand.
Cliton, through certain friends, by luck and stealth,
I have some *Extra-Strength* Brand Powdered Health.

CLITON
And it fights *death?*

DORANTE
 I've seen men in their shroud
Leap from their coffins, blinking but unbowed.
A friend was in the hearse, was getting buried?
One dash of Extra Strength—last week he married.
Own it, you own the elixir of the ages!

CLITON
I'll give you anything. A whole year's wages.
One bottle. Just a pinch. I need it! Please!

DORANTE
The problem is, the label's in Chinese.
The hidden powers are non-Chinese resistant.
How's yours?

CLITON
 What, my Chinese? It's non-existent!

DORANTE
Without Chinese the *jing-jong* don't react.

CLITON
You speak Chinese?

DORANTE
 Quite fluently, in fact.
I speak ten tongues. Kashmiri, Syriac,
Algonquin, Hebrew, High Bulgarian,
Pampango, Polish, Rastafarian,
And Volapük. Not always flawless syntax...

CLITON
Jing-jong...?

DORANTE
Jing-jong.

CLITON
You need ten tongues, an onion, and an axe,
The way that you make mincemeat of the facts,
Then dish them out to folks like Truth Tartare.

DORANTE
O ye of little faith.
(GERONTE ENTERS.)

GERONTE
Ah, there you are!

DORANTE
(Oh, God, not now.)

GERONTE
Dorante, I've had a thought.

DORANTE
Yeah, wow.

GERONTE
For given the wonder of that knot
That we call marriage, and the holy thunder
Of those old words, "Let no man..."

DORANTE
"...put asunder,"
Etcetera, yes.

GERONTE
And given my time of life,
I have a great desire to meet your wife.

DORANTE
My wife...? Oh, yes, my wife.

GERONTE
Are you attending?
(Takes out letter.)
I've penned this to her father, recommending...
Where is it... Yes. The point of this whole letter,
That she come here, and you yourself go get her.

DORANTE
Who? *I?*

GERONTE
Who else? It hardly warrants mention.
To send this blackguard [*i.e., Cliton*] would seem condescension.

CLITON
"Blackg..."?

DORANTE
He'd appreciate your politesse.
Too bad her Dad would never acquiesce.

GERONTE
Not acquiesce...?

DORANTE
I know he'd be beguiled.
But bring her *here*?

GERONTE
And you'd be reconciled.

DORANTE
I'd love to go. I'm *dying* to go. I'm wild.

GERONTE
Then why not leave forthwith?

DORANTE
My wife's with child.

GERONTE & CLITON
NO!

DORANTE
Yes! She's six months gone. No, thirty weeks.

GERONTE
My boy! What news! O, let me kiss those cheeks!
I'm floored! A grandfather...?

DORANTE
You.

GERONTE
I'm delirious!

DORANTE
But there are complications, some quite serious...

GERONTE
No, no, I wouldn't think of tempting fate.
I've bided this long. I'm content to wait.
O heaven, you heard an old man's imprecation!
I'd wait a year!

DORANTE
(That was the implication.)

GERONTE
Farewell. I'm going to pen a second note.
(Capering.)
Unless I die of joy!

DORANTE
(Check out the old goat.)

GERONTE
I'll send congratulations and my best
To him and to the mother, counsel rest...
You too must pen a note.

DORANTE
A long one. Roger.

GERONTE
Au 'voir!

DORANTE
Au 'voir!

(GERONTE EXITS.)

DORANTE
You have to love this codger,
With "imprecations" and his "notes to pen."

CLITON
Watch out, the codger's coming back again.

(GERONTE RE-ENTERS.)

GERONTE
I can't recall your in-law's name.

DORANTE
(not a clue)
His name...?

GERONTE
To put here on the envelope.

DORANTE
You frame
The note you want. I'll add his name and seal it.

GERONTE
Two hands might seem insulting. You don't feel it...?

DORANTE
The sentiment's what counts. He'll need a hanky.

GERONTE
Provincial gentry can be rather cranky.

DORANTE
He's very nonchalant.

GERONTE
Enough, Dorante.
What name?

DORANTE
Well, his own father is Menander.

GERONTE
No, not his father's name, but *his*!

DORANTE
Philander.

GERONTE
Philander! There! So simple!

DORANTE
No harm done.

GERONTE
(starts out, comes back immediately)
But didn't you say his name was Armidon?

DORANTE
On Tuesdays. Armidon's his *nom de guerre*,
His nickname from the war. He doesn't care,
Himself, how you address him, either name,
Philander, Armidon, it's all the same.
Philander'd be more proper, or more normal.

GERONTE
In my day we preferred to be more formal.
Philander, then. Au 'voir!

(GERONTE EXITS.)

DORANTE
Thanks for the chat!
You note how deftly I danced out of *that*?

CLITON
You better write these names inside your hat.

DORANTE
My wits will weave what memory can't supply.

CLITON
O, teach me, master! Teach me how to lie!

DORANTE
Teach you to lie...? But lying is an art.

CLITON
Truth's constipating me. The truth's a fart!
O, please, please, please?

DORANTE
                                        All right. Here's where you start:
All the world's a lie, and all the men and women
Merely liars, for each of them must play...

CLITON
                                        A part?

DORANTE
A role. This world's a scrim, Cliton, a fiction,
A richly tapestried, inch-thick depiction
Stretched over some mysterious cosmic hole.
You claim to be Cliton. How do I know?
Who's she, or he? Who is the whole back row?
How do I know the smallest thing? I can't.
No one knows anything. So people rant,
Protest, despair, take up astrology—
Each fearing deep in his biology
That life's a fraud, a fake, an empty vial.
Why else do people primp and pose? *Denial*.
That's where the liar comes in, because he knows
The truth, accepts the void, because he shows
Us the absurd commedia we're masked for.

CLITON
Ya know, this may be more than what I asked for.

DORANTE
He spins to poetry our daily prose,
Is given a turd and turns it to a rose,
Assembling like a magpie this, and this,
A gypsy wife, the Twillery, a kiss,
He plies his magic, his dark artistry
To dazzle us, reweave the tapestry
Unreeling colors from his endless spools.

He does what Nature does with Nature's tools,
For in a world where priests and princes lie
The liar blends in like a butterfly—
Defying gravity, his wits his wings,
He makes us take a second look at things.
Now try me. Ask me something. I'm at bat.

CLITON
You mean...?

DORANTE
Just try to catch me out. C'mon, chat.

CLITON
So where you from?

DORANTE
Japan.

CLITON
I didn't know *that*!

DORANTE
I'm not.

CLITON
Oh, *man*!

DORANTE
You note my air of ease?

CLITON
I half-expected you'd speak Japanese!
I'll get you this time.

DORANTE
Good. We'll start anew.

CLITON
Nice weather, huh?

DORANTE
I feel a drop...

CLITON
Me, too!
Damn it.

DORANTE
(peering at Cliton's face)
What's that...?

CLITON
Where...

DORANTE
Nothing. Just a pimple.

CLITON
A zit?!—God *damn* it!

DORANTE
Lying is so simple.
First: natural gestures. Keep your gravity low,
And centered.
(Hunching slightly, his weight low.)
See that? Everything must flow.

CLITON
("flowing")
So flow.

DORANTE
Most vital is the optic nerve.
Engage me.
(Points into his eyes.)
Don't allow your gaze to swerve.

CLITON
Don't swerve.

DORANTE
An easy tone, but with some verve.
So speak your speeches trippingly upon the tongue.

CLITON
(a rippling gesture before his face)
Tripping.

DORANTE
Let truth be told, but let your lies be sung.

CLITON
(bursts into lusty song)
With *verve!*

DORANTE
Irrelevant details are key.
(Tossing it off:)
"It was tenth of May at six-oh-three..."

CLITON

Gripping.

DORANTE
But sprinkle in some poetry.
(Airy gesture:)
"The bluebells were just fading now forsooth…"
And lastly—never, *ever* speak the truth.

CLITON

Lie.

DORANTE
So. Sum up the principles of lying.

CLITON

I can't remember.

DORANTE
Are you lying?

CLITON
No, I'm trying
To get them back!

DORANTE
That's very good! That's great!

CLITON

But I'm not lying yet, I'm…! Wait, wait, wait.
I got it. Principles of lying.

DORANTE
Go.

CLITON
(a gesture for each, rippling, airy, flowing, etc.)
Don't swerve. Be tripping. Poetry. Stay low.
Irrelevant details. With verve. But flow.

DORANTE

And?

CLITON
Never, ever tell the truth.

DORANTE
Bravò,
Cliton, bravò! You see how much you've mastered?

CLITON
Who, me?

DORANTE
You *liar*.

CLITON
Oh, I'm a lying bastard! C'mon, ask me anything.

DORANTE
Where are you from?

CLITON
Paris. *Japan*.

DORANTE
Wow.

CLITON
Smooth, huh?

DORANTE
/ succumbed. What city?

CLITON
Oh, you know...

DORANTE
Tokyo?

CLITON
Shanghai.

DORANTE
Brilliant. Now get thee forth and multip-lie.

CLITON
But getting back to plot, sir. You don't fret
This lie about your kid's the diciest yet?

DORANTE
Another rung upon my amorous ladder.
And here's a maiden who can aid the matter.
(ISABELLE ENTERS.)
Dear girl, in my transported attitude
I sadly failed to show my gratitude
When last we met. Well, scrimping's not my form.
I live to give. I am a fructifying storm.

I drench the hills, I inundate the plains.
Ask him. (Be quiet.) I shower the earth with rains.
(Takes out a coin.)
So here's a golden raindrop for your pains.

ISABELLE

O, sir, I must decline. I couldn't.

DORANTE

You must!
With all you've done?

ISABELLE

No, no, I'd be unjust.

CLITON

(aside to ISABELLE)
(What's all this garbage, "Sir, I must decline"?)

ISABELLE

(Butt out, pal. You make your rains, I'll make mine.)

DORANTE

(takes out another coin)
A second raindrop?

ISABELLE

(takes the money)
Sir, I'll tell you all:
It's definite. My lady's in your thrall.
She stayed up half the night because of you.
If you ask me, she's half in love with you.

CLITON

(We musta met her other half last night.)

ISABELLE

She can't *admit* she loves you, out of spite.
Those lies you lavished at the Twillery?
Four years a captain of artillery?
And what about Clarice? That pending suit?

DORANTE

I never sought Clarice. That suit is moot.

ISABELLE

My rainbarrel holds another ounce or two.

DORANTE

You mean...?

ISABELLE
I might have something here for you...
(She takes out a book and dangles it before his eyes.)
A bit of bait. Lucrece's private journal.
Now what was that about a rainshower, Colonel?

DORANTE
(tossing coins)
O Bella, Bella, buy yourself a gold umbrella!
(He grabs the book and reads.)

ISABELLE
(to CLITON)
Hello again.

CLITON
Oh, now you recognize me?

ISABELLE
Why wouldn't I?

CLITON
(offering his cheek to be slapped)
Okay. C'mon. Tenderize me.
Do it. Right there. Let fly.

ISABELLE
You are so hot.

CLITON
(My chance to lie! Okay. Let's take a shot.
Don't swerve. Be tripping. Poetry. Stay low.
Irrelevant details. With *verve!* And flow.)
("Flowing";)
Hi, there. The name's Clit...Jacques.

ISABELLE
Clit-Jacques.

CLITON
It's new to France.

ISABELLE
And what is that you're doing, modern dance?

CLITON
You know, I just arrived here from Peru.
My goldmines.

ISABELLE
Are you lying?

CLITON
Yes, are you?
Now ask me anything. Ask where I'm from.

ISABELLE
Nice weather, huh?

CLITON
Japan. Well, that was dumb.
D'ya feel a drop?

ISABELLE
No.

CLITON
No?

ISABELLE
What are you, simple?

CLITON
Say, what's that on your cheek? Is that a pimple?

ISABELLE
Here's what's on yours. [*Slaps him.*]

CLITON
Okay, I'm swearing off.

DORANTE
(finishes reading)
Ha, *ha!* Read this, my friend, and try to scoff.
It's love! Lucrece is a Dorantophile!

CLITON
You sure it's that same girl?

DORANTE
Cliton, the *style.*
Lucrece is mine. Enraptured and resistless.
Isabelle, take this letter to your mistress.
(HE gives ISABELLE the LETTER and returns the book.)

ISABELLE
Yes, sir.

DORANTE
(gives money)
Here's rain until the next installment.

ISABELLE

Yes, *sir!*

DORANTE

Report my uttermost enthrallment.

(ISABELLE EXITS.)

CLITON

(holds out hand)
I wouldn't mind a small emolument.

DORANTE

I'd better freshen up.

CLITON

Forget your honey.

SPARE CHANGE?

DORANTE

It's love! I don't have time for money.

(THEY EXIT. SCENE CHANGE.)

Scene Two

(Lucrece's drawing room. LUCRECE and ISABELLE.)

LUCRECE
So *tell* me, Isabelle. What did he *say?*

ISABELLE
You mean the master, or the weird valet?

LUCRECE
Either.

ISABELLE
He's yours.

LUCRECE
He loves me?

ISABELLE
Love? He's fiery.
But did you need to slip this guy your diary?

(She gives the book back to LUCRECE.)

LUCRECE
I had to test him. See he felt the same.
I still don't quite believe him. There's some *game*...
Or do I fear love? Am I just perverse?
Do *you* believe him?

ISABELLE
I believe his purse.

LUCRECE
Izzy. You didn't take some filthy *bribe?*

ISABELLE
Oh, yes. What better proof that you two jibe?
In this town, gold decides where north and south is,
So love will put its money where its mouth is.

LUCRECE
It's shameful. As if love was born from banks!

ISABELLE
(taking it out)
I have a letter from him.

LUCRECE

(snatching the letter)
                      Here's ten francs.

ISABELLE
What shall I say to him about his love note?
I'll say: it flew like pigeon to its dovecote.

LUCRECE
No. Say I tore the letter up unread.

ISABELLE
Oh, brilliant. You prefer to stay unwed?

LUCRECE
Tell him I shredded it with tranquil hands.

ISABELLE
Then goodbye raindrops, hello desert sands.

LUCRECE
Of course, mix in a sweetener, or three…

ISABELLE
"My lady loved your note, it's now debris"?

LUCRECE
Oh, you know what I mean. Blame women's nature.
Invest your text with sexist nomenclature.

ISABELLE
We're *moody*? Flighty?

LUCRECE
                    But in time we soften.
Imply that I might meet him, now and…

ISABELLE
                      Often?

(ISABELLE EXITS.)

LUCRECE
Tell him I tore it up!—Where was I now…
(Scans letter.)
"Joyrapturehappiness *accept my vow*
Of love." He loves me! Me, Lucrece! But *how*?
How could Apollo stoop to such as me?
And yet he seems to droop as much as me.
"Agonysorrowtorment *how I've yearned*
For you." That proves it, far as I'm concerned.

And yet it's odd how he extols my eyes.
He hasn't seen them! *"Lazuli at sunrise,"*
He calls them. Love y. So why analyze
What he... Yet here he says "Your lips, your face..."
He hasn't seen those either. "Your embrace
Is all I crave." I really have to shred this.
(She holds it as if to tear it up.)
Be brave, Lucrece. Well, after I've reread this,
Where is it, here, "Your delicate, warm hand
So pliant to my touch..." *Delicate hand*...
Well, *that*, for instance, I don't understand.
How could he know my hand is pliable?
The letter's really unreliable.
"Blahblahblahblah *your voice,* each note a pearl."
He's never heard it! So who *is* this girl?

(CLARICE ENTERS, followed by SABINE.)

CLARICE

Lucy, let me embrace you! What a morning!
A miracle!

LUCRECE

What's happened?

CLARICE

                Without warning
I find myself amidst the Great Event!

LUCRECE

You're pregnant?

CLARICE

No! Al's father came from Ghent!

LUCRECE

So you can marry!

CLARICE

Well...

LUCRECE

Why such a frown?

CLARICE

We have to wait for uncle to come down.
But once he does, we'll set the wedding date!

(Jubilation.)

LUCRECE
You were so worried. This should compensate.

CLARICE
Compensate? How?

LUCRECE
For having lost Dorante.

CLARICE
Ha, ha, ha, ha! Monsieur Dorante, the vaunted?
I never sought him. You're the one he wanted.
That's all dead wood now. I called him a beast.
Sabine?

SABINE
You did, Miss. Fifty times at least.

CLARICE
I'm only glad we got to get his goat.

LUCRECE
He just wrote *me* the most affecting note...

CLARICE
Oh, poor Lucrece. You don't believe this boy?
(Takes letter.)
"Joy, rapture..." Every word is pure trompe l'oeil!

LUCRECE
You don't say this, I'm sure, because he scorned you.

CLARICE
Believe him. Fine. Remember that I warned you.

LUCRECE
You think this isn't love, and I'm a sap?
All this is desperation?

CLARICE
It's a *trap!*
This isn't love, Lucrece! You're simply curious!

LUCRECE
If you and I weren't best friends, I'd be furious.
But let's stop here. Why hack through this "dead wood"?

CLARICE
Well, fine.

LUCRECE
We're understood.

CLARICE
How've *you* been?

LUCRECE
Good.

We're friends?

CLARICE
Oh, Luce...

LUCRECE
What were we *on* about?!
(They laugh about it all.)
Yet while he crushed your hand you heard him out.
Before this raging animosity.
So was that love, or "curiosity"?

CLARICE
Mere curiosity. A chance to laugh!
I *listened*, yes, awaiting some dumb gaffe.

LUCRECE
Just as I read this note. Amused. Aloof.
I read it as one takes some silly spoof.
"Joyrapturehappiness..."
I'm going to rip it up. The whole thing's spurious.

CLARICE
(taking the letter)
I don't see why you should, if you're just curious.

LUCRECE
Following your example, my wise friend.

CLARICE
(handing it back)
Well, then, let rip!

LUCRECE
(handing it back)
I will!

CLARICE
(handing it back)
Ta-ta!

LUCRECE
(ripping it up)
          The end!

CLARICE
Of course, to listen simply means you're civil.
Reading a note you lend yourself to drivel.

LUCRECE
Now, Claire…

CLARICE
    I can't leave you in some man's lurch!

LUCRECE
You know what I think? We should go to church.

CLARICE
A wonderful idea! Let's hear Mass.

LUCRECE
Then we'll forget that cad.

CLARICE
      That liar.

LUCRECE
          That ass.

SABINE
Are you two mad? Have you both lost the drift?
Madame, the gods have blessed you with a gift!
Do we so often yearn, so often burn
With passion for a man, that we should spurn
Him when he comes, or let him cause a rift,
However shifty this man's bent might be?
Hear this: each man's imperfect. *So are we*.

LUCRECE
Sabine…!

SABINE
    Good Christ, madame, *pursue* this youth!
Go now. Go find Dorante, surrender couth,
And wring from him what he thinks is the truth!

CLARICE
Yes, Miss.

LUCRECE
Yes, Miss.

SABINE
Or must I spank you both?

LUCRECE
Isn't love wonderful?

CLARICE
I take my oath.

(THEY EXIT. SCENE CHANGE.)

Scene Three

(The Place Royale. GERONTE ENTERS as PHILISTE ENTERS opposite, carrying a bouquet. PHILISTE heads for Clarice's house.)

GERONTE
What, is that you, Philiste?

PHILISTE
Monsieur.

GERONTE
Well met.
You know Poitiers.

PHILISTE
My birthplace.

GERONTE
Better yet.
Acquainted as you are—and in all candor—
Apprize me all you can of one Philander.

PHILISTE
Phil...?

GERONTE
...ander. From our home locality.
Just any facts. His personality,
His family, his fortune, fealty, fame....

PHILISTE
I'll tell you all: I've never heard the name.

GERONTE
You mean...? Well, yes, small wonder how you stare.
To you he's Armidon! His *nom de guerre*.
The father of Orphise? Whose beauty ranks
As high as snow upon the Pyrenees?

PHILISTE
No slander on Philander. Both are blanks.
(Turns to leave.)

GERONTE
So this is tact. You're sheltering my boy.
You've sworn to keep hush-hush about his joy.
Well, I know all. The watch, the pistol shot,
Her father forcing him to tie the knot...

PHILISTE
Dorante's a husband? Or is this a jest?

GERONTE
He's young, he's mine, I heard, I acquiesced.

PHILISTE
But—married? He?

GERONTE
              Here's more, if you're beguiled.
The two of them are going to have a child.

PHILISTE
Who told you this?

GERONTE
              Why, he himself! Dorante!

PHILISTE
I should have guessed. The story's so picante.

GERONTE
You mean to cast some doubt upon this tale?

PHILISTE
No, no. He has a gift in proud, full sail—
Your son's this world's most brilliant adapter.
No doubt in time he'll add another chapter,
Detailed, delicious, packed with derring-do—
At sea, perhaps, with magic herring, too.
He conjured an imaginary feast.
No doubt Orphise was baked from this same yeast.

GERONTE
I'll break your neck. I'll put your legs in splints!

PHILISTE
He must have shown you proofs, you're so convinced.
A license?

GERONTE
      No...

PHILISTE
      A portrait with her face?

GERONTE
He gave such rich details...

PHILISTE
> I rest my case.
As for this grandchild waiting at the sill,
I'll say but this: *I wouldn't change my will.*

(PHILISTE EXITS.)

GERONTE
A man of my age, taken by surprise.
Was it a dream, a cloud of buzzing lies,
This world I've walked in, blunt and sound as rock?
Myself I find turned to a laughingstock!
O wicked. Dastardly. Unkind. Felonious!

(DORANTE ENTERS, followed by CLITON.)

GERONTE (CONT'D)
Are you a gentleman?

DORANTE
> (Oh, no. Polonius.)
A gentleman? Of course I am, being thine.

GERONTE
You think that that's enough? To share my line?
Well, in the sink of lies you're swimming in,
As King of France you'd be no gentleman!

DORANTE
Has someone said I lied?

GERONTE
> Has someone *said*?
With L-I-A-R there branded on your head!
Remind me, if you can, of your wife's name.

DORANTE
Her name...?

GERONTE
> Her name, boy. Can you tell me that?

CLITON
(I told you, write these names inside your hat.)

GERONTE
Perhaps her father's name, or his estate?
Come, dazzle me. Invent a potentate!
Is he the King of Prussia? Duc de Guise?

CLITON

(Maybe try *flowing*, sir.)

DORANTE

(Be quiet, please.)

GERONTE

Do you recall the name *Orphise?*

DORANTE

Orphise.

GERONTE

What spawned such lies? Clarice, all that affair?
I scrapped that wedding deed, please be aware,
And you make me your fool, your goat?
Why? Have I held a dagger to your throat?
Why artifice? The watch, the gun, that anthem.
I blessed your marriage to a gypsy phantom,
How could you doubt I'd give my fond consent
To a flamingo, so you were content?
You've shown a loving father neither fear,
Respect, nor love. What *have* you shown? A sneer.
I wish to God I'd never bred nor known you.
So go, my son no more. I here disown you.

DORANTE

The truth is...

GERONTE

Truth! Will your lips let it pass?
The truth fits you as false teeth fit an ass.

CLITON

(Hee-haw!)

DORANTE

You see, I've met this girl... No, this one's real.
Her name's Lucrece, and she's my heart's ideal.

GERONTE

Lucrece? Her mother was a royal Briton...

DORANTE

The moment that I met her I was smitten.

GERONTE

And that was...?

DORANTE

Yesterday. No, please don't doubt me.

I didn't know then how she felt about me
But now she's written. Read this tender piece.
(Shows letter.)
I had to shed the yoke of dread Clarice
So, yes, I shammed, I told a thousand lies,
But now I beg, by every knot that ties,
Help me. If you still harbor any doubt
Believe Cliton. He knows me inside out.

GERONTE

Yes, after this extravagant ballet
I'll trust some lying, fraudulent valet?

CLITON

(I oughta...)

(DORANTE holds him back.)

GERONTE

Well, I'm a reasonable man, and just.
I'll see her father and attempt his trust.
But if I find that this is all some trick,
If your words and reality don't click,
You'll lie here pooled in blood as your reward
With justice rendered by your father's sword.

DORANTE

You wouldn't kill me...?

GERONTE

    Heavens, I have vowed it!

(GERONTE EXITS.)

CLITON

He'll do it, too. He'll slaughter you.

DORANTE

    I doubt it.

CLITON

Frankly, monsieur, you disappointed me.
You fooled him twice. I hoped you'd go for three.

DORANTE

Cliton, there's something nagging like a tooth.

CLITON

Remorse, perhaps, for having told the truth?
Or maybe that was all another wheeze
And you don't really love the fair Lucreze.

DORANTE
No, no. I *do*. At least—I *think* I do...

CLITON
You THINK?

DORANTE
Well, how should *I* know if it's true?
I've lied to everyone. To him. To you.
It's like I've grown this lying, inner elf.
What if my elf is lying to my self?
What if it isn't love, and I'm an ijjit?

CLITON
Hey, don't ask me. Consult your inner midget.

DORANTE
Look at Lucrece's friend. You know the minx.

CLITON
You mean the cougher who you called a sphinx?

DORANTE
How can I trust, should that girl ever speak,
That I won't fall for *her* within the week?
She had a certain grace and style and air.
Stand the two side by side, she's just as fair.
And she exuded such a *je ne sais quoi!*

CLITON
Back then you said she had a *je ne sais blah*.

DORANTE
Because she bothered me.

CLITON
Sure. Sheer frustration.

DORANTE
No, no, Cliton. Incipient fascination.

CLITON
One small detail? The minxy sphinx is took.

DORANTE
Alcippe.

CLITON
Her guy.

DORANTE
Thank God! I'm off the hook!
I'll take Lucrece, then. Given the situation.

CLITON
What is this, process of elimination?
And if you doubt her, why pile on more lies?
Your Dad just heard you praise her to the skies.

DORANTE
I may have overdone the vivid prose.

CLITON
Except this time, this isn't just a pose.
You sent him for her hand! You've tied the loop!

DORANTE
A holding action. Now I can regroup.

CLITON
Regroup? You're running out of options, fella!

DORANTE
Never. And look, here comes fair Isabella.

(ISABELLE ENTERS.)

ISABELLE
Monsieur.

DORANTE
You gave my note? She vetted it?

ISABELLE
Not quite.

DORANTE
You mean...

ISABELLE
I mean she shredded it.
She ripped it into strips, then bits, then glitter.
In short, she quickly made your letter litter.

DORANTE
You *let* her?

ISABELLE
Sir, my lady came unglued!
She's going to fire me.

CLITON
Okay, now you're screwed.

ISABELLE
And yet...

DORANTE
And yet?

ISABELLE
My hand has such a thirst...

DORANTE
(gives more money.)
And yet?

ISABELLE
She shredded it, but read it first.
Indeed, monsieur, she may well memorize it.

DORANTE
You're lying.

ISABELLE
It's truth!

DORANTE
Well, I can't recognize it!

ISABELLE
I see her coming with Clarice in tow.
Good luck, monsieur. You still may be her beau...
If not her husband.

(ISABELLE EXITS.)

DORANTE
"If not her husband..."?

DORANTE & CLITON
Whoa!

(LUCRECE and CLARICE ENTER, followed by SABINE.)

CLARICE
(Be strong. Speak out. No sidelong looks. No peeking.)

LUCRECE
(But if he lies?)

CLARICE
(You'll know.)

LUCRECE
(How?)

CLARICE
(He'll be speaking.)

LUCRECE
Monsieur...

DORANTE
You've come at last to grant my suit!
So call me foolish, call me absolute...
(Walking past LUCRECE to CLARICE.)
Until you are my bride I will not rest.

(He kisses Clarice's hand. Over his bowed head:)

CLARICE
(You'd think that it was *me* whom he addressed.)

LUCRECE
Monsieur...

DORANTE
(to CLARICE, ignoring LUCRECE)
Without you, how am I to be?

CLARICE
(His gaze appears to be affixed on me.)

LUCRECE
(A stray glance hit you, inadvertently.)
Monsieur...

DORANTE
(following CLARICE around)
And if today I felt the lack,
Another day and I'd be on the rack.
How could I bear my life if we don't mingle?
I beg you, be my wife! I swear I'm single!

(He throws himself down and follows CLARICE on his knees.)

CLARICE
(He pointed that at me. You did remark it?)

LUCRECE
(Perhaps if you stood wider of the target.)

CLARICE
(Stood wider of the target? I'm his aim!)

LUCRECE
Monsieur Dorante—

DORANTE
(to CLARICE)
I love you!

LUCRECE
(It's some game.)

CLARICE
(Why?)

LUCRECE
(*I* don't know! Perhaps to twist our plight
He chases you by day and me by night!)

CLARICE
(He's on his knees! I think he's plopped for *me!*)

LUCRECE
(showing the bits of her letter)
(But what about his note? Exhibit B?)

DORANTE
(to LUCRECE)
If I might interrupt
(To CLARICE:)
Your friend, madame,
Who otherwise is something of a clam,
Has found her tongue. I bear her no bad will,
But she has private cause to wish me ill.

LUCRECE
(A *CLAM?* I'll kill him. I'll rip out his nails.)

CLARICE
My friend has told me certain curious tales...

DORANTE
The troubled fancies of a jealous mind.
Your maid can tell you how my own's inclined.
(To SABINE:)
Just say it in the simplest words you can.

SABINE
I've had no conversations with this man.

DORANTE
She's mad!

CLARICE
(He's mad.)

LUCRECE
(He's mad.)

CLITON
(to SABINE)
You're *mad!*

CLARICE
Sir, you do recognize me? Know this face?

DORANTE
Good God, I'd have to be from outer space.
You whom I met near here just yesterday?
Whose hand I held, who…

CLARICE
Skip the resumé,
Blah, blah, blah, I'm your goddess, you're my slave.
But there's not someone *else* whose love you crave?

DORANTE
No! It's for you and you alone I swoon!

CLARICE
You said you'd rather wed a dead baboon!

DORANTE
Forget the ape! My feelings are profounder.
If I can't marry you, I'd rather wed a flounder!

CLITON
(Nice one.)

CLARICE
Lucrece, a word.

DORANTE
(Lucrece?!)

CLITON
(Lucrece?!)

DORANTE
(You heard?)

CLITON
(I said she was Lucrece. You wouldn't budge.
Okay, now, smart guy, who's the better judge?)

DORANTE
(But last night at the gate...)

CLITON
(The switcheroo!)

DORANTE
(One played the other...)

CLITON
(...and you pitched her woo.)

DORANTE
(What of the maid?)

CLARICE
Sabine, find Isabelle.

(SABINE EXITS.)

CLITON
(Sabine?)

DORANTE
(Sabine? And Isab...?)

CLITON
(Isabelle?)

(ISABELLE ENTERS and waves coyly to CLITON.)

CLITON (CONT'D)
(Well, that explains it.)

DORANTE & CLITON
(*Twin from hell!*)

CLARICE
Monsieur Dorante.

DORANTE
Madame?

CLARICE
My friend "The Clam"
Has told me all, and of your shameful sham.

Did you not court this girl with praise profuse
While heaping me with nothing but abuse?

DORANTE
I'm sorry, when was this?

CLARICE
Oh, you're so slick.

DORANTE
No, really, madam. Are you playing a trick?

CLARICE
Last night! What chasm is your memory cursed with?

DORANTE
But you're the only lady I've conversed with.

CLARICE
You didn't speak to her last night till two?

DORANTE
How could I—speaking as I was to *you?*

CLARICE
Me...?

DORANTE
You. You thought I wouldn't know your voice?

CLARICE
You knew?

DORANTE
Madame, you left me little choice
But to indulge your clever masquerade.
You played Lucrece, I played the courtly blade,
And just to baffle you in your attempt,
Each time you said "Clarice," I feigned contempt.

CLARICE
And your imaginary marriage meant—
What, when your father'd come to seek my hand?

DORANTE
My bogus bride helped wrap a wedding band
Around your finger, just as I had planned.

CLARICE
(shows her bare finger)
What band?

DORANTE
I thought you'd bought your bridal gown...

CLARICE
I will—once Uncle What's-His-Name comes down.

DORANTE
In any case, Alcippe need never know
You met in secret with another beau.
Alcippe's so sensitive. Protect him, will you?

LUCRECE
Well, speaking for *The Clam*, I still could kill you!
Oh, yes, it's well and good to speak of "fun."
Clarice? Clarice is not the only one
To like some fun. I like fun, too. I love it!
My name's Lucrece But your fun, sir, well *shove* it's
What *I* say. *Shove* it! For while you were aching
With laughter, certain hearts were busy breaking.
I speak of mine, sir. Mine. Your loving oyster.
The bivalve at the back whose eyes grew moister
At the mere mention of your name. What prize,
What goal could you have gained from all those lies,
And from entangling me in your wild skein?
Why write me, for example, this long strain,
Apparently sincere, on your devotion?
(Takes out the bits of his letter.)
It breaks my heart to hold it. What an ocean,
What a wide, warm sea I rode when reading it.
What malice must have gone to breeding it.
But was it malice? Here, sir, have a piece.
Have all. But answer: was it mere caprice?

DORANTE
My goal was simple. To win *you*, Lucrece.

CLARICE
Don't tell me you *believe* that...

LUCRECE
                    Peace, Clarice.

DORANTE
You lent your friend your name and garden lawn
To stage her fraudulent *divertissement*,
And doing so became one of her engines.
You tortured me, I had my petty vengeance.
Forgive a lover, wounded but devout.

CLARICE

Oh, *please*.

LUCRECE

No, no. I want to hear him out.
And at the Twillery? You seemed to flout
Me, bantering with her. Was that mirage?

DORANTE

You might say that Clarice was camouflage.
I was too shy, tonguetied by your resplendence
To bare my soul and offer love's attendance.
She may have shared my words. You shared my heart.

CLARICE

Now this is magic of the highest art.
It's smoke and mirrors, Lucy. Sleight-of-hand.

DORANTE

I'm so in love I'm out of sight of land.

LUCRECE

Yes, with a mollusk, thank you. Not a girl.

DORANTE

A mollusk at whose middle lies a pearl.
And you may be a bivalve, but you're *my* valve.
Lucrece, I swear...

CLARICE

I swear, this man's a tease!

DORANTE

Let me not to the marriage—

LUCRECE

No Shakespeare, please!

DORANTE

You're right—a fact I know is always true.
It takes a liar to know a girl like you
Whose gaze illumines me and makes me blush.
Forgive me, madam, that I did not rush
Into your arms the morning that we met:
What women know, men can take years to get.
Pardon my truancy, forgive my timing.
To make it clear, I'll say it without rhyming:
(Very simply:)
I love you, Lucrece. Whatever any man could hope for in a woman is in you. Beauty, tenderness, intelligence, amazing tits, I didn't mean that, passion, honesty, morality, the kind that can move even an idiot like me. You are what

most men only dream of. I say all this without knowing you very well. In fact, I don't know you literally at all, except about your ski chalet and your father's name, which I can't remember. You see how honest I'm being? These have been the most wonderful twenty-nine hours of my life! The hours that included you, I mean. Please, Lucrece, please let me try to deserve you. If you try to love me maybe I can grow up into the kind of man who's worthy of your infinite perfections. And your amazing tits. Yes? No? Yes? Dear God, I hope that you believe me *now*.

LUCRECE
Well... *WOW.*

DORANTE
Just question my *chargé d'affaires*.
(To CLITON:)
Did I not praise her style and grace and air?
Her *je ne sais quoi?*

CLITON
I swear— as God is law!

ISABELLE
And madam, this valet's veracity
Matches his master's late mendacity.
Monsieur Dorante is really fiercely fond.

LUCRECE
To bad the facts and he don't correspond!

DORANTE
But if I say my father, as we speak,
Has gone to yours, dispatched by me to seek
Your hand, would that prove my sincerity?

LUCRECE
It might—unless some fresh disparity
Pops your soufflée.

DORANTE
But look—Pop's on his way.

(GERONTE ENTERS.)

GERONTE
The match is made, so set your mind at ease.
We only need the say-so of Orphise.

LUCRECE
Orphise?! Who's she?

GERONTE
Lucrece, I mean. Apologies.
Too many brides. So you're the Aphrodite
Who's captured my son's heart?

LUCRECE
Well, sir. I might be...
Depending.

GERONTE
But it all depends on you!
See how my puppy bends his eye on you?
I'm sorry, have we met? Or do I err?

LUCRECE
Yes, you were trying to dump your pup on her.

GERONTE
Well, will you have him? Join the family phylum?
Or shall I take a cell in some asylum?

LUCRECE
Good sir, I have good reasons to revile him.
The reasons, like Dorante, are convolute.
But heart says love, and heart I can't refute.
I'll take him—*and* his brilliant little jokes.

(DORANTE and LUCRECE kiss.)

GERONTE
Looks like a marriage made in heaven, folks!

ALCIPPE (O.S.)

Clarice! Clarice!

(ALCIPPE ENTERS with PHILISTE.)

ALCIPPE
Your uncle says it all depends on you!

CLARICE
Time out while I experience *déja vu*.

ALCIPPE
Well? Yes or no? Don't stand there like some statue!
Sweetie.

CLARICE
Oh, Pug, what man on earth could match you?
Of course I'll have you!

(ALCIPPE and CLARICE kiss.)

GERONTE
Blessings on you all!

PHILISTE
One second! I, too, stand in someone's thrall.
(Pulls ISABELLE to him.)
Sabine, my queen, let's do it. Let's elope!

CLITON
(pulling ISABELLE back)
Sorry, pal. This queen's Isabelle. I hope...

(CLITON is about to kiss ISABELLE.)

PHILISTE
Isabelle...?

CLITON
What, you mean you didn't know—
The dual status of the status quo?
G'wan, show him, babe.

ISABELLE
(exiting)
Sabine!

CLITON
You'll think they fake it.

PHILISTE
You mean...?

CLITON
Buck up now. See if you can take it.

(He does a drum roll, and SABINE ENTERS, breathless.)

SABINE
Philiste!

PHILISTE
Sabine...?

SABINE
I didn't think I'd make it.

PHILISTE
You mean...?!

CLITON
Hey, talk about your *je ne sais quoi!*

PHILISTE
Sabine??!!

CLITON
Your wife is a *ménage à trois!*

DORANTE
My friends, here's to my Dad, without whose virtue
I'd not have known how fraudulence can hurt you!
(GERONTE begins to sob loudly.)
Pop, what's the matter? Why all the sighs, and tears?

GERONTE
Oh, how I've lied, I've lied for all these years!
This show of probity that's masked my sin!
To have begot, and then forgot, your twin!

DORANTE
My twin?

GERONTE
A tale far taller than your fakery.
I left him with some crullers in a bakery!
The cause of many a marital scrimmage.
Like you he has a birthmark in the image
Of a red rooster, crowing on his tongue.

CLITON
A what?

GERONTE
That's how I'd know that he's my young.
By that lost bird.

CLITON
Yeah, but—*my* tongue has always sung.
See that?
(Sticks out his tongue.)

GERONTE
Dorante, you heard?
(DORANTE sticks out his tongue, too.)
Two cocks—of matching colors!

CLITON
Not only that.
(Producing them:)
I've got your missing crullers!

GERONTE

Chanticleer's crowed! The truth has finally won!

CLITON

Are you my Dad?

GERONTE

Come greet your papa, son!

(GERONTE and CLITON embrace.)

ALL

Awww.

GERONTE

Have half my all, plus what comes from your mother.
Now, happy truth—embrace your lying brother.

(DORANTE and CLITON embrace.)

ALL

Awww.

DORANTE

(to us)
How liars are punishèd by their own lies!
Was not *the moral of this exercise—*
But rather how, amidst life's contradictions,
Our lives can far out-fick the finest fictions.
A son and brother spun from a valet,
Four marriages at once (with ski chalet),
Plus other warps and wooves within this matrix,
Two sets of twins, a blushing dominatrix.
Yes, sometimes life is lively, sometimes duller,
Sometimes it's cruel, sometimes a missing cruller.
What things aren't possible in God's creation—
With a small push from the imagination!
And I? Well, given how sham's my benefactor,
Perhaps I'll go onstage and be an actor.
Maybe Corneille will write me up a play.
Or maybe, with my gifts and disposition,
I'll emigrate and be a politician.
But think, before you hit the parking booth,
How this was all a lie—and yet the truth.
Impossible? Don't hurt your spinning head.
Just hie thee happily home and lie—in bed!

CURTAIN

DAVID IVES

The Heir Apparent

adapted from *Le Légataire universel*
by Jean-François Regnard

Commissioned by:

 SHAKESPEARE THEATRE COMPANY
Recipient of the 2012 Regional Theatre Tony Award®
Artistic Director Michael Kahn
Managing Director Chris Jennings

as part of its ReDiscovery Series.

The commissioning and world premiere production of *The Heir Apparent* was made possible by the generous support of The Beech Street Foundation

Comedy Tonight
or: Meeting Monsieur Regnard
by David Ives

Voltaire said, "Whoever doesn't enjoy Regnard doesn't deserve to admire Molière."

Now that's a puff line to put on a theatre marquee.

Consider these tidbits from the life of Jean-François Regnard: first, that as your average young man of 23 gadding about the world he was taken prisoner in 1778 by Algerian pirates, sold into slavery, did six months' hard labor, got ransomed, and when he arrived home hung his slave-chains on the wall in his Paris house. Second, that after a cushy Treasury job, he launched himself as a comic playwright at age 38 and became the Next Big Thing after Molière. Third, that after he'd been buried 125 years, some kids found his skeleton when his church was being renovated and used his skull as a projectile.

In other words, Regnard had an archetypal career as a playwright: a slave while alive, a football when dead.

Add to this that he was beloved by all who knew him, that he made a great portion of his fortune on a gambling spree, and that, passing through Lappland, he caused a furor because of his uncontrollable laughter at a typical Lapp funeral. His name is cognate with renard, the French word for fox, and he lived up to it. "*Il faut, par notre esprit, faire notre destin*," Crispin says in *The Heir Apparent*. "It's with our wits that we create our fates."

The buoyancy with which Regnard lived is so intrinsic to his art that the man and his work are one. The play at hand (from 1708, titled *Le légataire universel*) is worldly, utterly honest, satirical without being condemnatory, ofttimes bawdy, sometimes scatological, now and then macabre, and it craves jokes as a drunkard craves his pint. Like a drunkard, the play will do anything to find the pint as Regnard goes off on knockabout detours hunting for laughs—not out of desperation but out of brio. Granted, some of *Heir* is a shameless rip-off of Molière's *Imaginary Invalid*. But is there anything in the *Malade imaginaire* to match Crispin's (i.e., Regnard's) inspired impersonations?

Because Regnard was writing as French classical theatre was heading into a century of much different character, the verse dialogue is more conversational than Molière, the concerns more bourgeois, while the farce is turned up (as they say in *Spinal Tap*) all the way to eleven. One can draw a straight line from *Légataire* to Feydeau's middle-class nightmares, and straight from there, or should I say down from there, to TV sitcoms. And what could be more up-to-date than his characters' almost feral obsession with money?

When Michael Kahn sent me *Légataire* to look at for possible adaptation for the Shakespeare Theatre, I had never heard of Regnard. Yet, just as when Michael had sent me Corneille's *Le menteur* two years previously (which became *The Liar*, which became Michael's priceless production of last season, which turned out to be the most fun I ever had working on any play) I needed only a single reading to know I had to take on the piece. The off-color jokes made me howl even while I marveled at Regnard's facility at rendering them in such graceful couplets.

How to bring the play into English? I took it as my job, while pruning some of his more extravagant asides, to mirror Regnard's restless inventiveness and tumbling action. As with *The Liar*, I took my liberties. Among other things, I beefed up Isabelle and Madame Argante, both of whom disappear in the original for the bulk of the play. Geronte held such delicious comic possibilities I probably almost doubled his part. I extended the Geronte-versus-Eraste marriage complication and embellished the impersonations that are the play's set pieces. Finally I attempted a more satisfying ending, since the original—like many French plays of that period—simply stops, abruptly, just when we expect a final cascade of unravelings and recognitions.

Working with (I won't say "on") Regnard has been a delight, for he's been, as he was in life, the best of company. As Lady Mary Wortley Montagu said of Henry Fielding: "It is a pity he was not immortal, he was so formed for happiness." Wouldn't it be wonderful if Regnard could be raised from his tomb—not to be a plaything this time, but to take his rightful place in the English-speaking theatre as a natural master of comedy, for gaiety ran in his veins as his birthright.

"*Les gens d'esprit n'ont point besoin de précepteur*," says Crispin in a line I didn't include. "True wits don't need a tutor."

Regnard Resurgent
by Drew Lichtenberg

Why is Jean-François Regnard (1655-1709), so popular in his own time, so obscure to modern audiences? Widely recognized in Paris as the first comic master since Molière, Regnard died at the peak of his powers, after a night of heavy drinking, perhaps celebrating the runaway success of his final play and masterpiece, *Le Légataire Universel* (1708, translated by David Ives as *The Heir Apparent*). Why was he forgotten?

Perhaps it has to do with the profound shift in taste and culture over the course of the 18th century. France, no longer a global hegemon, was knocked off her perch as cultural arbiter of Europe, and confectionary comedies of Regnard's stripe came to seem decadent, immoral if not obscene. They were self-consciously artificial, reveling in theatricality. They employed sudden and improbable reversals, flouting the rules of *vraisemblance*. Most damningly, they were peopled with characters designed (horror of horrors!) to elicit laughter rather than sympathy. To Enlightenment thinkers such as Diderot, Lessing and Voltaire, Regnard's work embodied the style of a previous generation.

In other words, Regnard evoked the social world of the Bourbon kings, not the Sans-Culottes. In his Preface to *The Marriage of Figaro* (1778), Beaumarchais epitomized an age of moral sentiment when he noted, "if Regnard had named his *Légataire*, *La Punition du celibate* (*The Punishment of Celibacy*), the piece would have thrilled us." Whereas Regnard finds the miserly Geronte to be a figure of fun, Beaumarchais can only see a life squandered. Instead of arriving at the morally didactic (and gruesome) punishments of the French Revolution, Regnard keeps things light by constructing an emotionally satisfying payoff.

If we look at what was actually onstage, however, Regnard never went out of style. His plays were acted in theatres of distinction across the continent right up to the age of Revolution. They were adapted into English by David Garrick's company at the Drury Lane. They were included in the Weimar repertory of Mr. Germany himself, Johann Wolfgang von Goethe. (Lessing actually began his playwriting career with 1748's *Der Spieler*, a rhymed verse translation of Regnard's *Le Joueur*.)

Today, *Le Légataire Universel* is a chestnut of the French repertory, having been performed at the Comédie Française over 1,000 times, and the penultimate "Crispin's will" scene is regarded as one of the great comic set-pieces in all of French drama. But Regnard remains obscure to modern American modern audiences, a victim of historical circumstance and the winds of taste. The fact that this play, his valedictory masterpiece, is similarly unknown is all the more reason for its rediscovery as one of the world's most beloved comedies.

Ever since Aristotle and Horace, theoreticians have been concerned with comedy's uncomfortable ability to bring us close to vice, to make us have fun at bad behavior. Many great thinkers still rail against comedy, ranking it below tragedy because of its capacity for licentiousness. When looking back at history, we tend to take the long view, elevating "serious" art and demoting the merely silly, the fun, the frivolous, the entertaining.

We still have these biases today. In modern times: Paul McCartney, the singer of "sappy love songs" is often underrated in comparison to John Lennon, the angry young man; Charlie Chaplin is seen as less transgressive than his contemporaries the Marx Brothers; Raymond Chandler's postwar novels are filled with just as much humor and existential dread as those of Nabokov, but you will not find them side-by-side on many college syllabi.

Perhaps this is the way it will always be. Form will always lose out to content, plays with profound "meaning" will always get the historical leg up on plays that are simply, sublimely entertaining. Like McCartney, like Chaplin, Regnard had no patience for history. He was an entertainer who wrote entertaining plays. Anyone who has worked in the theatre knows how fiendishly difficult this is, to engineer a maximal amount of entertainment within a minimal amount of space and time. And anyone reading or seeing this play can sense how profoundly this play still "means," to today's audiences as well as in 1708.

In David Ives's brand new "transladaptation," Regnard has met his match. For Ives does not simply translate the play, brilliantly and wittily. He also unearths the acute social anxieties animating Paris in the early 1700s. *The Heir Apparent*, it turns out, dramatizes a theme of excruciating relevance to the period's *haute bourgeoisie*. Indeed, tensions over inheritance, primogeniture and France's engrained class system would boil over in the revolutionary currents of Beaumarchais' time. But Regnard solves this social problem cathartically, through art, through a miracle of the theatre. His ingenious solution lends the play its farcical fascination, but to say any more would be spoiling.

Beaumarchais was wrong about the title of this play needing to be rewritten. There is perhaps no other comedy in the French canon that speaks so universally, so simply, and so elegantly across the ages. We are all Regnard's heirs.

About Jean-François Regnard

Aristotle writes that comic characters are "meaner" and "uglier" than the average man, "though not altogether vicious." Aristotle is writing, in fact, about morality, which he considered part of a character's cosmetic appeal. Comic characters are more immoral than you or I, but not hatefully so. In comedy, Aristotle seems to be saying, it all comes down to viciousness, i.e. vice.

There is perhaps no French playwright more associated with vice—both in his life and in his work—than Jean-François Regnard. His eight great verse comedies, written a few decades after the death of Moliere in 1673, all feature heroes indulging in vice to a gleeful degree, suggesting a French corollary to the rakes and fops of the contemporary Restoration Drama in England. Titles such as *The Gamester* (1696) and *The Distracted Husband* (1697) illustrate Regnard's central interest and strategy.

Unsurprisingly, Regnard himself was meaner than the average man, although not altogether vicious. A lifelong gambler who squandered away his large inheritance, Regnard spent his twenties traveling, playing cards and partying. In 1678, after a voyage to Italy, he was captured onboard a British frigate by pirates and sold into slavery in Algiers before being ransomed back to the French consulate. In 1681, Regnard traveled across Scandinavia. The publication of his travel diary, featuring scandalous accounts of the Laplanders, introduced much of continental Europe to Finland.

After returning to Paris, Regnard tried his hand at playwriting. From 1688 to 1696, he wrote a series of racy (some would say obscene) one-act sketches for the Italian troupe at the Hôtel de Bourgogne. In 1696, he made his first attempts at verse, launching a brief but meteoric career at the Comédie Française. In 1709, at the height of his powers and popularity, Regnard died unexpectedly, "of indigestion," in his country *chateau*. Some suspected foul play, as Regnard's tendency to lift plots and jokes from others had made him many enemies in the theatrical community. It's more likely, however, that his dissipated lifestyle was to blame.

Despite his libertine biography, Regnard was a playwright of virtuosic skill and intelligent craft. His work is not remarkable for the originality of plotting (much of it plagiarized from Moliere and others), but rather for the economical craftsmanship of his storytelling and the remarkable ingenuity of his language. Regnard's plays are "ballets of words" in which the speaking characters suspend stage reality. They abound in complex rhetorical devices—rapid-fire exchanges, internal rhymes and rhymed refrains, passages both alliterative and assonant, hurtling along at a breakneck speed. Regnard's ping-pong way with words is echoed by the headlong pace of his plotting, which brims with clockwork reversals, roundabouts and unexpected resolutions. The overall effect of a Regnard play is one of ecstatic freedom paired with intense discipline—a fitting epitaph for a playwright who saw and appreciated so much of the world.

Like his Restoration contemporary George Farquhar, Regnard resurrected the laughing comedy of an earlier age. A gambler and a distracted man he may have been. But he was also the heir apparent of a profound and rich tradition.

This adaptation of *The Heir Apparent* was first performed by the Shakespeare Theatre Company at the Lansburgh theatre in Washington, D.C., where it opened on September 12, 2011, under the direction of Michael Kahn.

Original cast
(in order of speaking)

CRISPIN
Carson Elrod*

LISETTE
Kelly Hutchinson*

ERASTE
Andrew Veenstra*

MADAME ARGANTE
Nancy Robinette*

GERONTE
Floyd King*

ISABELLE
Meg Chambers Steele*

SCRUPLE
Clark Middleton*

* Member of Actors' Equity Association,
the Union of Professional Actors and Stage Managers

Original production team:

Director
Michael Kahn

Set Designer
Alexander Dodge

Costume Designer
Murell Horton

Lighting Designer
Philip Rosenberg

Composer
Adam Wernick

Sound Designer
Christopher Baine

Casting
Stuart Howard and Paul Hardt

Resident Casting Director
Daniel Neville-Rehbehn

Voice and Dialect Coach
Ellen O'Brien

Literary Associate
Drew Lichtenberg

Assistant Director
Jenny Lord

Stage Manager
Joseph Smelser*

Assistant Stage Manager
Benjamin Royer*

The Heir Apparent **Characters**

ERASTE, our young hero, in love with:

ISABELLE, our charming and beautiful heroine

CRISPIN, a crafty young manservant, in love with:

LISETTE, a down-to-earth maid

GERONTE, miserly old uncle to Eraste

MADAME ARGANTE, Isabelle's dowager mother

SCRUPLE, a lawyer who is very, very small

The setting is Paris, the house of Geronte. Spring, 1708.

PRONUNCIATIONS:

Crispin: kree-*SPAN*

Lisette: lee-*ZETT*

Eraste: uh-*RASST*

Argante: ahr-*GAHNT*

Geronte: zhur-*AHNT*

Eulalie: *YOO*-luh-lee

NOTE: For purposes of the verse, "Madam" without an "e" is pronounced MADD-um; when it's spelled "Madame" with an "e," it's pronounced muh-DAMM. For purposes of height and slightness, Scruple may be played by a woman.

This play is for Michael Kahn

in gratitude and admiration

and because it made him laugh.

— David Ives

ACT ONE

(Paris, 1708. The parlor in Geronte's house. A spring morning. A door at right to the rest of the house and doors up center toward a foyer. A window left with curtains and shutters. A large thronelike armchair. Some bottles and glasses filled with colored liquids. On shelves, decades of accumulated stuff. Prominent are "The Box," an ornamental chest chained to an altar-like pedestal; and a tall and odd-looking clock.)

(The clock whirrs and chimes with a strange, agitated farting sound. LISETTE ENTERS from right and throws open the curtains and shutters.)

CRISPIN (O.S.)
Lisette...?
(HE ENTERS from center, breathless.)
Lisette...!

LISETTE
What's up, Crispin?

CRISPIN
(embracing her)
My energizer!

LISETTE
Well, well. Since when are you an early riser?

CRISPIN
Since working for the nephew to your miser.
And there is hell to pay today, my pet.
The old man hasn't kicked the bucket yet...?
Geronte's alive? Please say he isn't dead!

LISETTE
If you can call it life, he's out of bed.
So yes, alive and hoarding breaths like francs.

CRISPIN
I know I never pray, but—God? My thanks!

LISETTE
Well, God nor gold will help the old man thrive.
I thought last night would be his last alive.
Twenty-two times he fell into a swoon
And lay as limply as a pitted prune.
He only lived thanks to these brews I craft.

CRISPIN
(picks up one of the bottles)
Your über-laxative? That healing draft?

LISETTE
I irrigated him both fore and aft.
He popped up blinking, did a quick pavane,
And hopped a polka to the closest john.

CRISPIN
Ironic talent, making dead men dance.

LISETTE
I'm high colonic mistress of all France.
But what's this interest in the old man's health?

CRISPIN
My master's urgent need for all his wealth.
The gold is safe?

LISETTE
(indicating the The Box)
    Locked in its air-tight chest.

CRISPIN
With luck, my master's well-deserved bequest.

LISETTE
Dream on, Crispin. With nephews thick as flies?
Who each would rob, maim, kill or pulverize
To get your master's piece of the estate?

CRISPIN
Yeah, but Eraste's this money's proper mate!
And not just 'cuz he's up to here in bills.
There's now *Madame Argante*.

LISETTE
    I'm getting chills.

CRISPIN
Two years he's pledged in stealth to Isabelle?
Last night Eraste decides it's time to tell.
What happens but her dragon-headed Mom,
The dread Madame Argante, explodes *this* bomb:
Unless Eraste is named Geronte's lone heir,
I mean *sole solitary single* heir,
Isabelle's history and Eraste can rot.
How'll you and I afford to tie the knot?
How'll we run off to sunny Mandalay?

LISETTE
Then say some prayers. He makes his will *today*.
And would you like to hear how deep's his greed?
To save on writing up this crucial deed
He hired a lawyer no taller than a creeper
As if—because he's short?—he might come cheaper.
But wait a sec... She's here!

CRISPIN
Madame Argante?

LISETTE
Since sunrise she's been holed up with Geronte.
They locked the door and blocked it with a chair
But just "by chance" I *did* hear...

CRISPIN
Yes?

LISETTE
"Sole heir."
Plus lots of talk of wills and deeds and money—
With Isabelle's name, neck-and-neck.

CRISPIN
Oh, *honey!*
You don't know what that means? Farewell to dread!
They're raining money on my master's head!

(ERASTE ENTERS from center. A NOOSE hangs around his neck.)

ERASTE
My friends—no, please don't try to cheer me up.
All night I drank of sorrow's weary cup,
Tempted by poison, gunshot and the rope.
(Shows the noose's label.)
The cheapest noose they had. The brand-name? *"Hope."*

CRISPIN
Roll up your clothesline, sir. Prepare to marry.
Madame Argante's in there.

ERASTE
So?

CRISPIN
Cash and carry!
Why would your uncle hang with such a pill
Unless to craft a wedding-deed-slash-will?

ERASTE
You mean I'll get to marry Isabella?

CRISPIN
(removing the noose)
Today you're Paris's most happy fella!

ERASTE
So we'll be one?! [Gives out a celebratory howl.]

CRISPIN
Yeah, hey, the wedding's bliss,
But—Isabelle aside?—you'll have all *this*.
And stocks...and bonds...

ERASTE
...and gold...

CRISPIN
...the plate, the crest...

ERASTE
That ugly clock, this ornamental chest...
He'll settle all on me?

CRISPIN
You wanna bet?

ERASTE
(collapsing into Crispin's arms)
Crispin, my heart!

CRISPIN
Hang on. You can't die yet.
Wait till you're solvent, in a gold pavilion.

LISETTE
Riding through Paris on a silver pillion.

ERASTE
Why not? The old man's worth *an easy MILLION!*

ALL THREE
A million! A million! A million!

ERASTE
Thank God! Since each day's mail brings some new threat.
(Takes out some LETTERS.)
"Monsieur, I'll throw you into jail for debt."

Or this: "Your date with the Bastille is nigh."
But uncle's will could put them off me. Why?

ALL THREE

A million! A million! A million!

ERASTE

But wait. What if this whole deal comes unsprung?
Some hitch, some cog, some tiny cam, or camlet?
You know my uncle. What if...

CRISPIN

          Hey. *Prince Hamlet*.
The Battleaxe is in there on your side.
You got a Cadillac to smooth your ride.

(MADAME ARGANTE ENTERS from right, unnoticed by ERASTE.)

ERASTE

You're right. He hasn't got a snowball's chance.
She'll turn him into stone with one chill glance!
This *is* the basilisk, Madame Argante!
She whom the Prince of Darkness couldn't daunt.
She next to whom a rock looks nonchalant.
Who makes Godzilla seem a mad bacchante.
To whom Attila is a dilettante.
She who...

MADAME ARGANTE

    Monsieur Eraste.

ERASTE

        Madame Argante.

MADAME ARGANTE

I know what you want. Words that might unmuddy
What I've been up to in your uncle's study,
An explication of our *tête-à-tête*.
You love my daughter, don't you? Better yet,
You crave at any cost her satisfaction?

ERASTE

Oh, madam, I would brave Ulysses' action!
To win her bliss I'd ape Achilles' test!
Great Vulcan's flame...

MADAME ARGANTE

         Sir, lay this noise to rest
And more important don't intone to me
Names each of which is quite unknown to me.

Your friend Ulysses visits which salon?
This Vulcan's not in *my* arrondissement.

ERASTE

The only purpose of my earthly zeal
Is this: to broker an unearthly deal
And see my Isabelle to holy marriage.
All worldly riches I hereby disparage!
What are they to the treasures in her look?

MADAME ARGANTE

Such ardor is so precious—in a book.
Yes, knights and mincing ladies, lovers true,
Phloxes and chocolate boxes... I could spew.
No matter. I just framed in there a pact
Which leaves your every lavish dream intact
And renders you my Isabella's savior.
Don't thank me, please. You know I loathe *behavior*.

ERASTE

But how much...?

MADAME ARGANTE

    As I loathe being stopped when speaking.
You note this love'y wedding deed?
(Produces a paper.)
          No peeking.
Regarding love and marriage, pounds and pence
There is an art to building up suspense.
I will say this: the stocks, the bonds...

ERASTE

    The ancient crest...?

MADAME ARGANTE

That ugly clock, this ornamental chest...

ERASTE

They're all included?

MADAME ARGANTE

    In a clean account
Climaxing here [*a spot in the document she keeps close*]
in an obscene amount
Set off in its own box, in bright vermillion.
I won't say what it is.

ERASTE

    A mill...?

MADAME ARGANTE
A million.
I'm off to her and, if you don't refuse,
I'll bring Belle back to celebrate the news.

ERASTE
Refuse, madame...?

MADAME ARGANTE
Fine, fine. Just please don't *babble*.

LISETTE
This way.

MADAME ARGANTE
I'll see myself out, thank you— *Rabble!*

(MADAME ARGANTE EXITS center.)

CRISPIN, ERASTE, LISETTE
A million! A million! A million!

LISETTE
Congratulations, sir, from social scum!

ERASTE
Bless you, Lisette.

CRISPIN
I hope you'll fling a crumb
The *rabble's* way when once you're in your palace.

ERASTE
Crispin, I'll be a font. A brimming chalice.
A bottle ever tipped to pour a toast.
I'll pass out lucre like a priest the Host!

CRISPIN
You'll front me dough so I can wed my crony?

ERASTE
And rent the Pope to head the ceremony.

LISETTE
Perhaps I could be maid to your fair dame?

ERASTE
And paid in pearls. But have I lost all shame?
While sniffing francs like some fine muscatel

I utterly forgot my Isabelle!
Who glows with rays bright Aphrodite speckles!

CRISPIN
And who you'll lose if you don't get these shekels.
'Cause don't forget, you still don't own the till.
Not till your uncle writes and signs a will.
So keep him stoked. A hundred things could screw this.

LISETTE
A lawyer's on his way here to pursue this
And since he's late, Crispin, go fetch him, pronto.

CRISPIN
Aye, aye, commander.
(To ERASTE, hand raised Indian-style:)
    Kemo sabe!

ERASTE
(ditto)
    Tonto!

CRISPIN
Wait, where's this lawyer, what's his name again?

LISETTE
You cannot miss the guy. He's two-foot ten.
Around the corner, by the name of Scruple.

CRISPIN
How droll. A lawyer no bigger than a loophole.
I'm gone!

(CRISPIN EXITS center.)

LISETTE
    He's right, sir. Till this will is signed
You have to keep your uncle's mind inclined.
What with his moods, we don't want some kerfuffle.

ERASTE
Today my uncle's fur shall go unruffled.
My sole intent will be to acquiesce,
My every syllable some form of *"yes."*

LISETTE
I hope it works.

GERONTE (O.S.)
Lisette!

LISETTE
He's coming, sir. God bless.

(GERONTE ENTERS from right in a shabby nightshirt and robe, leaning on a cane, hacking and coughing. He wears a tight cap with fur ear-flaps.)

GERONTE
Good morning, nephew.

ERASTE
Uncle—*absolutely!*

GERONTE
I beg your pardon?

ERASTE
Yes! As you astutely
Proclaimed: "*Good morning!*" So we're in accord!
What better good can any morn afford
Than greeting you, my luminary *unc?*
A model for us all! What spark! What spunk!
So full of...

LISETTE
Mucus?

ERASTE
...life.

GERONTE
What are you—drunk?

ERASTE
Yes. No! Oh, please, not there, sir. This is cozier. [*Leading him to the chair.*]

GERONTE
Don't touch me.

ERASTE
There. I've never seen you rosier.

GERONTE
No?

ERASTE
No. Yes! I detect distinct improvement.

GERONTE
Then you can thank the twenty stinking movements
Induced by *her* to keep me from my grave.
A stream of ordure black enough to pave
A road from Paris to the far Crimea.

ERASTE
But otherwise, how...

GERONTE
Diarrhea! Diarrhea!

ERASTE
But...

GERONTE
Diarrhea! Say it.

ERASTE
Diarrhea...

GERONTE
Diarrhea! After that, I should be proud?
Another night like that, just buy my shroud.
A *cheap* one. Nothing gaudy. Nothing sunny.

ERASTE
How are you now?

GERONTE
Who cares? How is my *money*?
Lisette!

LISETTE
Monsieur?

GERONTE
Investigate *The Box!*

LISETTE
The Box is chained up fast.

GERONTE
The Box's locks?

LISETTE
Secure, monsieur.

GERONTE
Now bring *The Box* to me!

LISETTE
For that, Lord Paranoid, I'll need *The Key*.

(He takes out a KEY fastened to an endless string around his neck. She takes it and, trailing line across the room, frees the moneybox.)

GERONTE
For gold I deem no safeguard too extreme.
But this reminds me... Yes! I had a dream!
For taking flight last night on wings I flew
Up from my bed and over Paris, through
The air where cloudlets dangled, draped in swags—
Plump, saffron clouds all shaped like moneybags!
Beyond the sun, a glittering louis d'or,
I reached the stars, a spray of silver ore
Strewn on the jeweler's velvet of the skies!
But then I knew I'd gone to paradise.
For lo! A road before me, lined with banks
Where I was reunited with...

ERASTE
Your wife?

GERONTE
My francs.
(Lisette hands him The Box and he hugs it.)
My first centime! Oh, happy, trusty chest!

(Gives LISETTE back The Box, who re-secures it while he hacks and coughs.)

ERASTE
But sir, these ills of yours must be addressed!

GERONTE
You mean buy pills? And pile up bills from docs?
Don't you know what's important, boy?

ERASTE
The Box?

GERONTE
The Box!
Some quack should charge ten sous to stoke my gut?
Two francs to poke a plunger up my butt?
It's criminal! Extortion past endurance!
Of course if we had national health insurance...
But this is seventeen-oh-what?

ERASTE
Oh-eight.

GERONTE
I wouldn't pay for it at any rate!
I'd rather bid the Reaper come and visit—
And if he had a ring I'd kneel and kiss it!

ERASTE
And so would I!
(With a cry, GERONTE slumps over the arm of his chair, still.)
        But—uncle? Sir? What is it?
Lisette, what is this? One of his attacks?

LISETTE
It *was* one.

ERASTE
        So he's dead?

LISETTE
        Relax. Relax.

GERONTE
(sitting back up)
I thought I saw a coin between those cracks.
But boy, you greet me on a special day.
Where is this lawyer? Lisette?

(CRISPIN has entered during this.)

LISETTE
        Crispin?

CRISPIN
            He's on his way.

ERASTE
("innocent")
But why do you need a lawyer?

GERONTE
        To write my will.

ERASTE
Oh, sir, don't even say the word! A chill
Runs through me at the sound. The thought's appalling!
"Testament." "Legacy." Each word recalling
The passing of the dearest man alive.

GERONTE
Who?

ERASTE
You. Whose death I doubt I could survive.

GERONTE
I feel the same, but we're both sentimental.

ERASTE
Of course, a will is good, it's fundamental.

GERONTE
Yes—given the sharks who're circling me like chum.

ERASTE
You don't mean...?

GERONTE
Fortune-hunters!

ERASTE
Sir, I'm *dumb*!
There're parasites who're chasing for your gold?
Your stocks, your bonds, the real estate you hold,
Your tapestries, your plate, your ancient crest,
That ugly clock, this ornamental chest...?

GERONTE
Have you had all my property assessed?

ERASTE
Yes. No! But when you pen your final sentiments
Let not my love for you be an impediment
To anything you plan to leave, or settle.
My feelings for you need no precious metal.

GERONTE
You're good to me, my boy. You're...

ERASTE
Heaven-sent?

GERONTE
And since you're here, I'll tell you my intent.
I'm going to name one individual
Who'll get it all. The full residual.

ERASTE
One person, uncle? I don't mean to quiz...

GERONTE
Oh, I know who that special person is.

(Taking Eraste's hand;)
One close to me, with power to love and please.
That person I shall leave, for life, at ease—
With francs that dance a solid gold cotillion!
Do you know what I'm worth?

ERASTE, CRISPIN, LISETTE
A mill...?

GERONTE
A million.
Think that's enough to fund a happy life?
A sum sufficient to support...*a wife?*

ERASTE
(kissing Geronte's hand)
I love you, sir. I love you! That's my story.
I don't ask much. A small memento mori.
Just ten centimes, to think on you and hold—
A souvenir of you, to thwart the cold.

GERONTE
You disagree?

ERASTE
No!

GERONTE
Find my plan too dire?

ERASTE
Of course, you have to do as you desire.
The larger family, though, might feel some ire...

GERONTE
They wish me nothing and I'll parrot them.
I'll leave them zip! I'll disinherit them!

ERASTE
Oh, sir, you have to leave them *something*. Do!
It's simple human charity.

GERONTE
Not a sou!
These money-sniffing dogs, all preened and oiled,
What better pleasure than to see them foiled?
To see it, I'd float down off my heavenly cloud.

LISETTE
Unless you're roasting with a toastier crowd.
(KNOCKING, OFF.)

GERONTE
Ah, there's Madame Argante and her coquette.
Let them in. First, though, my best wig, Lisette.

LISETTE
"Best wig," monsieur? That thing's more like a pet.
God knows what animals hooked up to breed it.
You shouldn't put it on, sir. You should feed it.

GERONTE
I'll wear my hair no matter how you jig—
And swear I'll wear it, missy, in my wig.

LISETTE
Well, I'll swear, too, and it's no perjury:
What *you* need's drastic plastic surgery.

ERASTE
Enough, Lisette. You're torturing the man.

GERONTE
I'll fetch my wig myself.

LISETTE
              It's in the can,
Next to your girlie mags.

GERONTE
              You're venomous!
And not one word to them about my enemas!

(GERONTE EXITS right.)

ALL THREE
A million...! A million...! A million...!

(LISETTE EXITS center to answer the front door.)

ERASTE
The virtues of agreeability!
Forget to-be-or-not-to-be-ity.
Suck up! Eat crow! That's all one has to do.

CRISPIN
To thine own pocket. Sorry. *Self* be true.

ERASTE
Now where's this lawyer?

CRISPIN
He'll be here any sec.
Or rather—*shortly*, since the man's a speck.

(ISABELLE runs in from center, embracing ERASTE.)

ISABELLE
Darling!

ERASTE
Oh, Isabelle!

ISABELLE
So how's it *going*?
What do you think our chances are?

ERASTE
They're glowing!
My uncle's like some madcap, lavish aunt.

ISABELLE
We'll get enough to wed?

ERASTE
Enough to flaunt!
He's going to leave it all... Madame Argante.

(MADAME ARGANTE has entered from center with LISETTE.)

MADAME ARGANTE
Good day again, Monsieur Eraste... [*Noting CRISPIN.*] ...and so on.

ERASTE
A joyful day, by what I have to go on.

MADAME ARGANTE
Yet sad, the settling of a patrimony.
And then to think of adding matrimony!

ERASTE
How could a marriage our gladsome spirits douse?

MADAME ARGANTE
You wouldn't say that if you'd known my spouse.
That pillar of the church, that foe of whoredom,
That undisputed lord of bedroom boredom.
(ERASTE and ISABELLA clinch and kiss.)
STOP THAT.

(GERONTE RE-ENTERS in a fluffy wig with his earflapped cap over it.)

GERONTE
Madame Argante, forgive my tardiness.
My maid's too-typical fool-hardiness
Arrested me in grooming for our chat.

LISETTE
Monsieur, there's something nesting in your hat.

GERONTE
Welcome, Georgina, to my humble cell.

ISABELLE
If you mean me, sir, my name's Isabelle.
I understand you passed a doubtful night?

GERONTE
Mere gossip, mademoiselle, from ghouls who'd fright
Me prematurely to my grave to rot.
I *did* make twenty visits to *The Pot*.
A stream of ordure…

ERASTE
Uncle? Bad idea.

GERONTE
You're right. It's wrong to mention diarrhea.
A stream of ordure 's hardly social grist.

LISETTE
And enemas are strictly off the list.

GERONTE
They are! We will not enter that morass.
As for my piles…

ERASTE
I think we'll let that pass.
Where were we in our beatific meeting?

GERONTE
Just don't believe the lying, thieving, cheating
Hucksters who'd have you think me at [*cough, spit*] death's door.

ISABELLE
You, sir? Life's living, breathing metaphor?

GERONTE
That's what I am! No thanks to those piranha
Who'd grab my gold through drams of belladonna.

ERASTE
But, uncle, no one here wants to deprive you.
And see, you've this madonna to revive you!
One glance from whom is like a waking kiss.

GERONTE
I've noticed how you gaze on this young Miss.
Ahhh, pungent funk of feminine attraction!
The girl's beguiling, is she?

ERASTE
                      To distraction.
Praising her wildly would comprise detraction.

GERONTE
She has the stuff to bless a husband's house?

ERASTE
With every virtue of a perfect spouse.
Beauty to burn. Unmatched intelligence.
An ideal fit of wit and elegance.

GERONTE
She's young.

ERASTE
           Her age presents no barrier.

GERONTE
Who wouldn't grasp this lass?

ERASTE
                    And like a terrier.

GERONTE
One needs substantial means to carry her.

ERASTE
She's like the Nile. She's rich without a source!
She's fire and light! An elemental force!
Yet strong as oak. No wind or change can vary her.
I love her!

GERONTE
      Good. I'm going to marry her.

ERASTE, ISABELLE, CRISPIN, LISETTE
You *what?!*

GERONTE
I said I'm going to marry her.
At three o'clock this afternoon. [*To ISABELLE:*] My saint!

ISABELLE
If you'll excuse me, all, I'm going to faint.
(She does so, into Eraste's arms.)

GERONTE
Poor girl. No doubt the rapture was too strong.

ISABELLE
(waking immediately)
I fainted, sir, because this plan is *wrong*.
We—*wed*?

GERONTE
Today at three.

ISABELLE
You've lost a screw!

GERONTE
Yes, I agree. Let's move it up to two.
Oh, kitten...!

ISABELLE
Kitten?

GERONTE
See how like two pills
Your brilliant eyes have remedied my ills,
Your smoothing curves my soothing anesthetic!

ISABELLE
My body, sir, is not your paramedic.

GERONTE
You're my elixir! Promising a cure
Stronger than Bromo Seltzer—and more sure.
I have no doubt, thanks to your healing syrups
I'll soon be back inside the manly stirrups,
Erect upon the saddle, hot to trot,
And in nine months we'll see a screaming tot.
My features, naturally. Mouth, lyrical...

LISETTE
This babe would also be a miracle.
For pardon, sir, but you, who're plugged with phlegm,
Whose every cough proclaims a requiem,
With stones to pass, a bloated spleen, a limp,

With gas enough to float a German blimp,
You who're asthmatic, rheumatic, and myopic,
Smegmatic, aspermatic, misanthropic,
Sclerotic, cirrhotic, phlebotic,
Thrombotic, neurotic, necrotic,
You'd put on gloves and spats and play the groom
Who need but one small leap to reach the tomb?

GERONTE
I gather that you somehow disapprove?

LISETTE
Your bowels are the only parts that move!

GERONTE
I let her fling these barbs designed to slay me.

LISETTE
Yeah, free speech being the only thing you *pay* me.
Monsieur, if Satan's tempted you to wed
Pick someone apropos—like someone *dead*.
Leave her a guy who doesn't buy his hair.
About this tall, brown eyes, quite debonair,
A hundred fifty pounds and tightly assed—
Someone remarkably like young Eraste.

GERONTE
Eraste?

LISETTE
    Eraste.

GERONTE
       What's he to my Georgina?
I know my needs.

LISETTE
A bowl of hot farina?

GERONTE
A second self! A mate! That's what will mend me.
A nurse who day-in day-out can attend me.
An aide-de-camp who'll damp my tiniest sneeze,
Empty my slops and rid my shorts of fleas,
Twenty-four-seven she'll be on her knees,
Succoring me.

ISABELLE, ERASTE, LISETTE, CRISPIN
WHAT?

GERONTE
Succoring, I said.
But showing her zeal, too, in the master bed.
Why leave my gold to some finagling ferret
When I've a wife to dangle such a carrot
In front of? She who'd gladly bear the brunt of
My little moods and piddling peccadilloes,
Whose arms will wrap me like two weeping willows,
Whose hands will keep my household spic-and-span.
Who'll be all things unto a needy man!

LISETTE
Yeah—hooker, housemaid and prescription plan.

ERASTE
My uncle's right.

ISABELLE
He's what?

ERASTE
He's an *adult*.

LISETTE
I'll say.

ERASTE
Who're we to jib and not exult?
Yes! I say let him marry whom he please!
Perhaps *Madame Argante*, though, disagrees...?

MADAME ARGANTE
I? Not at all. I find this prospect thrilling.

ERASTE
There's not *another beau*, who's right and willing?

MADAME ARGANTE
No.

ERASTE
One who loves her?

MADAME ARGANTE
No.

ERASTE
Who'd kneel in thanks?

MADAME ARGANTE
No beau I know who has a million francs.

ERASTE
You asked one if he craved her satisfaction.

MADAME ARGANTE
And now she gets it! Why? Does this transaction
Distress you somehow? Give you cause for pain?
What other suitors lose is Bella's gain.
True, gold's no substitute for love's rich spread,
But where's the sandwich when there ain't no bread?

ERASTE
But sir, you said you'd name a legatee
Who loves you.

GERONTE
           As Georgina here loves *me*!
Why? Do you somehow blanch at my design?

ERASTE
No! Sir, your plan's infernal, it's so fine!
You want to marry? Why should *I* feel sorry?

GERONTE
I'm going to leave you that memento mori.
You know—your sentimental souvenir?
Indeed, I'll leave you ten centimes *a year!*
So there, Madame Argante. We've done our task.

ISABELLE
May I say something? I, who wasn't asked
About the fitness of this wedding plot?
Remember me? "Georgina"? Who I'm *not*?
I, the sad puck in Mamma's game of hockey?
The lucky slave who'll fumigate your jockeys,
The blot put here on earth to dab your nose,
Affix your dickey, mend your flealess clothes,
To sport with you with "*zeal*," not grin and bear it,
The succorer of any dangled carrot?
And let me get this straight: as for your gold
It only comes with *you*, to have and hold?
I have to buy this show or have to hike it?
Must swig your Kool-Aid any way you spike it?
Must sing your song no matter how you mike it?
Is that your quid pro quo?

GERONTE
           I knew you'd like it.

LISETTE
Monsieur Eraste, speak for this mademoiselle!

ERASTE

I still say uncle's right.

LISETTE

                He's booked for *hell!*
He's seventy! He's dull! He's asinine!

GERONTE

Excuse me, please. I'm only 69!

ISABELLE

So you advise me to go through with this?

ERASTE

I urge you to, and wish you every bliss.
Think of liquidity. Think of expedience.
Dismiss your id. Think filial obedience.

GERONTE

Exactly.

ERASTE

          Swallow personal disgust.
So what if, when he urinates, it's dust?

GERONTE

That happens.

ERASTE

                So what, his every ailment?

GERONTE

(long sheet of paper)
I've got a list of them, for your regalement.

ERASTE

Or if he's to his hips in River Styx?

GERONTE

It's nothing that a trip to Lourdes can't fix.

ERASTE

The die is cast! It's destiny! It's fate!
Behold your perfect, predetermined mate!

ISABELLE

Well, sir. You're eloquent as this man's shill.
You think that I should marry him? *I will!*

GERONTE

I knew she would.

ISABELLE
                        I'll brave those wedding choirs
If they must pry "I do" from me with pliers!

MADAME ARGANTE
See there? Give her a task, she'll never shirk.

GERONTE
But I sense Mother Nature hard at work.
Digestive tract, you know. I'm off to stool!

(GERONTE EXITS right.)

LISETTE
Behold the bottom of the dating pool.
And sir, you'd leave your filly to this fool?

MADAME ARGANTE
Come, daughter.

ERASTE
                   No, madame, with all due deference,
Did you not swear to me I'd be your preference?
Did you not promise me your daughter's hand?

MADAME ARGANTE
Provided *you* provided gold and land.
Is it my fault your spending powers are spent?
That you're one of the Ninety-Nine Percent?
Rejoice! The gold and land are Isabella's!

ERASTE
By wedding *him?*

MADAME ARGANTE
                  So call me overzealous.
That happens, acting on one's children's part.
I'm really just a soccer mom, at heart.

ERASTE
You'll do this, mademoiselle, you'll be his toy?

ISABELLE
I am amazed, monsieur, my fount of joy
By you of all the world should come in question.
Did you not bid me disregard digestion
And swallow giving *succor* to Geronte?
Filial obedience? Was that not your taunt?

ERASTE
You missed how, on the inside, I was winking?

ISABELLE

Your inner tic escaped me. I was blinking—
Thanks to some prickly tears that blocked my view.
Well, I have a trousseau to buy. Adieu!

(ISABELLE EXITS center.)

ERASTE

Madame Argante—what if I changed his mind?
Produced a will that named *me*, underlined,
Sole heir to all my uncle is possessed of?
Would you accept that as a fitting test of
My worthiness to have your daughter's hand?
Give me one day. One hour. One grain of sand
Trickling into an hourglass and I'll do it.

MADAME ARGANTE

You have till two o'clock. But if I rue it,
This rash and most untypical compassion,
You will have fucked yourself in royal fashion.
(MADAME ARGANTE EXITS.)

ERASTE

Okay, I'm ready. I'm fired up. I'm *scorchin'!*
But, Christ! How can I pull this off? Cruel Fortune
Wants me a gerbil puffing on its wheel.
Fortune—which kicks its gate and turns its heel,
Slamming the door on opportunity.

CRISPIN

So slam it back, and with impunity!
Don't give me Fortune's wheel and Fortune's gates—
It's with our wits that we create our fates.
So *va fungoo* the Unforeseeable!
And hey, nice job there, bein' agreeable.

ERASTE

Some drops of oil to grease a squeaky strut!

CRISPIN

There's lubrication, sir, and kissing butt.

ERASTE

You're right, Crispin. To truckle is to suck.

LISETTE

He's coming back.

CRISPIN

Be firm.

ERASTE
I will.

LISETTE
Good luck.

(GERONTE RE-ENTERS. During the following, ERASTE "firms up" and seethes, working up his anger.)

GERONTE
Well, that was certainly inopportune,
All to eject one small black macaroon.

LISETTE
Thank you for that.

GERONTE
My guests, they showed no pique?

LISETTE
No, you might say they turned the *other* cheek.
I have to tell you, not to be a smarty,
That was one hell of an engagement party.

GERONTE
A party! Yes—that puts in mind, Lisette,
We'll need some kind of festive marriage fete.
But nothing too expensive. Nothing gaudy.

LISETTE
An undertaker, to collect the body?

GERONTE
Musicians—half a score or so, or nine.
Or six, or three. A soloist is fine.
What player comes cheap who's worthy of my wife?

LISETTE
A flatulist who blows a penny fife?

GERONTE
Good, good. And food. But simple, off the cuff.

LISETTE
A bean sucked off our sleeve, is that enough?

GERONTE
I'll pay one franc. Anything more is thieving.

LISETTE

Great. Where's the franc?

(GERONTE takes out a purse, take a purse out of the purse, takes a purse of out that purse, and tries to pry a coin out of its depths.)

GERONTE

Right here. Right here. Right here…

[*Weeps.*]

LISETTE

Monsieur, stop *grieving*!

ERASTE

No! I say it's absurd! It's creepy! Sick!

GERONTE

I beg your pardon?

ERASTE

What a filthy trick!

GERONTE

You seem upset.

ERASTE

Oh, DO I?

GERONTE

With what cause?

ERASTE

The way you'd flout both God's and Nature's laws
By wedding while you're in the Reaper's jaws!
And then to think of generating tots
When your machinery lacks the jigawatts?
It's ludicrous. It's humorous. It's sad.
And by a woman *whom I love*, I'd add,
And who requites me in that sentiment.
What you need, sir, 's a Final Testament.
Wed pen to paper. Copulate with ink.
Beget a will. I'll say it, I won't blink.
Will will will WILL. And under "legatee"?
A single sentence designating ME.
The race goes to the fit? I'm here for christening!
Well, uncle?

GERONTE

Sorry, lad, I wasn't listening.
About this wedding…

ERASTE
Sir, I must protest.
Do I not rate at least a small bequest?

GERONTE
Yes, that reminds me—I've two relatives
Who both need economic lenitives.

ERASTE
You mean a legacy?

GERONTE
They're of my breed.

ERASTE
You said you'd not support these buzzards' greed!
Don't you detect a huge disparity?

GERONTE
But as you say—it's simple human charity.
First, there's a nephew starving in New York,
Second, a widowed niece who married pork—
She wed the Count Cochon, pig breeder fine
Who lent a true nobility to swine.
They'll get, as members of our family's flanks,
A small memento. Twenty thousand francs.

ERASTE, LISETTE, CRISPIN
What?!

GERONTE
Twenty thousand francs.

ERASTE
All told?

GERONTE
Apiece.

ERASTE
I didn't even know you *had* a niece!

GERONTE
Nor I, until she wrote me this epistle. [*Takes out a LETTER.*]
"Dear sweetest Uncle Jerry. How I bristle
To think of you alone..."

ERASTE, LISETTE, CRISPIN
(Alone?)

GERONTE
                            "...up there and ill.
I hope that you'll include me in your will.
Love, Widow Julie." Look, a paste-on piglet
That wags its curly pig-tail when you wiggle it.
(He shows the wiggling piglet.)
Isn't that cute?

ERASTE
               So she gets twenty thou
For sticking on a picture of a sow?
And I don't get enough to buy a loin?

GERONTE
"P.S., I thought you'd like this shiny coin."
(Shows COIN and kisses it.)
Sweet Julie.

ERASTE
           Well, then, hell, I'll give you two!
And wiggle like a whole damn petting zoo!

GERONTE
Nephew, this is unkind! How can you think this?

ERASTE
How? Twenty thousand francs is how!

LISETTE
(gives GERONTE a glass)
                                Drink this.

GERONTE
I'm strewing gifts! For this I get a dig?
(He drains the contents of the glass.)

ERASTE
She sent you half a sou and Porky Pig!

GERONTE
This niece and nephew need some leverage.
So I... Lisette—Lisette, what was that beverage...?
My guts are a volcano hotting up!

LISETTE
I call that cocktail *"Drano."* Bottoms up!
(GERONTE EXITS right, fast.)
Well, now that we're alone, thanks to my brew,
What—short of turning Buddhist—do we do?

ERASTE
I tried aggressiveness, I tried détente...

CRISPIN
Try *brain power*—something lacking in Geronte.
First thing, we get back what has been bereft you
From Widow Porkfat and this New York nephew.

ERASTE
Crispin, he'll never budge. You saw him bust me.

CRISPIN
When he comes back, just keep him stalled—and trust me.
For this day is the Feast of St. Crispin!
Once more unto the breach! *I have a plan!*
(CRISPIN starts out, but comes right back. To US:)
Okay, so do we understand the plot?
The will, Madame Argante, the wedding knot?
You got all that? Good.
(To a couple in the audience:)
                    You two look confused.
Let's backtrack, just to keep us all enthused.
Do you remember how, a couple times,
(Amidst our author's brilliant, supple rhymes)
Geronte spoke of a New York nephew? Yes?
A widowed niece who's raising pigs, no less?
He wants to leave them money. Did you cop that?
Well, we three needy bastards need to stop that
And I might save us from the frying pan—
For this day is the Feast of St. Crispin!
Once more unto the breach! *I have a plan!*

(CRISPIN EXITS center as ISABELLE runs in from there and embraces ERASTE.)

ISABELLE
Oh, darling!

ERASTE
Love!

ISABELLE
Forgive me, if you can.

ERASTE
No, me.

ISABELLE
No, me.

ERASTE
No, me.

ISABELLE
No, me.

ERASTE
Enough. We have a glitch.

ISABELLE
Besides not marrying or being rich?

ERASTE
He's leaving 20,000 francs apiece
To a Yankee nephew and some fleecing niece.

ISABELLE
I'll massacre the bitch!

LISETTE
Call off your dogs.
Miss Julie's in the country, raising hogs.

ISABELLE
Can't one of us devise some brilliant plan?

LISETTE
One of us has. Resilient, wise Crispin.

ISABELLE
We're out of danger?

ERASTE
If this plan pans out.

ISABELLE
We'll need a back-up plan, to ban all doubt.
Something with all its t's crossed, all i's dotted.

ERASTE
Something ingenious...

LISETTE
Something sly...

ISABELLE
I've got it!
I've just had what the French call a *trouvaille!*
But wait a sec. I *am* French!

ERASTE
So am I!

ERASTE & ISABELLE
(abruptly in a French film)
Ah, mon amour!

ISABELLE
Je t'aime!

ERASTE
Je t'aime!

ISABELLE
La lune!

ERASTE
Le soir!

ISABELLE
Mais quoi?

ERASTE
Mais toi!

ISABELLE
Tu m'aimes?

ERASTE
Quand même!

ISABELLE
Au 'voir!

LISETTE
(sobbing.)
(So beautiful.)

(ISABELLE runs out center as GERONTE RE-ENTERS from right.)

GERONTE
That was a filthy trick on your employer.
Now where's my tardy teentsy-weentsy lawyer?

ERASTE
(improvising)
He...said...he had...some documents...to...skim...

GERONTE
Fine! He won't come to me, I'll go to him. [Starts out.]

ERASTE

No! Uncle!

GERONTE

Well? What is it? What's the matter?

ERASTE

You can't.

GERONTE

Can't what?

ERASTE

Can't visit him. An adder!
They found an adder in his attic.

GERONTE

What?!

ERASTE

A spitting cobra. Sounds dramatic, but
I saw the beast myself. As thick as this.
It had these two long fangs, and did it hiss!
You should've seen that python writhe and rankle.
It bit me, too.

GERONTE

It bit you?

ERASTE

On the ankle.
I'm feeling it, Lisette! The poison's working!

LISETTE

Don't panic, sir! Not yet!

ERASTE

See that? That jerking?

GERONTE

Help him, Lisette!

LISETTE

I can't without the...stuff...

ERASTE

The anecdote.

LISETTE

The *antidote*.

ERASTE
It's tough—
I mean, to die without a legacy...

GERONTE
Poor lad.

ERASTE
I say, *without a legacy*.

GERONTE
What's dying like?

ERASTE
Dying? It's like...Tennessee...

GERONTE
What? Tennessee?

ERASTE
("delirious")
Tennessee! Tennessee!

LISETTE
Stand back, sir. Tennessee means curtains.

GERONTE
Shocking!

ERASTE
Is that you, Mamma? Holding me and rocking?
But what's this river? What's this darkling shore?
Dear God...!
(LOUD KNOCKING, offstage. Suddenly calm:)
Is someone knocking at the door?
(LISETTE RUNS OUT center. ERASTE springs to his feet.)
I feel much better now. Just lost my poise.

GERONTE
(hears shouting offstage)
But what the devil's all that bloody noise?

(CRISPIN ENTERS from center dressed as an American backwoodsman, with a drooping moustache and carrying a blunderbuss. On his head, he wears a STUFFED DOG. LISETTE follows him in.)

CRISPIN/AMERICAN NEPHEW
Aloha from New York!

GERONTE
New York?

CRISPIN/AMERICAN NEPHEW
(ignoring GERONTE, addressing ERASTE only till noted)
Bon giorno!
Is this here Paris, home to whores 'n' porno?

GERONTE
Good God.

CRISPIN/AMERICAN NEPHEW
Jeez, I been poundin' on yer portal
Fer a month o' Sundees! Wondered if a mortal
Man, dawg or woman were alive in here!
Don't smell like it. That is some atmosphere
You folks got in Paree. Whoo-*ee,* that's funky!
Stinks like the backside off a Rhesus monkey.
(Still to ERASTE:)
Yer hand, sir! Je sweez on-shit*tay*. Beau-coo!
(It's me! Crispin!)

ERASTE
(I thought it might be you.)

CRISPIN/AMERICAN NEPHEW
You don't smell that? It's downright homicidal.
Did one Ga-*ront*, live at this domicidal?

GERONTE
I am Geronte.

CRISPIN/AMERICAN NEPHEW
Well, unkie, hush my snoot!
I thought I'd find you in a funeral suit
Wrapped up and ready fer yer trip to Jesus!
Put 'er there, boy!
(Pumps Geronte's hand till further noted.)
I'm sorry 'bout the Rhesus.
Just shootin' off my trap as I will do.

GERONTE
Monsieur, who *are* you?

CRISPIN/AMERICAN NEPHEW
What's that?

GERONTE
Who are *you?*

CRISPIN/AMERICAN NEPHEW
Guess it's no mystery, you cain't place my mug.
We never met before! Gimme a hug.

GERONTE
Get off of me! Explain yourself, you varlet!

CRISPIN/AMERICAN NEPHEW
(leveling his blunderbuss)
Them's fightin' words and you should now be scarlet.
I'd blast ya if my Maw were not *yer sister*.

GERONTE
My sister? You?

CRISPIN/AMERICAN NEPHEW
    I'm not yer sister, mister.
My *mother* were yer sister. I'm her kid.
A' course, she wasn't married yet. She did
Get hitched months later. Is that yer affair?
My Maw's a round-heel whore? Hey, *I* don't care!

GERONTE
This is my sister, sir, of whom you're speaking.

CRISPIN/AMERICAN NEPHEW
Okay, her timing needed tweaking!
(To LISETTE:)
          Hi!

GERONTE
So nephew, you came all this distance?

CRISPIN/AMERICAN NEPHEW
(leveling the blunderbuss again)
         Why?
You doubt my word?

GERONTE
  No!

CRISPIN/AMERICAN NEPHEW
        You poltroon! You dastard!
I am yer nephew if I *am* a bastard,
As sure as y'er a geriolatric stork.

GERONTE
I only meant, you don't seem from New York.

CRISPIN/AMERICAN NEPHEW
Oh, y'er some geographic referee?

GERONTE
I thought you might have stemmed from...Tennessee.

ERASTE
Tennessee! Tennessee!—Excuse me.

CRISPIN/AMERICAN NEPHEW
So you got in-bred ijjits, too, huh. Nasty.
But hang on, you must be my cousin Rasty!
Whoa, handsome guy! I thought he'd be a mutt!

GERONTE
One question, sir. When are you leaving?

CRISPIN/AMERICAN NEPHEW
WHUTT?!

Hey, I arrive here slav'rin' for your cash
And you sit there alive and unabashed?
I am be-destitute becuz o' *you!*
So I ain't leaving till I see 'em screw
Yer coffin shut and tup it down some shaft.
As fer yer will, see here, I brung this draft
That says I get it all upon your *de*-mize.
(Produces paper.)
Nor don't go stuffin' nothin' in yer Levi's,
'Cuz I will dig you up with my bare claws!

GERONTE
Monsieur, had I the use of these two paws
I'd heave you out that window.

CRISPIN/AMERICAN NEPHEW
Who, sir, me, sir?

GERONTE
Yes, sir, you, sir.

CRISPIN/AMERICAN NEPHEW
Haw, haw! You stupid geezer!
You cain't treat me like some vile denizen.
This here's my walls and floors and dens y'er in!
It's only out the goodness o' my heart
That you ain't livin' in a shoppin' cart!
(CRISPIN motions to ERASTE to jump in, but ERASTE doesn't understand the signal.)
So whatcha say? CLICK!
(Levels gun and cocks it loudly.)

GERONTE
I promise! You'll inherit!
The hour I'm gone you'll get the lot. I swear it!

CRISPIN/AMERICAN NEPHEW
Okay, how long d'ya plan to be alive?

GERONTE

I doubt I've ten days left.

CRISPIN/AMERICAN NEPHEW

I'll give ya five.
Till then I'm gonna need a pide-a-terre
So me 'n' this fine pair on yer au pair
Can gnaw the prod'gal calf down to the bone!
(He grabs LISETTE.)

LISETTE

("damsel in distress")
Help! Help!

CRISPIN/AMERICAN NEPHEW

And by the way, I need a loan.
Ten thousand, or I burn this house to earth!

ERASTE

You devil!

CRISPIN/AMERICAN NEPHEW

HUNGH?!

ERASTE

What hellhole gave you birth?
How dare you speak that way to uncle? Vanish,
Beelzebub, and be forever banished
Not only from this house but from...

CRISPIN

(Your land?)

ERASTE

...our land!

CRISPIN/AMERICAN NEPHEW

Oh, please, sir, please, suspend yer wrathful hand!
I dint mean nothin' mean to ol' Geppetto!
See? Y'er so tough I'm talkin' in falsetto!

ERASTE

Now go! Or must I drive you out in Latin?

CRISPIN/AMERICAN NEPHEW

No, sir. I'm gone. Get thee behind me, satin!
And damn the man who stops me or impedes me.
If anybody asks, *America needs me!*

(CRISPIN EXITS center.)

ERASTE
Well, that should be the last of that grandee.

LISETTE
Your sister must have mated with a tree—
And not the brightest gingko in her garden.

GERONTE
That creature's not my nephew!

ERASTE & LISETTE
                                        Beg your pardon?

GERONTE
My sister was as fine as Belgian crape.
How could she generate the Hairy Ape?

LISETTE
He looked like you.

ERASTE
                    The traits were undeniable.

GERONTE
He wore a dog! He's certifiable!

LISETTE
Another reason he deserves no boon!
Leave money to some transatlantic loon?

ERASTE
Whose whole demeanor, sir, was one big F-You?
No, I cannot support my fellow nephew.

GERONTE
Perhaps you're right. But if he was a fake...

LISETTE
All Yanks are like that, sir! For heaven's sake!
Ruffians who need to go to school again!

ERASTE
They don't know wine or cheese.

LISETTE
                                  They're hooligans!
They'll cover this whole planet with their stench!

ERASTE
Steal film from who invented it!

ERASTE & LISETTE
The French!

ERASTE
So he's a fake? It's esoterica!

GERONTE
You're right! I disinnerit all America!
I'll give his cash to someone not unruly.
To someone who deserves it!

ERASTE
Me?

GERONTE
                              Niece Julie!
I'm sure she could use double gold in scores.

ERASTE
But, sir, if you'll excuse me, I've some chores...

(ERASTE EXITS center, quickly.)

LISETTE
You did note how your nephew saved the day?

GERONTE
Yes, and I'll compensate his brave display.
In view of prowess he evinced in plenty
I'm going to up his ten centimes to twenty.
The gall of that would-be acquisitor!
(KNOCKING, offstage.)
What's *this* noise, now? Another visitor?
(LISETTE EXITS center.)
Unless that's Lawyer Scruple, I don't want...

(CRISPIN trips in as NIECE JULIE, wearing an enormous padded dress and sausage curls. LISETTE follows.)

CRISPIN/NIECE JULIE
Excuse me, sir. Are you Monsieur Geronte?

GERONTE
Good God!

CRISPIN/NIECE JULIE
Oh, uncle, what a pleasure! Truly!
What, you don't recognize me, sir? IT'S JULIE!
COUNTESSE DE LA COCHON? CHATEAU DE SWINE?

GERONTE
You needn't shout at me. My hearing's fine.

CRISPIN/NIECE JULIE
Your other senses? Don't tell me they're failing!
(Waving, from six inches away.)
I'm over here!

GERONTE
I *see* you.

CRISPIN/NIECE JULIE
You're not ailing...?

GERONTE
This time of year a cold gets in my head.

CRISPIN/NIECE JULIE
That's queer! Some neighbors told me you were dead!
How wonderful to find they were mistaken.
But I forgot my gifts!
(Producing them from a capacious bag:)
A side of bacon...
A bag of pork rinds and some sausage twirls...
They're off the same hog as my sausage curls.

GERONTE
(aside to LISETTE)
(Her note was sweet, but could this girl be gaucher?)

LISETTE
(I'll tell you this: she isn't strictly kosher.)

CRISPIN/NIECE JULIE
And as proof positive of who I am,
Check out my portrait on this Polish ham.
All for a man I honor like my Mommy—
Oh, and some cutlets and a small salami.

GERONTE
A kin at last who's kind and not a fool.
A chair for her, Lisette.

CRISPIN/NIECE JULIE
Oh, just a stool.
A mound will do. A tiny bump. A bevel.
I, sit with uncle on a single level?
(LISETTE brings her a stool.)
No, that's too tall.

LISETTE
("don't give me any crap, okay?")
                        Yeah, well, *it's all we have.*

GERONTE
My little niece, you are a healing salve.
(As "JULIE" loudly bursts into tears.)
But why these tears?
("JULIE" moans.)
                        This moan?
("JULIE" sighs.)
                                  That sigh so sweeping?

CRISPIN/NIECE JULIE
You called me *little*, sir. That's why I'm weeping!
I *was* once brittle as a fishing pole
But victuals, kids and pigs will take their toll—
For they with Life conspired like vicious plotters
To turn me to this mincing ham on trotters.
Just look at me, a sow in patchy twill,
So poor that I'm reduced to eating swill!
(A snorting sob into a hankie.)
Oh, oinkle, *uncle*, then there was my marriage—
Dear Cyril, whom I'll let no man disparage!
Too bad the S.O.B. kicked off so young.
He left me dirt poor, and my boobs behung
With nine small infants like some sucking necklace.

GERONTE
You have nine children?

CRISPIN/NIECE JULIE
                        Ten. So call me reckless.
Then when he's dead two years, to top our sins,
Out pops a complimentary set of twins!

GERONTE
Twins? Two years after?

CRISPIN/NIECE JULIE
                        Oh, Cyril was virile.

GERONTE
But, niece, what brings you to my door unbid?

CRISPIN/NIECE JULIE
To see you, sir! My motives are unhid!
And to appall you with my tale of woe
So you in turn can leave me all your dough.
Your stocks, your bonds, what's hidden in your closet.

(Takes out a large piggy bank.)
See there? Miss Piggy's ready for deposit!

GERONTE
I? Leave you all...?!

CRISPIN/NIECE JULIE
Oh, sir, I pullulate,
I levitate, I ululate with thanks!

GERONTE
But all I've left you's 20,000 francs!

CRISPIN/NIECE JULIE
You're joking. Twenty thousand? Why, it's piddling!
Anything less than everything's belittling.
You think I'd breed or suckle any brat
If I'd not get the goods your will begat?
Ah, well. I'll have to play my own rewarder—
By serving you with this restraining order. [*Shows a paper.*]

GERONTE
Restraining what?!

CRISPIN/NIECE JULIE
It's inescapable.
You see, it says here you're incapable.

GERONTE
Incapable? You crocodile! You dare?

CRISPIN/NIECE JULIE
How else am I to get my proper share?

(KNOCKING, offstage.)

GERONTE
Goddamit, what's that bloody noise out there?

(ISABELLE ENTERS, also as JULIE, in a fat dress and sausage curls.)

ISABELLE/NIECE JULIE
Excuse me!

GERONTE
Help me, Jesus!

ISABELLE/NIECE JULIE
Uncle Jer!?
You mean that you're not dead? You shock me cruelly!

But what's the matter, sir? It's me! [*Oink, oink.*] It's Julie!

GERONTE
Yes, but... Yes, but...

ISABELLE/NIECE JULIE
But what?

GERONTE
Is that you, too?

(*ISABELLE sees CRISPIN, and screams.*)

CRISPIN/NIECE JULIE
Who is this creature?

ISABELLE/NIECE JULIE
What is *that*?

GERONTE
It's *you!*

CRISPIN/NIECE JULIE
Yes, I! The rightful heir to this man's plenty!
I've twelve sick children. [*Oink.*]

ISABELLE/NIECE JULIE
Really? I have twenty. [*Oink.*]

CRISPIN/NIECE JULIE
We live inside a barn. [*Oink.*]

ISABELLE/NIECE JULIE
You have a roof? [*Oink.*]

CRISPIN/NIECE JULIE
We dine on husks.

ISABELLE/NIECE JULIE
You opera-bouffe Tartuffe!

GERONTE
Enough, enough! But, niece, you haven't brought
Some nasty old restraining order...?

ISABELLE/NIECE JULIE
What?
Of course not, uncle! That thought's not arisen.
No, I've a warrant ordering you to prison. [*Produces a paper.*]

GERONTE
Prison?

ISABELLE/NIECE JULIE
Till I get all the gold I want.
Why else bring Lady Piggy on this jaunt?
(She produces an even larger piggy bank.)

GERONTE
I don't know where I am.

(ERASTE ENTERS, also as JULIE in a fat dress and sausage curls and carrying a still larger piggy bank.)

ERASTE/NIECE JULIE
Uncle Geronte!

GERONTE, ISABELLE, LISETTE, CRISPIN
Good God!

GERONTE
Oh, let me guess. You're Julie, too?

ERASTE/NIECE JULIE
Or Three. [*Oink.*]

GERONTE
I see you brought your trusty bank.
Well *I* say you three piglets *all* are rank!
Nor do I care which is my sibling's daughter.
Remove your shanks and take your banks to slaughter!
You'll not feed off my gold! I'm not your fork!
I disbequeath you all! And swear off pork!

(GERONTE EXITS right, followed by LISETTE.)

CRISPIN/NIECE JULIE
Oh, sir, you treat me like this—me, a widow?

ISABELLE/NIECE JULIE
And me, a widow!

(Fading mountain echo, as he goes:)

ERASTE/NIECE JULIE
Ditto!

CRISPIN/NIECE JULIE
Ditto...!

ISABELLE/NIECE JULIE
        Ditto...!

(GERONTE is gone. Jubilation.)

ERASTE
Were we amazing?

ISABELLE
        We were brilliant, kiddo!

CRISPIN
Well, those usurping relatives are finished!

ISABELLE
We've still got work.

ERASTE
        My hopes are undiminished.
I snap my fingers in the face of dread.
Some angel's guiding me, with wings outspread!

LISETTE
(runs in)
Monsieur, monsieur...!

ERASTE
        He's on The Pot?

LISETTE
        He's dead.

ERASTE, ISABELLE, & CRISPIN
He's *what?!*

LISETTE
        Stretched on the bed, completely still.
Sans breath, sans warmth, sans heartbeat...

ISABELLE
        ...and sans will.

ERASTE
A temporary swoon, that's all it is.

LISETTE
Monsieur, this isn't just a lack of fizz.

CRISPIN
One of your magic laxatives can't spark him?

LISETTE
The only question now is where to park him.

(They weep and wail, crying "NO! NO!")

CRISPIN
Hang on now, kids. Okay, we lost the fox.
But he left one thing in his hole.

ALL
THE BOX!

ERASTE
Lisette—the key!

LISETTE
It's bonded to his leash!

ERASTE
Well, see if it can reach here from his niche!
(LISETTE runs out right.)
                                            Eesh!

ISABELLE
                                            Eesh!

CRISPIN
                                            Eesh!

LISETTE (O.S.)
I've got it!
(LISETTE runs back in trailing the chain, but slams to a screaming halt just shy of The Box.)
No! We're short about one grommet!

ERASTE
Then to the Mount we'll bring the dead Mohammed!

(ERASTE and CRISPIN run out right.)

LISETTE
(to us)
Okay, I grant you, it's a bit macabre.
It's not the way we'd *like* things. It's a *job!*

(ERASTE and CRISPIN reappear, carrying the limp GERONTE.)

CRISPIN & ERASTE
Corpse coming through!

ERASTE
I'll get the key. You prop him.

(ERASTE digs the key from Geronte's shirt and frees the moneybox while the others struggle to hold up the body.)

CRISPIN
I've got him.

ISABELLE
Someone brace his knees.

LISETTE
Don't drop him!

ISABELLE
We're losing him! We're losing him!

CRISPIN
You stop him!

ISABELLE
I have to sneeze. *ACHOO!*

GERONTE
(waking for a second)
Gesundheit!

ISABELLE
Thanks.
But wait! You're sure he's dead?

LISETTE
As lumbered planks.

ERASTE
The Box has been unchained!

CRISPIN, LISETTE, ISABELLE
HURRAY!

ERASTE
And in a jiff...
The Box has been unlocked!

CRISPIN, LISETTE, ISABELLE
HURRAY!

CRISPIN
Let's lose the stiff.

ALL—INCLUDING GERONTE
HURRAY!

(ERASTE and CRISPIN carry the body off. LISETTE and ISABELLE falls on their knees before The Box.)

LISETTE & ISABELLE
Almighty Box, for whom we have a yen,
Please make us filthy stinking rich. *Amen!*

(ERASTE RE-ENTERS.)

ERASTE
My friends, attend the blossoming of our scheme!
One million francs!

ISABELLE
Oh, darling, it's a dream!

(ERASTE slowly opens The Box and looks inside.)

CRISPIN
Well, sir?

ERASTE
(producing them)
One coin. One note. *"My First Centime."*

(They weep and wail, tearing their hair, crying "NO! NO!")

CRISPIN
Stop! STOP! We know this million must be close.
Let's be *more* motivated, not morose.
Lisette, sew tight your lips and watch the door.
Monsieur, we two will search beneath the floor
And frisk the place for any stray dinero.
Mamselle, go home and be a chirping sparrow
Unto your Mom, the radar dowager—
Who if she finds he's dead will be a howitzer.
(They join hands, Four Musketeers-like.)
Now all for one, and one... The rest you know.
And here's to holy matri-money!

ALL
Matri-money!

                              CRISPIN
                                                              GO!

(They scatter as the clock whirrs and makes its agitated, farting chime.)

THE CURTAIN FALLS

END OF ACT ONE

ACT TWO

(The same, a while later. Everyone back in their own clothes. As the curtain rises, CRISPIN is searching the room for money.)

CRISPIN
Nothing in there... Nope. Nope. Nothing behind...
(Calls to next room:)
You'd think we'd hit it, two of us combined...
(ERASTE ENTERS from right, carrying wads of paper.)
What's that?

ERASTE
The only treasure I could find.

CRISPIN
Don't look so miserable! At least you *got* some!

ERASTE
I had to wreck his potty for this flotsam.
The total compensation for our caper?
A measly 40,000 francs—in *paper*.
Some IOU's, a ream of ancient stock...
(The clock whirrs and makes its agitated, farting chime, striking One.)
If I had a pistol, I would cream that clock.

CRISPIN
And he's still in there, really...*you* know...dead?

ERASTE
He didn't grumble while I dredged his bed.
Three hours I've searched, expecting glittering eyefuls.
What do we get? Some promissory trifles!
(He tosses the notes into The Box.)

CRISPIN
What trifles? We can float on forty K!

ERASTE
One drop of what a proper will would pay.
What of the sea of money I expected?
The ocean of centimes that he collected?

CRISPIN
(showing the centime they found in The Box)
His first memorial coin could come in handy.

ERASTE
What for? To bribe my jailers? Buy some candy?
(Tosses the coin out the window.)

You know, this isn't avarice, or greed.
I'll tell you what it is Crispin...

CRISPIN

You mean the rise of the bourgeoisie and a proto-capitalist society
devoted to competition, consumerism, and cut-throat
self-promotion?

ERASTE

                                It's *need*.
That million would have let me marry! Breed!
I'm talking chromosomes! Man/woman! He/she!

CRISPIN

Yeah, sure, the propagation of the specie.
Species, I mean.

ERASTE

Alas, my friend! We're pigs in Fortune's poke,
Our fertile dreams going up in sterile smoke!

CRISPIN

You've just gone bonkers chasing after riches.
You think you're bad? Check out *these* sonsabitches.
(He indicates the audience.)
What can you do but hitch your pants and man up?

ERASTE

But didn't you say you'd think some brilliant plan up?
How do we find my uncle's treasure hoard?

CRISPIN

Hire a psychic? Fire up the Ouija board?

ERASTE

Oh, thank you for that wisdom.

CRISPIN

                         Anytime.

(LISETTE ENTERS from center.)

LISETTE

Monsieur Eraste the lawyer's here.

ERASTE

                            Sublime!
Each awful moment sires a fouler sibling.
So what's he doing?

LISETTE
He's a lawyer: quibbling.
Should he come in left foot or right foot first?
And could he sue you if he trips?

ERASTE
I'm cursed!

LISETTE
Oh, he's a tetchy one, thanks to his size.
A Kaiser's ego in a pygmy's guise.

ERASTE
Does he know uncle's terminal condition?

LISETTE
Not yet. But isn't it the law's tradition
Not to care, long as he can send a bill?

ERASTE
Not when a dead man *has to write a will!*
Not when his client's *morto-tissimus*,
Uploading boulders next to Sisyphus!
Crispin!

CRISPIN
Monsieur!

ERASTE
Alas!

CRISPIN
Alack!

ERASTE
For woe!

CRISPIN
How could a dead man write a...write a...*WHOA!!!*

LISETTE
The juice is loose, monsieur! Crispin is thinking.

ERASTE
How can you tell?

LISETTE
See that? That manic blinking?

CRISPIN
(thinking and blinking furiously)
Wait wait wait *wait*. It's crazy, but... Why not...?

ERASTE
Crispin, is it a plan?

CRISPIN
Plan? It's a *plot!*
A vision sent by God!

ERASTE
Of what?

CRISPIN
Of clover—
And we're all in it! Wait! It's clouding over!

LISETTE
Oh, damn this vision!

ERASTE
Vision, please! Return!
Dream on, Crispin Dream! Glow! Enkindle! Burn!

CRISPIN
I got it! Yes! If I, if ne... That's clever...
Then you, then me... Not bad! But then... However...

LISETTE
This lawyer isn't gonna wait forever.
(CRISPIN is still lost in complicated mental planning.)
Crispin! We got some bank books to enhance!

CRISPIN
Would you excuse me, babe? I'm in a trance.
(Goes back into it:)
So he says *blah*-blah...I say cha-cha-*cha*,
He does the thing...I do the tra-la-la...
It's coming, kids, it's coming...! *YES! TA-DAA!*
My friends, I have outdone the algebra,
Out-thunk all thinkers Anglo, Frank or Teuton
Including Ike (that's what I call him) Newton.

LISETTE
What is it?

CRISPIN
An idea that's so ace
I bet you five you're gonna kiss my face.
Lisette, I need a set of Scrooge's clothes.

One of those sacks he wears, the bagged-out hose,
And don't forget the wig and fuzzy helmet,
That weird-ass front that hangs down like a pelmet,
For I shall be a hail-miser-well-met.

LISETTE

But you don't mean...?!

CRISPIN
                Hey, darlin', shall we dance?

LISETTE
(grabbing his face and kissing it)
You living treasure! This was worth a trance!

(LISETTE EXITS right.)

ERASTE
You'll reunite my future and my lady's?

CRISPIN
Boss, it's my *job* to pluck you outta Hades.
Get ready to be named sole legatee.

ERASTE
Crispin, you are a genius!

CRISPIN
        C'est la vie.

ERASTE
For this you shall be blessed for years in scores.

CRISPIN
I've only one request.

ERASTE
        Name it. It's yours.

CRISPIN
Don't let them hang me, sir! I'm just a pawn!

ERASTE
Hang you? For what, Crispin?

CRISPIN
                Oh, sir. Come *AWN*.
The crime that you're about to perpetrate!
Of course, they'll hang you first...

ERASTE
Who, me?

CRISPIN
Too late!
Here comes Lisette with all the needed trappings.

(LISETTE RE-ENTERS with a pile of Geronte's clothes.)

ERASTE
They're going to *hang* me?

CRISPIN
Sir, if you'd stop yapping
And lend a hand, our little show can start.

LISETTE
One of his robes and caps.

CRISPIN
Oh, very smart.
See there? I touch his stuff and it's seismotic!
I suddenly feel sclerotic, phlebotic,
Thrombotic, neurctic and necrotic.

(With their help, CRISPIN dresses in Geronte's clothes.)

LISETTE
As long as with the old man's seedy raiment
You're not infected by his dread of payment.
You will remember poor Lisette, now...?

CRISPIN
(Geronte's voice:)
Who?
Where are my fetid slippers? You, sir! You!
Fetch me a neckerchief and make it snappy!
(His own voice:)
These duds are magic. Geez, I'm feeling crappy!
My lungs are like a slough, my head's all snot.
And now this urge to merge with yonder pot...
(LISETTE pulls him back. Takes cane and walks like GERONTE.)
So what d'ya think, sir? Will I pass inspection?

ERASTE
Oh, you've transcended that. It's resurrection!
The old man as he walked, or limped, in truth.

LISETTE
You want to make some bread, set up a booth
And raise the dead for people for a living.

CRISPIN

You powers of hell, whom men call unforgiving
Send back a spirit from your haunted deep!
Restore to us Geronte, the king of cheap!
(He does thunder and lightning as GERONTE stumbles in from right, looks around in a daze, and stumbles back out.)
Okay, I'm set. Lisette, bring on the shyster.
(LISETTE EXITS center.)
Monsieur—the shutters. I may be a meister
Of transformation, but I need my light.

ERASTE

(closes curtains)
Hermetically sealed up, all nice and tight.
Now pray to Venus that she's philanthropic.

CRISPIN

I pray to Christ this lawyer is myopic!

(He sits in Geronte's chair. LISETTE ENTERS from center.)

LISETTE

Your lawyer, sir.

CRISPIN/AS/GERONTE

Send in the clown! He's late!

(SCRUPLE ENTERS from center. He is very short—the result of walking on his knees, which are cased in little shoes. He drags the train of a legal robe behind him.)

SCRUPLE

Monsieur Geronte?

CRISPIN/GERONTE

Ah, there you are! But wait...
Lisette, where is he?

SCRUPLE

Here, sir.

CRISPIN/GERONTE

Where's this lawyer?

SCRUPLE

I'm here.

CRISPIN/GERONTE

What, did you leave him in the foyer?
Go search the house and find the S.O.B.!

SCRUPLE
Monsieur Geronte!

CRISPIN/GERONTE
I hear a voice.

SCRUPLE
That's me!

CRISPIN/GERONTE
Good God, what's that? Who're you? Speak up, you're far!

SCRUPLE
I am Scruple—giant of the Paris bar!

CRISPIN/GERONTE
A giant?

SCRUPLE
To my clients and the courts,
A titan in the world of wills and torts!
You note this golden chain, my ruby ring?
Gotten by vetting *every tiny thing*.
I am a beagle, sir, being such a stickler
The Legal Board calls me "The Great French Tickler."
For, winkling out what's doubtful in a suit,
I eat minutiae!

CRISPIN/GERONTE
Well, you're minute.
But have we met before? You know my mien?

SCRUPLE
You don't recall you hired me sight-unseen?

CRISPIN/GERONTE
You're *still* unseen!

SCRUPLE
Of course, I know you faintly.

CRISPIN/GERONTE
My greed? My oddball cap?

SCRUPLE
To put it quaintly.

CRISPIN/GERONTE
Well, as you know, I'm soon to reach our saintly...
Hello?

SCRUPLE
I'm here, monsieur.

CRISPIN/GERONTE
...our saintly port.
And time being (like you, Titan) rather short,
I need a will, sir, terse and to the topic,
And *no small print*. Forget you're microscopic.
Write BIG!

SCRUPLE
I'll make a note.

CRISPIN/GERONTE
LARGE aspirations!
[*Cough.*] You've read my memoir? [*Spit.*] "Great Expectorations"?

SCRUPLE
I don't believe...

CRISPIN/GERONTE
Be quiet. I've just one fret:
That I'll kick off before this will is set.
Who knows but fixing it in inky black
Won't spark some freakish terminal attack?
(Has a wild "heart attack," slumps over "dead," then immediately rises.)
Yes! Given the document we have in mind,
I want to live to see this deed is signed.

SCRUPLE
On that account, sir, set your cares at rest.
I know no man who's not survived the test
Of setting down his ultimate desires.
(CRISPIN "dies" during:)
It's not as if one's...bank of...mortal fires...
Could be extinguished by the mere... *Monsieur?*
(CRISPIN wakes, only to start "dying" again.)
...mere writing of a will. The act's a cure!
Why, I've seen men who'd been the near-departed
Rise up anew from their... *Monsieur!*

CRISPIN/GERONTE
("coming alive")
Who farted?

SCRUPLE
If you don't mind, I think we'd best get started.
(Noting ERASTE and LISETTE peering over his shoulder.)
But lest we generate some legal cloud,
No lookers-on, of course, can be allowed.

LISETTE
I can't leave him alone. This man's a baby!

CRISPIN/GERONTE
Gah-gah!

ERASTE
I'd happily leave, but uncle, maybe...

CRISPIN/GERONTE
These persons, sir, are so discreet, so sage,
They shred my every confidential page
By eating them like epicurean dishes.

SCRUPLE
They eat your...?

CRISPIN/GERONTE
Papers.

(He gives paper to ERASTE and LISETTE, who chew unhappily.)

SCRUPLE
As the client wishes...
You swear to God you are this will's testator? [*"Tes-TAY-tor."*]

CRISPIN/GERONTE
How dare you, sir! I am a *what?!*

SCRUPLE
Testator.
You hold the rights to vest what's vestable?

CRISPIN/GERONTE
I am the holder of the testicle.
You're here to show how best one can invest it,
And keep my testicle from dying intestate!

SCRUPLE
Yes, well, we start with standard boilerplate,
As, "I, Monsieur Geronte, do hereby state..."

CRISPIN/GERONTE
Hey! HEY! Did I not say let's hit the gas?
I'm dyin' up here!

SCRUPLE
All right, we'll let that pass.

CRISPIN/GERONTE
I'm passing some right now.
(Pauses, to pass the gas.)
                                                 All right, I'm set.

SCRUPLE
Now, are there any monies owed, or debt?

ERASTE
Sir, given my uncle, we need hardly fret...

CRISPIN/GERONTE
No, wait wait wait. I have some IOU's.
(Digs out some filthy, crumpled papers.)
From Gaston's Bar, two francs and forty sous...
This one's for booze down at The Horny Goat,
Three francs and ten centimes...

SCRUPLE
                                         I'll make a note.
Now to your obsequies? Your burial?

CRISPIN/GERONTE
Oh, that. Just stick me in a carry-all.
Dump the cadaver in the nearest pit.
Nephew, you hear my wish?

ERASTE
                              I'll see to it.

CRISPIN/GERONTE
And nothing fancy, mind you. Nothing gaudy.
Forget the carry-all. Just toss my body
Into a cab and tell the driver *GO*.
It'll be half a mile before he'll know.
To *stiff* a cabbie from beyond the grave!
To think of all the tips I might've saved
By riding dead! Ah, well. Too late to fix that.
But pay for funeral expenses? Nix that.
I wouldn't have it on my conscience...*Up There*...
Anyone ran a tab on this affair.

SCRUPLE
I'll make a note. Now, any legacies?

CRISPIN/GERONTE
This part's a breeze. It is my ecstasy
And privilege to name sole testatee,
Leaving to him all goods, gold, property,
Deeds, ready money, furniture, rugs, plate,
All income payable to my estate,

My signet and the wiglet on my pate,
My dentures and what's hidden in my sock,
That ornamental chest, that ugly clock,
Also including, for nostalgia's sake,
That agitated, farting noise it makes, [*imitates the clock*]
While disinheriting all uncles, aunts,
Americans, cousins, nieces, potted plants,
As well as any bastards I've been blessed with
And several women I'd the joy to nest with,
In short all I possess, present or past,
I give my nephew (what's his name?) Eraste.

ERASTE
O bitterness too bitter! Heavy cross!
O spite! That I must gain but by your loss!

SCRUPLE
That's all?

CRISPIN/GERONTE
    Not quite.

ERASTE
    Not *quite*?

CRISPIN/GERONTE
    In recognition
Of five long years of good coition... [*Corrects himself:*] ...nutrition,
I leave unto my faithful maid Lisette...

LISETTE
Oh, thank you, sir!

CRISPIN/GERONTE
    Girlfriend, don't thank me yet.
To her, whose tits are like some crystal *palais* [*"PAL-ay"*],
That she may wed Crispin, that faithful valet [*"VAL-ay"*],
And be insured against financial crash,
I leave her...

ERASTE
    Yes?

CRISPIN/GERONTE
    A thousand francs in cash.

ERASTE
What?!

CRISPIN/GERONTE
Make that *new coins* in a handy tote.
You got that, Scrupulous?

SCRUPLE
I'll make a note.

LISETTE
Heaven bless you, master, with eternal light!

ERASTE
So much for extra legacies.

CRISPIN/GERONTE
Not quite.
I leave Crispin…

ERASTE
Crispin? You've lost your mind!

CRISPIN/GERONTE
Nephew, you've left your inside voice behind?
To *said Crispin*…

ERASTE
Who causes only *grief!*
The man's a libertine, a brazen thief!

CRISPIN/GERONTE
…a lad whose only flaw's being overzealous,
To him, despite the whinings of the jealous,
I leave a miniscule gratuity…

ERASTE
Which is…?

CRISPIN/GERONTE
Two thousand francs annuity.

ERASTE
Two thou…? It's madness! It's fatuity!

CRISPIN/GERONTE
Or would you rather that I made it three?

ERASTE
No! *No!*

CRISPIN/GERONTE
I *could* leave four, if three's too mingy.

Hell, make it *five!* I'm tired of being stingy!
What's more, without that clause this will is void!
Nephew, your thoughts?

ERASTE
Oh, sir, I'm overjoyed.

CRISPIN/GERONTE
Now have I any other pals who're needy…?

ERASTE
(I'll kill you.)

CRISPIN/GERONTE
…no. Why subsidize the greedy?

SCRUPLE
So is that all, monsieur?

CRISPIN/GERONTE
Yes, read that back.

ERASTE
(Not one more magnanimity attack.)

SCRUPLE
Now let me see here. "I, monsieur," and so on.
"One debt to Gaston's Bar…"

(GERONTE wanders in from right. He and CRISPIN are dressed exactly alike.)

ERASTE & LISETTE
AAAAAAAAAAHHHH!

SCRUPLE
What is it?

(Before he can see GERONTE, LISETTE and ERASTE stand blocking the old man from sight.)

CRISPIN/GERONTE
Go on.

(During the following, GERONTE weaves about the stage as ERASTE and LISETTE try to herd him back toward his room.)

SCRUPLE
"…to Gaston's Bar, two francs and forty sous…
The Horny Goat, etcetera, for some booze…
Testator's burial should run up no tab…

To be effected in a taxicab..."
I'll skip down to the major transferee.
"I name my major" (not sole) "testatee
Leaving to him all goods, gold, property,
Deeds, ready money, furniture, rugs, plate,
All income payable to my estate,
My signet and the wiglet on my pate,
My dentures and what's hidden in my sock,
That ornamental chest, that ugly clock..."

(GERONTE plops himself in his chair on Crispin's lap, hiding CRISPIN from Scruple's view.)

GERONTE
Where am I...?

SCRUPLE
Beg your pardon, sir?

GERONTE
Where am I?

SCRUPLE
You're in your sitting room. Remember?

CRISPIN/GERONTE
(working Geronte's arms like a puppet, from behind)
Damn! I Forgot! Read on, read on.

SCRUPLE
"...that ugly clock, Including..."

GERONTE
Who are you?

(SCRUPLE looks up. GERONTE and CRISPIN are still.)

SCRUPLE
"...that ugly clock,
Including also for nostalgia's sake,
That agitated, farting noise it makes..." [*He imitates the clock.*]

GERONTE
Who are you?

SCRUPLE
Sir, I am your lawyer, Scruple!
The *fleck* there at the center of your pupil?
Oh, you can't see me? I'll approach the chair...

CRISPIN/GERONTE
(waving him back with Geronte's hand)
No, stay right where you are.

SCRUPLE
Now, I was where...?

GERONTE
Who are you?

SCRUPLE
Damn it, sir, I've had my fill!

CRISPIN/GERONTE
You keep this up, how can I make my will?

(MADAME ARGANTE ENTERS from center, followed by ISABELLE.)

MADAME ARGANTE
Monsieur Eraste! What is this? What's going on here?
I know that something's up. My daughter's *cheer*
Is so non-stop it must be artificial.
I sniff a plot—some sneaky interstitial
Attempt to pull whole sheep over my eyes!
Hello, Monsieur Geronte.
(CRISPIN waves Geronte's hand. Seeing GERONTE alive, ISABELLE screams. To ERASTE:)
You won't disguise
This ruse, and somehow I've a deep suspicion
Your uncle's health's the news—that his condition
Is terminal and you've concealed that fact.

GERONTE
Who're you?

MADAME ARGANTE
You see? His brain's gone non-intact!

GERONTE
Who're you?

MADAME ARGANTE
Monsieur Geronte, it's Eulalie!

GERONTE
Who're you?

MADAME ARGANTE
It's EULALIE!

CRISPIN/GERONTE
Eulalie? Trulily...?

MADAME ARGANTE

                                                                     Trulily!

(To ERASTE:)
He's ready for his funeral eulogy!

(Unnoticed by her, GERONTE gets up and wanders the room again.)

SCRUPLE

(seeing two Geronte's)
Good God!

MADAME ARGANTE
        What's that?

SCRUPLE
        I think I'm seeing duple!

MADAME ARGANTE

(indicating SCRUPLE)
What is that creature?

ERASTE
        That's the lawyer, Scruple.

SCRUPLE
The Greek colossus of the Paris bar!

MADAME ARGANTE

You're an *iota*, sir, that's what you are!
(To ERASTE:)
You let him lapse into this senseless haze.
Well, I will sue your *ass*, to mint a phrase.

ERASTE

But what you see's the existential daze
That comes of having written up one's will!

MADAME ARGANTE

You mean…it's made?

ERASTE
        That's why he seems so ill!
Exhausted from the act of mere bequeathing,
From facing his mortality, he's seething
With questions all of us in time must face.

GERONTE

Where am I?

ERASTE
Who am I? What is my place
In this mad universe *which I must EXIT?*
Exit, I say, must exit *exit, EXIT!*

(GERONTE staggers out right. LISETTE follows him.)

ERASTE
As for this will, you wouldn't want to hex it...

MADAME ARGANTE
You're hopeful? And your hopes are testable?

ERASTE
Madame, I am my uncle's testicle!
Or, if not testicle, say, golden cup.
Is that not true, monsieur?

SCRUPLE
Well, not...

ERASTE
Shut. Up!
And just to show I beat the long phalanx,
Consider this.
(Opens the The Box.)
Some 40,000 francs!
In paper, but a rich engagement gift.

MADAME ARGANTE
My boy, please pardon me if I seemed miffed
Or chastened you beneath your future roof.
He's left you *all*, you say...?

ERASTE
Is this not proof?

MADAME ARGANTE
I know it's merely scrip and paper stocks
But may I...for a moment...grip...*The Box?*
(ERASTE puts it in her arms. We briefly hear an ANGELIC CHOIR.)
I feel as if I've peered beyond the veil!
But if this all turns out to be some tale...

CRISPIN/GERONTE
Madame, I vow you'll not be disappointed.
Eraste's my sole (well, almost sole) anointed.

MADAME ARGANTE
"Al*most*"...? He's not the only legatee?

CRISPIN/GERONTE
Small gifts to servants to remember me...

MADAME ARGANTE
To *servants*?

CRISPIN/GERONTE
Plus what I've bequeathed to *you*...

MADAME ARGANTE
You left something...to *me*?

CRISPIN/GERONTE
Yes, you! The glue
Unto my greed, the paste of my tight fist!

SCRUPLE
You left her what? Monsieur, I must insist—

CRISPIN/GERONTE
That as to what it is we all stay dumb?
(The woman's mad!) That we conceal the sum?

MADAME ARGANTE
Don't tell me. No, just let me dream and want!
That you should leave me something...? You, Geronte?
You who know stocks and bonds and how to pick 'em?
You who are stuck to gold as if with stickum?
That you, who'd only part from it with shears,
Give *me* a piece of what to you adheres...?
O, sir, I am not worthy of this debt!
The figure is irrelev... What'd I get?

ERASTE
The will is sealed.

MADAME ARGANTE
No matter. I divine it.

SCRUPLE
One last formality. Monsieur must sign it.

(LISETTE ENTERS from right.)

LISETTE
Excuse me, sir, but I've just had a tweet.
He's dead at last.

MADAME ARGANTE
Who's dead?

ERASTE
　　　　　　　　　　　Her parakeet.

MADAME ARGANTE
Stuff the damn bird! Bring me a quill and ink!

(LISETTE gets one.)

CRISPIN/GERONTE
I don't know why, I feel about to sink...

MADAME ARGANTE
You'll not die now! Take this and sign that, mister!

CRISPIN/GERONTE
I can't! I'm weak! I'm limp! I have this blister!

MADAME ARGANTE
What would compel your hand to get this signed?

CRISPIN/GERONTE
The Kama Sutra somehow comes to mind.
But *would* you grant a dying man a favor—
A final sign of friendship I might savor?

MADAME ARGANTE
I'll do it, yes! Whatever size or flavor
If it will help you sign and keep me CALM!

CRISPIN/GERONTE
Good. Rub your head and belly with your palm.

MADAME ARGANTE
I beg your pardon, sir?!

CRISPIN/GERONTE
　　　　　Ah, what a balm
It were unto a sickly man to view that!
You know? Like this...? [*He demonstrates.*]

MADAME ARGANTE
　　　No, I will not do *that!*

CRISPIN/GERONTE
(laying down the quill)
Well, I won't beg...

MADAME ARGANTE
(rubbing belly, patting head)
　　　　　　　　　How's this?

CRISPIN/GERONTE
Oh, yes, that's good!
Waggle your tongue!
(MADAME ARGANTE goes "La la la la la.")
Now maybe if you stood
On just one leg! Now Scruple! Everybody!
And counterclockwise! Eulalie, you're muddy!
All right, I'll sign!
(All stop and gather around as he signs the paper very slowly.)
"G...E...R..." Guide my hand.

MADAME ARGANTE
(moving his hand for him very quickly)
"...O...N...T...E."

SCRUPLE
The witnesses.

(ERASTE and LISETTE sign in record time.)

MADAME ARGANTE
The sand.
(She dumps sand all over the signatures.)

CRISPIN/GERONTE
Wow, that was fun! And look at you, all sweaty.
I swear to God, I'm semi-cured already!

ERASTE
Lisette, you want to tend your little pet?

SCRUPLE
I'm not a PET!

ERASTE
Her parakeet.

LISETTE
You bet.

(LISETTE EXITS.)

SCRUPLE
May I please go?

ERASTE
Bravó, monsieur! Well done!

SCRUPLE
As chaos, yes, perhaps this was well run.
A travesty in every other wise.

Humiliated but aerobicized
I'll take my leave now if you've no objection
And bring a copy back for your inspection—
That is to say, *if you can make me out.*
Should you have codicils—please! Take me out
And drill me with a pistol shot or two,
Then hail my corpse a cab to Katmandu! Adieu!

(SCRUPLE EXITS center, LISETTE EXITS right.)

MADAME ARGANTE
Though miniature, he casts a major damper.
Well, Isabelle and I must also scamper.
Oh, please don't worry for this little box.
I'll put it somewhere safe and oil the locks.
You have no need for it, there's nothing pressing.

(CRISPIN signals "don't let her take The Box!" MADAME ARGANTE notices the gestures and CRISPIN turns them into a sign of the Cross.)

ERASTE
But look, my uncle's giving us his blessing.

MADAME ARGANTE
Monsieur, you've made a worthy couple rich!

CRISPIN/GERONTE
My dear, you are an avaricious bitch!

MADAME ARGANTE
Thank you.

CRISPIN/GERONTE
I've but one wish I wish were gratified:
A tiny parting peck from nephew's bride...?

ISABELLE
With all my heart.

CRISPIN/GERONTE
Where are you...?
(CRISPIN grabs ISABELLE and gives her a good one.)

ERASTE
All right, fella!

CRISPIN/GERONTE
I can die happy now!

MADAME ARGANTE
Come, Isabella.

(MADAME ARGANTE EXITS center.)

ISABELLE
I couldn't stop her, she was on a tear.

ERASTE
Well, let her rip. Come grip your millionaire.

ISABELLE
Ah, mon amour!

ERASTE
Je t'aime!

ISABELLE
Tu m'aimes?

ERASTE
De tout mon coeur!

Tu pars?

ISABELLE
Je dois!

ERASTE
Au 'voir!

ISABELLE
A tout à l'heure!

(ISABELLE EXITS center.)

CRISPIN
Well, I don't care what anybody says.
I am a one-man Comédie Française!
(Getting out of Geronte's clothes.)
This wig did me so well, I'm sad to doff it.

ERASTE
Who knew that you would don it to such profit?
What were you thinking? An *annuity?*
Five thousand francs?

CRISPIN
A superfluity.

ERASTE
A thousand to Lisette?

CRISPIN
It's chicken feed!

ERASTE

Grade-A organic!

CRISPIN

Well, my chick's in need.

ERASTE

And so will *I* be, bankrolling your squeezes.

CRISPIN

It's *love*. It's *charity*. Take some tips from Jesus.
But hey, this will is not to your desire?
We'll call him back and toss it on the fire!
Lisette! Get Scruple!

ERASTE

No!

CRISPIN

You're satisfied?

Lisette!

ERASTE

No, wait!

CRISPIN

You're good?

ERASTE

I'm *gratified*.

(LISETTE ENTERS from right, obviously upset.)

LISETTE

Monsieur...!

CRISPIN

You know, though, this "near-death" experience,
Which was right up there with your best Shakespeareans...

LISETTE

Crispin...!

CRISPIN

It's put me in a pensive mood.
(One sec.) It's fed my tendency to brood.
You know—the tears in things, life's evanescence...

LISETTE

Monsieur!

CRISPIN
What are we? One brief day's florescence!
Just look at Uncle G. Alive at dawn
(One moment, hon) and now he's "G" for *gone*.
This poor old man whom nothing can revive...

LISETTE
Crispin...

CRISPIN
What is it, darling?

LISETTE
He's alive!

CRISPIN & ERASTE
GHHAAAAAAAAHHHHHHHH!

LISETTE
I go in there, he's ice-cold on the bedding.
Next thing I know, he's dressing for his wedding!
His Sunday shirt and shoes, a coat to match.

CRISPIN
Oh, *Jeez*! You mean we gotta start from *scratch*?

ERASTE
Remember those gendarmes arresting you?

CRISPIN
Hey, I was kidding! I was *testing* you.

ERASTE
We'll visit you in jail. We'll bring you food.

CRISPIN
You'll visit *me*...?

ERASTE
That tendency to brood
Might help you when you're climbing up the scaffold.

CRISPIN
You mean this was some kinda *crime?* I'm baffled!

LISETTE
Monsieur Eraste, you know you're in this, too.
And now our standard question...

ERASTE, LISETTE, CRISPIN
What to do.

CRISPIN
O Fate! O Fortune! Fie this effing fettle!

ERASTE
Lisette is right. We have to show our mettle.
I'll show you mine.

LISETTE
And mine.

ERASTE
Crispin? Be bold!

CRISPIN
Okay. I only hope our mettle's gold.

GERONTE (O.S.)
Eraste?!

LISETTE
(to Eraste, who's leaving)
What are you doing?

ERASTE
Saving my skin!

(ERASTE EXITS center.)

CRISPIN
Well, that was fast. My master's mettle's tin.

(GERONTE ENTERS in a dandy outfit, all spruced up.)

GERONTE
Good morning, all! Or is it afternoon?
One-thirty, is it! Lord, was that a swoon!
Like getting sucked into a dirty funnel!
But wait... Now I recall a long, dark tunnel
Opened before me! At its end bright lights—
And Grandmamá, in very strange white tights...
At which I woke and thought, *Lord*, what a dummy!
I'm rich as God yet live here like a mummy!
For what, this urge to scrimp and hoard and save?
It's not as if I'll splurge when in my grave.
But what's the news? Don't let my chatter bar you.

LISETTE
One question, sir.

GERONTE
Yes, ask away.

LISETTE
Who *are* you?

GERONTE
A man reborn to this world's lofty scene,
Inhaling life's proverbial coffee bean.
But wait a moment... Why're the shutters closed?

CRISPIN
What shutters? Those?

GERONTE
(sees Crispin's costume left lying)
I don't recall these clothes...

LISETTE
What clothes? Oh, *those?*

GERONTE
That was the implication.
Perhaps you could provide an explication
Of everything that passed here during my swoon?

LISETTE
Pure pandemonium, sir. The house bestrewn,
Just as you see, the moment it befell you.
You'd not believe the... Well, Crispin can tell you.

CRISPIN
Who, me? Oh, sir, you'd not believe the scene.
Me, madly shutting shutters shut, to screen
Your rolling eyes. You, tearing off your clothing
While shouting *"Lies! Lies! Lies!"* as if in loathing
Of your old odious personality.
"Burn these!" you cried. *"They're greed, they're malady!"*
(A very handsome suit there, by the way.)
Your nephew doing CPR, to stay
The hand of death and lengthen out your days.
Lisette here, plotzing... You would be...

GERONTE
Amazed?

CRISPIN
Amazed.

GERONTE
Where *is* Eraste...?

LISETTE
   Ah, sir, you're going to shiver.
Thinking you dead, he threw himself...

GERONTE
      The *river?*

LISETTE
The foyer. Totally inconsolable.
The grief? The weeping?

CRISPIN
   Uncontrollable.

GERONTE
Well, bring him in. I long to see the boy!
If nothing else so he can share the joy
Of seeing me wed to...

LISETTE
   Isabelle.

GERONTE
         Christina...?
Serena...?

LISETTE
   ISABELLE!

GERONTE
   Thank you. *Georgina.*

CRISPIN
I'll lead my master, sir, to the arena—
Half-dead himself, no doubt, from sheer despair.
If not half-bald from tearing out his hair.

(CRISPIN EXITS center.)

GERONTE
But this reminds me. My estate! My heir!
Did Scruple come?

LISETTE
   No. Yes.

GERONTE
   "No? Yes?" Which is it?

(KNOCKING, offstage.)

LISETTE

See that? His punctuality's exquisite,
For there's the little bastard now.

GERONTE

                Well? Run!

(LISETTE EXITS as CRISPIN ENTERS leading a reluctant ERASTE.)

LISETTE
(aside to CRISPIN as she goes)
(I'll stall the lawyer. You stall Number One.)

CRISPIN

Come, master, come. Behold this boon we've won.

ERASTE

Alas, what bliss, what happiness unbounded.
How mis... How wonderful to find our fears unfounded.

GERONTE

Dear boy, these transports come as no surprise.
I know your bent to sentimentalize.
But you were right!

ERASTE

        I was?

GERONTE

              To play my proctor.
To hell with price, I'm going to find a doctor!
I'll live to ninety if I mind my health!

ERASTE

Well, death could always visit you by stealth...

(ERASTE is about to strangle GERONTE. CRISPIN restrains him. LISETTE RE-ENTERS during the following.)

GERONTE

But listen, why dwell on mortality?
I'm tubing toward connubiality!
In light of which (ah, there you are, Lisette)
I'm going to guarantee you *get yours yet*.
Leave you some few centimes? What was I thinking!
I have some 40,000 francs, not clinking
But safe in paper, hidden in my commode.
A sort of "privy purse."
Lisette, where are you slinking? Find that lode.
They're for Eraste, in honor of my nuptial!
What's wrong? You look aghast.

ERASTE
                              Oh, sir, my cup shall
O'erflow with...something at your wedding vows.
But that's reward enough, seeing you espoused.
What use have I for 40,000 francs?

GERONTE
To live life well! So please—no specious thanks.
Bring them, Lisette.
(LISETTE goes into slo-mo.)
                         Arriba, la Paloma!

LISETTE
Monsieur, I think it's my turn for a coma.

GERONTE
Shall I go? Fine. Then so I will—with speed.

ERASTE
No, uncle—uncle, really, there's no need.
I swear, sir, I don't need them...overly.

GERONTE
Are you three putting something over me?

LISETTE
Over you?

CRISPIN
     Over you?

ERASTE
Who, uncle? *Us?*

(SCRUPLE ENTERS from center.)
SCRUPLE
Monsieur Geronte?

GERONTE
              Who's *this* homunculus?
Oh, Scruple, is it? For our rendezvous?
SCRUPLE
Yes, I am Scruple, sir, but...who are *you?*

GERONTE
I am Geronte.

SCRUPLE
        Oh, please. These eyes can see.
May I request some personal I.D.?

GERONTE
It's true we've never met.

SCRUPLE
Not met?

GERONTE
Not yet.

SCRUPLE
Whom did I meet?

GERONTE
Meet when?

SCRUPLE
My previous jaunt.

GERONTE
Your previous…? Sir, I tell you, I'm Geronte!

SCRUPLE
Somewhat transfigured.

GERONTE
So? I *am* your client!

SCRUPLE
I marvel that reality's that pliant.

GERONTE
I marvel at how long you've kept me waiting.

SCRUPLE
Some half an hour?

GERONTE
Some half a *day*, debating
Whether I'd ever find you in my sight.

SCRUPLE
If that's another crack about my height,
I'll leave right now! *"Hello? Hello? Where ARE you?"*

GERONTE
You're so bizarre I'm shocked they don't disbar you.
I hope you've cleared your offices of snakes.

SCRUPLE
Snakes?

GERONTE
Pythons! Cobras! *Fangs*, for heaven's sake,
Damning to Tennessee young healthy men!

SCRUPLE
Tennessee?

ERASTE *(a brief mad fit)*
Tennessee!

SCRUPLE
Well, here we go—again.

GERONTE
Again 's a bit obscure, but I'll ignore it.
Besides, I want no conflict. I deplore it
Still more today when all that's cruel or snide
Subsides before the joy of groom and bride—
A girl whose beauty every ill acquits.

SCRUPLE
(indicating LISETTE)
You mean this woman and her crystal tits?

GERONTE
No, I mean ME! That is, my wife-to-be.

SCRUPLE
You didn't mention any wife to *me*.

GERONTE
I didn't mention when?

SCRUPLE
This hour just past!

GERONTE
Sir, your obscurity leaves me aghast.
No matter. Business calls, so grab a quill.
You know the task at hand. I need a will.

SCRUPLE
You need...?

GERONTE
A will.

SCRUPLE
(producing a document)
This will...?

GERONTE
Good Lord, you're sloppy!
My *own* will, sir, not someone else's copy!

SCRUPLE
This *is* your will.

GERONTE
I *have* no will, you wen!
How could I?

SCRUPLE
So, you want...a *new* will, then...?

GERONTE
Fine! Call it new! I've just one major fret.

SCRUPLE
That you could die before the will is set?

GERONTE
How did you know?

SCRUPLE
You *said* it, FIE ON *ME!*
Now what're you gonna do? Go DIE ON ME?
(He imitates Crispin's wild heart attack.)
Would that be your response? Your fun retort?

GERONTE
The price one pays for hiring someone short!
But wait. Are lookers-on like these allowed?
Might they not generate some legal cloud?

SCRUPLE
But aren't these persons so discreet and sage
They shred your every confidential page
By gobbling them as snacks? Or were they faking?

GERONTE
What medication, sir, have you been taking?
They *eat* my documents? Pray tell, what for?

SCRUPLE
A question I'd've asked in days of yore—
When I was sane. Before these brain attacks
Made me see two of you on double tracks.

GERONTE
I will ignore your mad hallucination
To finish this before my inhumation.
My debts no doubt come first. Well? Is it true?

SCRUPLE
Monsieur, you are a course in *déjà vu*.
For I foresee your words as from afar.
Debt obligations? Sure!
(Takes out bills.)
                                  There's Gaston's Bar...

GERONTE
There's *what?!*

SCRUPLE
                   Your bills for booze.

GERONTE
                                  My bills for WHAT?
Where did you get these things?

SCRUPLE
                                From YOU, you BUTT!
What of your burial in a city cab?
Oh, you've decided you don't want that? FAB!
You note I'm crossing out IN BOLD? *Small hint.*
For God forbid there be the least *small print!*

GERONTE
What is that, what's that document you're scratching?

SCRUPLE
The testament you spent this morning hatching!

GERONTE
I wrote my will?

SCRUPLE
         You did.

GERONTE
                Today?

SCRUPLE
                          Of course!
Apparently you've since had buyer's remorse!

GERONTE
Eraste, you saw me write this?

ERASTE
What?

GERONTE
This deed?
You're down here as a witness to the screed.

ERASTE
I have no legal training on this head.
I pass, and let Crispin speak in my stead.

GERONTE
You saw me write this?

CRISPIN
You mean, did I "see" you?
Well, not exactly. Some man who could *be* you...
Vaguely...was here in something like that chair.
A sort of *aura*, far as I'm aware.

SCRUPLE
That *he* says he was here, well, that's the jackpot!
I've *never met this man!*

CRISPIN
This, from a crackpot
Who said we scarf your papers with a spoon?
Plus don't forget, sir, don't forget *your swoon*.

GERONTE
It's true, I had a transient caesura...

LISETTE
Monsieur, your seizure was bravura!
You *do* remember sending for this loon...?

GERONTE
I do.

LISETTE
This deed?

GERONTE
I don't.

LISETTE
Well, there's your swoon!

CRISPIN
And you remember your Kentucky cousin?

And Lady Pig, who littered by the dozen?

GERONTE
I do.

CRISPIN
And leaving me some trifling boon?

GERONTE
I don't.

CRISPIN
Your mind got stifled by the swoon!

GERONTE
How odd. I must have been completely blotto!

ERASTE
And that explains this lawyer's obbligato!
Apparently you wrote this thing, you see?
Behold your signature. Fait accompli!

CRISPIN
It's good enough for me.

LISETTE
And me.

CRISPIN
'Nuff said.

(MADAME ARGANTE and ISABELLE ENTER from center. MADAME ARGANTE is carrying the moneybox.)

MADAME ARGANTE
I just now heard the news. So is he dead?

GERONTE
Not yet.
(Seeing him alive, MADAME ARGANTE and ISABELLE scream.)
Do I seem pounding on death's door?

MADAME ARGANTE
But one acquainted with facts here swore
She saw you stretched as if in effigy.

GERONTE
It was a momentary lethargy,
A swoon from whose effects I'm reeling still.
It seems while thus cocooned I wrote my will.

MADAME ARGANTE
You did.

GERONTE
I did?

MADAME ARGANTE
Sir, am I not your glue?
Your trusty mucilage to all that's true?
Of course you wrote it, and it's so well-written!

GERONTE
I left it all to Kitten?

SCRUPLE
STOP! *What kitten?*

GERONTE
Georgina here, the miss with whom I'm smitten.
My lawyer, Scruple.

MADAME ARGANTE
We met, previously.
I hope you'll pardon devious old me,
But you said *smitten* in that tangled thread.
Does that portend you still intend to wed?

GERONTE
Of course I do! I wonder you should ask it.
But don't you want to check that clumsy casket?

MADAME ARGANTE
If you don't mind, I'd rather cuddle it, please.

GERONTE
I've one just like it.

MADAME ARGANTE
(darkly, to ERASTE)
Really? *Quelle surpreeze.*

GERONTE
Well, since this will is made I may as well hear it.

ISABELLE
And God forbid there be some snag to queer it.
(Are we about to die?)

ERASTE
(Or something near it.)

GERONTE

Well, Scruple?

SCRUPLE

No! I disavow this deed!
For I suspect there's something fishy...!

GERONTE

Read!

SCRUPLE

It's not just fishy, s r—it's *WHALE-SIZE* fishes!
Fine. You see nothing shady, or suspicious.
To *"hit the gas"* we'll skip name, place and date...

ISABELLE

Oh, no, please read it! I love boilerplate!
I gorge on formulaic legal prose.
Who else?

CRISPIN

Me!

LISETTE

Me!

ERASTE

Me!

ISABELLE

Me! Since none oppose...

CRISPIN, LISETTE, ERASTE

Boilerplate! Boilerplate!

GERONTE

Let's get this done before my final rest.
Forgo the filler. What's my first bequest?

SCRUPLE

"In recognition of five years' coition..."

GERONTE

Coition?!

SCRUPLE

Pardon me. "Of *good* coition."
Pardon me. Wrong again! "Of good *nutrition*,
I leave Lisette a thousand francs in cash."

GERONTE

I *what?!*

LISETTE

Sir, I am speechless, I'm abashed!
I never dreamed with my bad attitude
You'd show such lavish gratitude.

GERONTE

A thousand francs?!

SCRUPLE

"Delivered in a tote..."

GERONTE

A *tote?!*

SCRUPLE

No tote?

GERONTE

No tote.

SCRUPLE

I'll make a note.

CRISPIN

Monsieur, it may seem incongruity.
You left me too a small gratuity.

GERONTE

How much?

CRISPIN

Five thousand francs annuity.

GERONTE

Five *THOUSAND?*

CRISPIN

See? I also was amazed.
But hey—what can you get for that these days?

GERONTE

I am amazed I missed this spectacle.

SCRUPLE

You want to hear about your testicle?

GERONTE

NO!

SCRUPLE

You endowed with a legacy.

GERONTE

Fine. Read me that

SCRUPLE

"It is my ecstasy
To designate as major legatee,
Leaving to him all goods, gold, property…"

GERONTE

Skip that!

SCRUPLE

Etcetra…"Hidden in my sock,
My ornamental chest, that ugly clock." [*Imitates the clock.*]

GERONTE

Enough!

SCRUPLE

It's there, you see? Straight off my plume.

GERONTE

Just tell me, pray: I leave this all to whom?

SCRUPLE

"My nephew, what's his name, Eraste."

ISABELLE

That swoon…

GERONTE

Enough of swoons!

CRISPIN

Or maybe you were plastered.

SCRUPLE

And then you disinherited your bastards.

GERONTE

My what? So I have bastards in the bargain?

ERASTE

That word, sir? "Bastards"? That's just legal jargon.

SCRUPLE
Then we all rubbed our heads and wagged our tongues.
(They all show how, going "La la la la la.")

GERONTE
Has my whole frontal cortex come unslung?!

SCRUPLE
"Signed by Geronte, as witnessed by..." and so on.

CRISPIN
Well done, sir! *This* is why you've got that glow on.
Because you've done good deeds for those you love.

GERONTE
(To SCRUPLE)
You plotted this with them. You're hand in glove.

SCRUPLE
I write what's said! I'm an amanuensis!

GERONTE
But why would I, unless I'd left my senses,
Bequeath a bounty to a scamp like this,
A pile to her, or in parenthesis,
Leave everything to him from bonds to bedding
Intended for this woman whom I'm wedding?
Why leave to lunatics whole grand estates
For rubbing abdomens and patting pates?

MADAME ARGANTE
Pardon, sir. No. Your senses weren't bereft.
This was conspiracy! Extortion! Theft!
For while you languished, void of any motion—
Knocked out no doubt by some rare Chinese potion
Or hypnotized by thugs from Samarkand—
No matter. They, monsieur, they forced your hand!

GERONTE
By thugs from Samarkand?!

MADAME ARGANTE
                      It was a *crime*.
I marvel that your nephew's marked with grime,
But Izzy here's on fire to say "I do."

GERONTE
Thank God, at least there's one of you who's true.

ISABELLE
Good sir, I too deserve your righteous thunder
For I was also party to this plunder.

GERONTE
You'd decimate me with so cruel a taunt?
Those 40,000 francs—that's what I want!

ERASTE
They're gone, sir.

GERONTE
Gone? Gone where?

ERASTE, ISABELLE, CRISPIN, LISETTE
Madame Argante!

GERONTE
Am I in France, or pirate-strewn Siam?
Is there *no one* here who's innocent?

SCRUPLE
I am.

ERASTE
Sir, didn't you just now claim you'd needs be mad
To give away so blindly all you had?
Well, I maintain you hadn't lost your senses—
You'd found them. In your swoon, without defenses,
You showed your *true* self: liberal, generous, kind.
You had regained, not lost, your natural mind.

GERONTE
To leave one sou to you were gross miscarriage.

ERASTE
Well then my true loss isn't gold, it's marriage.

GERONTE
Marriage? To whom?

ERASTE
Georgina. *Isabelle.*
Whose infinite appeal, sir, you know well
From having been yourself her beauty's victim.
Who just by being turns love into a dictum.

GERONTE
So you mean *marriage* sparked this mad display?

ERASTE & ISABELLE
It did.

CRISPIN & LISETTE
Us, too.

GERONTE
Why didn't you all just *say*?
Confer with me, inform me, make me wiser?

CRISPIN
Because you were a rotten, stinking miser!
As blind as money! Deaf as any ox!
(Impersonating GERONTE, as before:)
Lisette, my gold! Invigorate The Box!
What's that, sir? Help the world? Improve man's lot?
You want me, I'll be curled up on The Pot!

SCRUPLE
Ah-HA! My well-known insight leaps the gap:
You were that man (or someone) *in a cap!*
The elephant in here at last comes clean!

GERONTE
That elephant's irrelevant! [*To CRISPIN:*] You mean...
That's what I was? So keenly cold? So tart?
My eyes are opened through this servant's art!
And let me toss this thought into the cup:
If people hope you dead, you have *Fucked Up*.
So now as Lazarus twice or thrice reborn
Let me spill you your due from Plenty's horn!

CRISPIN
You mean I'll get that small annuity?

GERONTE
As payment for your ingenuity.

LISETTE
I get my thou, to check in at the Ritz?

GERONTE
Two thou, to compensate those crystal tits.

ISABELLE
Monsieur, what of our marriage? Not to force you...

GERONTE
My darling *Isabelle*, I here divorce you
And pass you in my stead to this bad seed—
Who'll blossom richly, thanks to this mad deed.

And given my current urge to dance and sing
I don't care if the fairies wrote the thing.
So Scruple, file this instantly at court,
And pray excuse my having been so short
(So to speak). Blame that swoon. My head was spun.

SCRUPLE
Oh, *may* I stay, please, for the dénouement?
Why, the suspense, monsieur, is killing me!
I know it seems absurd—unwilling Me,
Lord Have-You-Seen-My-Ring-And-Golden Chain,
Requesting more non sequiturs, more pain.
But Christ, this place is fun! A wondrous mess!
I wish my every day knew such excess.
For I who spend my days tilting for fees
Feel up on stilts instead of on my knees!
Oh, please, please, *please*. I'll be as still as clay.

GERONTE
You're very strange.

SCRUPLE
I am!

GERONTE
All right, then, stay.

SCRUPLE
Thank you!

GERONTE
For wedded bliss is now our theme.

ERASTE
But, sir, you only left us one centime.

GERONTE
You ransacked my whole house, you heartless youth?
I'm only joking, lad, for here's the truth:
There's so much gold you'll run amok with it.

ERASTE & CRISPIN
But *where?*

GERONTE
That clock is chockablock with it!

ERASTE
Your fortune's in its chronologic pocket?

GERONTE
Drop in that old centime and you'll unlock it.

ERASTE, CRISPIN, LISETTE, ISABELLE, SCRUPLE, MME. A
Where is THE COIN?

ERASTE
Out there!

(ERASTE leaps out the window.)

CRISPIN
(sports announcer)
More tension, folks,
As our young hero, caught in Fortune's spokes,
Looks for the damn centime!

(ERASTE comes leaping back into the room, with COIN.)

ERASTE
The coin is here!

CRISPIN
I *told* you you should keep it!

ERASTE
All stand clear!

(The clock whirrs and begins its farting chime as ERASTE takes the centime and drops it in a slot and pulls a crank. Immediately the strangled chime starts to ring out loud and clear—and a fortune in gold coins pours out as if the clock were a one-armed bandit.)

ALL
A million! A million! A million!

ERASTE
That thing gave birth like some great golden bunny!

GERONTE
You know the old expression: "Time is money."
The loot was *here*. You didn't need to roam!

CRISPIN
Well, like they say...

CRISPIN, ERASTE, ISABELLA, LISETTE, SCRUPLE
(as in The Wizard of Oz)
There's no place like home, there's no place like home…

MADAME ARGANTE
But wait! This treasure straight from Tiffany
Has sparked in me a rare epiphany!
For see how money caused that strangled chime—
As down the ages *Gold* has jangled *Time!*
Clogged history's onward march with wars of greed,
Usurped the common good for private need,
Transforming me into a heartless vulture
Who as a blushing maid craved art, and culture!
Who played bad folk songs wearing purple tights,
Smoked weed, and argued for the people's rights!
Well, I'll no more be slave to money's chains,
But do what mere humanity ordains!
SOCIALISM!

(SHE tosses COINS into the audience.)

GERONTE
Eulalie...

MADAME ARGANTE
SOCIALISM NOW!

GERONTE
This is America! [*Corrects himself.*] France! You'll start a row!

ISABELLE
Amazing, Mom! Your character's been inverted!

MADAME ARGANTE
Today I've been alchemically converted.

GERONTE
So you abjure all use of legal tender?

MADAME ARGANTE
Are you insane? I'll just be *nice*—in splendor.

GERONTE
We're soulmates, then! You know we rhyme, Argante?

MADAME ARGANTE
Betokening, you think, some mutual...want?

GERONTE
(kneels, producing a HUGE RING)
Would you...

MADAME ARGANTE
I do!

GERONTE
Friends, greet Madame Geronte!

ALL
HURRAY!

CRISPIN
Well, this is where we'll end our tender fable,
With Cupid not just crowned but wearing sable.
And if you need a moral, sample this:
Don't try to take it with you. Spread some bliss.
For here's what's chief: that life, like Scruple here, is brief.
It's we conjoined, not coins, that mend our cares.
Now live, and thrive, as this earth's loving heirs.

CURTAIN

END OF PLAY

DAVID IVES

The Metromaniacs

adapted from *La Métromanie* by Alexis Piron

Commissioned by:

 SHAKESPEARE THEATRE COMPANY
Recipient of the 2012 Regional Theatre Tony Award®
Artistic Director Michael Kahn
Managing Director Chris Jennings

as part of its ReDiscovery Series.

The commissioning and world premiere production of *The Metromaniacs* was made possible by the generous support of The Beech Street Foundation

Metromania Mania
by David Ives

Frankly, I fell in love with the title.

Having enjoyed myself enormously adapting two French comedies of the 17th and 18th centuries for Michael Kahn and the Shakespeare Theatre Company, I was casting around for a third. In the course of reading in and about that period, I stumbled again and again upon mention of an obscure play from 1738 with a superb title: *La Métromanie*. It means, more or less, *The Poetry Craze*. ("Metro" from "metrum," Latin for poetic verse, and "mania" from… Oh, never mind.) As it happens, Drew Lichtenberg, STC's omniliterate literary manager, had noticed the title as well: potentially a real find for STC's wonderful ReDiscovery series, dedicated to bringing to light classic plays that had remained too long in undeserving darkness. It was via the ReDiscovery series that Michael and I had developed our two previous happy collaborations, *The Liar* and *The Heir Apparent*.

So I ordered the French text from the Internet and it arrived in a blurry offprint of an 1897 edition with an English introduction by a huffy scholar who heartily disapproved of the play and all its characters. Now I was interested. When I read that the play's author, one Alexis Piron, had failed to make the Académie Française because he'd written a lengthy poetic *Ode To The Penis*, I was really interested.

So what kind of play did the Bard Of The Hard-On write?

A very chaste and wonderfully delightful one. Upon inspection *La Métromanie* turned out to be a farce based on a brilliant idea, if given sometimes to long-winded declamations on Art. Its world is the airy, unmoored, Watteau-ish one that Piron's contemporary Marivaux would also put onstage. There's not much like realism in *The Metromaniacs*. We're in a levitated reality that's the exact counterpart of the vernacular, set-in-an-inn comedies the English were writing at the same time. This is champagne, not ale. Since it's about people who are mad for poetry, champagne is apropos, as is the fact that it's in verse. To dump this delicate play into prose would be to clip the wings of Pegasus and harness him to a plow.

The play was a lip-smacking scandal in its time, spinning into art what had been real-life comedy. It seems that all Paris had fallen in love with the poems of one Mademoiselle Malcrais de La Vigne, a mysterious poetess from distant Brittany (read: Appalachia). The celebrated satirist Voltaire publicly declared his love for the lady and her great works, only to have it revealed that Mlle de La Vigne was a guy named Paul Desforges-Maillard, very much living in Paris and taking his revenge on the poetry establishment for not appreciating his genius. Needless to say, Voltaire wasn't pleased when Piron's satire showed up (and showed him up). Worse than that, the show was a hit.

The premise was comic gold. The structural mechanics, I have to confess, turned out to be something else. Piron was a wit and a poet but not much of what I'd call a *farcifactor*, often content to let his characters intone his ravishing couplets without paying much attention to who just exited where or why anybody's doing anything. Besides those fatal disquisitions on Art, the play had not one but two male leads, a lackluster female ingénue and, like so many French plays of the period, it simply came to a stop rather than resolving. This is all by way of saying I've fiddled a good deal with Piron's masterpiece in bringing it into English. (The first English version ever, to my knowledge, but I'm open to correction).

When my friends ask me what it's about, I always say that *The Metromaniacs* is a comedy with five plots, none of them important. On the other hand, that's the beauty of the play, its purpose and part of the source of its delight. We go to certain plays to inhabit a world elsewhere, and *La Métromanie* is that kind of play in spades. Piron doesn't want plot. He wants gossamer and gorgeousness, he wants rarified air and helpless high-comic passion. A purer world. Characters drunk on language, fools in love with love. In other words, the way the world was meant to be.

Given what's in our newspapers day by day, a few yards of gossamer may be just what the doctor ordered. So gossam on, *mes amis*, gossam on...

Lost Inside a Dream
by Drew Lichtenberg

The Metromaniacs opens on a special kind—a uniquely 18th-century kind—of scene. A well-to-do gentleman, one well-off enough to own an urban manse above the grime and grit of Paris, is putting on an amateur theatrical in his salon *des arts et des lettres*. The subject is *amour*, the play a dreamy device designed to reach his dreamy daughter. 100 suitors, a number drawn as if from Homeric myth, have gathered at the home in order to court her, but she is more interested in *Parnassus* (the literary magazine). The daughter, you see, prefers imagined romance to the real thing. So the father has fronted the money and written a play himself (*mais oui!*) to bring her back to reality. This may sound like a ludicrous if not downright fantastical scenario, but it is one that our author, Alexis Piron, bases upon close and accurate observation of Parisian literary life in the mid-1700s.

As Derek Connon points out, Voltaire's circle was fond of just such aesthetic larks. At the country house of his lover and patroness, Madame Du Châtelet, Voltaire frequently staged dramatic readings of his new plays. One reporter records, in 1734, the partial rehearsal and performance of 44 separate acts of plays and operas for an audience of aristocratic aesthetes—all within a 48-hour span. As *The Metromaniacs* testifies vividly, these events could often result in hilariously terrible art. Madame Du Châtelet may have translated Newton's *Principia Mathematica* into French, but according to one eyewitness, her attempts at acting were horrific enough to "induce vomiting."

There have always, it seems, been rich people convinced they were great artists, just as there have always been penniless poets in need of a patron. Our play's hero, Damis, is one such would-be genius. He has arrived with "two empty pockets and some ten-franc words," as his servant puts it, as well as a pseudonym befitting his ambitions and hiding his penury. He is one "Cosmo de Cosmos," just like the man born François-Marie Arouet, but known to the world as "de Voltaire."

Our milieu, in fact, *is* the Paris of the young Voltaire. This play—the talk of the town in 1738—was ripped from the headlines by Alexis Piron, a popular writer of low-brow potboilers and satiric farces. Piron seized on a literary scandal involving a poetry magazine, some cross-dressing in verse, and the red-faced Voltaire himself. It is a fragile and insulated ecosystem, this salon cosmos of the idle rich and their artistic hangers-on. Piron shows us characters at a remove from life. They build Edens on their parquet floors and escape into literary daydreams, living a life of fantasy. In short, their heads are stuck firmly up their aesthetic *derrieres*.

The France of the 1730s was one in which taxes on the middle-class had never been higher, nor their opportunities for social mobility more circumscribed. The royal coffers were bankrupt, depleted by the wars of the now-deceased "sun king," Louis XIV. His son, Louis XV, who took over the throne in 1715 at the age of five, was now well into his thirties, and still employing surrogates to rule in his ineffectual stead. Piron's own career reflects the changing times. Unwilling or unable to play the game of appeasing his patrons, he was exiled from the halls of *academe* and into the artistic (though financially profitable) purgatory of the unregulated fairground theatres. As an outsider to the artistic and political establishment, he was the ideal writer to provide a satirical portrait of a society in decadent decline.

But if *The Metromaniacs* is a social satire, it is a magnanimous one. This play is filled with memorable characters, all of them ultimately lovable, all of them redeemed by the engagement of their fertile imaginations with the sensual reality of their fellow human beings. Damis, intoxicated by ideas, meets his soul-mate in Francalou, flighty father and author of the amateur theatrical. If indolence is to be scorned, refulgence is to be celebrated. Within these woods, everyone can be who they really are by pretending, and theatrical transformation results in a strange kind of truth.

In other words, what begins as a social critique transfigures into the stuff of aesthetic daydreams, and vice versa. Piron mixes upstairs and downstairs, muddling the classes until he ultimately transcends them. The play's characters skirt the edge of optimistic allegory, and its cascade of ever-complicating plots overflows the theatre's tidy unities. Like Cervantes' *Don Quixote* or the *Gulliver's Travels* of Jonathan Swift, Piron's cross-channel contemporary, *The Metromaniacs* delights in a fantasy world commenting obliquely on its own society.

Did Voltaire, so embarrassed by this play, learn any lessons from it? Could it have been swirling in the ether when he wrote his own allegorical-satirical-fantastical masterpiece, *Candide*, over two decades later, in 1759? We'll never know. Courtesy of David Ives, let's give the last word to our *ami*, Damis:

> Unlike those chatterers who speak in herds,
> We speak the best of all possible...words.

About Alexis Piron

One of the most widely produced comic writers of the 18th century, Alexis Piron (1689-1773) lived a life dogged by controversy and topicality, rivalry and ribaldry. Indeed, Piron, who once said that he "farted epigrams," was as well known for his personal feuds as his satirical writings. His ability to make powerful enemies, combined with his Falstaffian zest for the low life, helps to explain his contemporary obscurity. For every creative triumph that flagrantly flouted the rules, Piron seemed to run into direct conflict with the Parisian cultural establishment. The life of the party in his own times, he is all but forgotten today.

Born in 1689 in Burgundy, Piron showed an early knack for poetry and knavery. Witness his "Ode to the Penis," an enthusiastic epistle addressed to his member, written when he was still a teenager. Though his father wanted him to study law, he moved to Paris to write for the stage, shortly after the death of Louis XIV in 1715.

Instead of writing, however, for the Comédie Française—the officially sanctioned theatre of the French ruling classes—Piron made his debut at the unofficial fairground theatres located outside the city. At these *théâtres de la foire*, Parisians came to have a naughty good time, classical decorum be damned. They were periodically closed down by the Comédie Française, which eventually obtained a bizarre legal injunction that forbid fairground authors from employing more than one speaking character.

In *Arlequin Deucalion* (1722), Piron solved this restriction ingeniously. Harlequin, the lone survivor of a biblical flood, entertains himself by acting out scenes from the underwater Comédie Française, sprinkling in satirical jabs at 18th-century plays, actors and authors. Part sketch comedy, part literary ventriloquism, part enraging satire, the play established Piron as an unofficial enemy of "high art" and an anarchic, dangerous wit.

Over the next decade, Piron would move confidently from one mongrel, "low-brow" genre to another. In 1738, however, Piron produced his unexpected masterpiece, at, of all places, the Comédie Française. Inspired by a real-life literary scandal involving Voltaire, *La Métromanie* satirizes the literary pretensions of the ruling classes, bringing poetic delusions of honor and glory down to the parterre of public opinion. "What is this *Métromanie* by that maniac Piron!" Voltaire wrote a friend when hearing about the play. "I fear this will not be pleasant." The play was a popular success, and one that Voltaire would not forget.

In 1753, Piron was nominated to the famed Académie Française (of which Voltaire was a member). Louis XV vetoed him, citing the impropriety of his adolescent *Ode a Priape,* though many believe the reasons were more personally motivated. Though he lived a long life of material comfort, Piron was never produced again at the Comédie Française. For his epitaph in 1773, Piron wrote his final, and most famous, couplet:

>Ci-gît Piron, qui ne fut rien
>Pas même académicien.

As David Ives translates it:
>Here lies Piron, a nothing, an anatomy.
>He couldn't even make the French Academy.

This adaptation of *The Metromaniacs* was first performed by the Shakespeare Theatre Company at the Lansburgh theatre in Washington, D.C., where it opened on February 9, 2015, under the direction of Michael Kahn.

Original cast
(in order of speaking)

FRANCALOU
Adam LeFevre*

LISETTE
Dina Thomas*

MONDOR
Michael Goldstrom*

DAMIS
Christian Conn*

DORANTE
Tony Roach*

LUCILLE
Amelia Pedlow*

BALIVEAU
Peter Kybart*

* Member of Actors' Equity Association,
the Union of Professional Actors and Stage Managers

Original production team:

Director
Michael Kahn

Set Designer
James Noone

Costume Designer
Murell Horton

Lighting Designer
Mark McCullough

Sound Designer
Matt Tierney

Composer
Adam Wernick

Period Movement Consultant
Frank Ventura

Voice and Dialect Coach
Ellen O'Brien

Casting Director
Laura Stanczyk, CSA

Resident Casting Director
Carter C. Wooddell

Literary Manager/Dramaturg
Drew Lichtenberg

Assistant Director
Craig Baldwin

Production Stage Manager
Bret Torbeck*

Assistant Stage Manager
Elizabeth Clewley*

The Metromaniacs Characters

Metromaniac. Noun. A person addicted to poetry, or to writing verses. (From Latin metrum, poetic meter + Greek mania, madness.)

DAMIS, a young poet

DORANTE, a young man in love with Lucille

LUCILLE, a young woman in love with poetry

LISETTE, Lucille's maid

MONDOR, Damis's valet

FRANCALOU, Lucille's father

BALIVEAU, Damis's uncle

The setting is the ballroom of Francalou's house in Paris. Spring, 1738.

FRANCALOU	*Fraynk*-a-loo
LISETTE	Lee-*zett*
MONDOR	Mahn-*dorr*
DAMIS	Dah-*mee*
DORANTE	Dor-*ahnt*
BALIVEAU	*Bal*-a-voe
MERIADEC	*Mair*-ya-deck
PEAUDUNCQVILLE	Po-dunk-*veel*
BOUILLABAISSE	*Bool*-yuh-bezz
COMEDIE	Ko-may-dee
FRANCAISE	Frahn-sezz
MELPOMENE	Mel-*pom*-a-nee
ST. SULPICE	Sann-syool-*peece*
STUMM	Shtoom (keep it quiet)

Note: Parenthesized dialogue indicates an aside to the audience.

For scansion, the words "poet" and "poem" sometimes count as two syllables, sometimes one depending on the verse. Ditto "didn't," "isn't," and "even." "Poetry" is sometimes two syllables, sometimes three.

Once again, for Michael Kahn:

The Metromaniacs' *perfect host.*

— *David Ives*

ACT ONE

(Spring, 1738. The ballroom of Francalou's house in Paris, most of it concealed right now by a show curtain. FRANCALOU and LISETTE ENTER through the audience.)

FRANCALOU
(trumpeting as he enters; then:)
A fanfare! Good! To spark the celebrations.

LISETTE
It's touch and go. There could be complications.

FRANCALOU
But what about our *show*? The stage is set?
The actors and musicians, they've all met?

LISETTE
Yes, sir.

FRANCALOU
All right, then. Curtain up, Lisette!

LISETTE
You said you wanted something magical…

(LISETTE opens the curtain, revealing a "wood" of painted trees and a couple of "rocks." A full "moon" hangs over it all.)

FRANCALOU
I love it! *Yes*! What's more theatrical
Than this: an artificial sylvan wood
Where yesterday my Paris ballroom stood?
These trees, this Eden sprouting from parquet—
A perfect setting for my humble play!

LISETTE
You've got some dappled shade, bright-fading moon.

FRANCALOU
It just wants fawns with pan-pipes playing a tune.
My guests, now, and my daughter, they'll go where?

LISETTE
I thought we'd put the audience out there. [*Points to audience.*]

FRANCALOU
Brilliant! They'll stroll in here, digest, relax—
And we'll serve up *The Metromaniacs*!
Of course, I only wrote it for a laugh.

But here and there's a joke, a paragraph,
A rhyme or two I might not call un-juicy.
What a choice welcome-home gift for my Lucy!

LISETTE

She won't be shocked to see herself portrayed?
And played by me, monsieur?

FRANCALOU

                       Well, you're her maid!
Who else could send her up with such finesse?

LISETTE

You know she likes to wear that rosy dress?
I forged a copy that will make us *blur*.
In costume, sir, I swear you'll think I'm her.

FRANCALOU

You'll do her languid slouch, the drawl, the twirl?

LISETTE

(twirling a lock of hair)
You mean *Whatever, Dad...*"?

FRANCALOU

                       Yes! That's my girl!
With luck, by seeing herself she'll come alive,
Re-find her natural energy, revive!

LISETTE

Maybe if Lucy didn't read all day...

FRANCALOU

The remedy's right here! This very play!
My comedy will cure her foul ennui,
Make her the hurricane she used to be!
What's all her indolence but ignorance
That life's for laughing and that we're its jests?
Maybe she'll find a mate amongst my guests.
A hundred men might warm her virgin winter.

LISETTE

You might find someone.

FRANCALOU

         I?

LISETTE

                       A willing printer.
For, sir, with all the poems and plays you write—
You scribble all day long and half the night!

FRANCALOU
The Muses have bestowed on me an itch.

LISETTE
If you could just get published...

FRANCALOU
                        Oh, that's rich!
HA, HA, HA, HA!

LISETTE
Monsieur? Hello? Do I detect some glee?

FRANCALOU
Yes, but the laugh's on this, Lisette, [*shows MAGAZINE*] not me.
Parnassus, our top literary rag.
I send them poems and they do what? They *gag*.

LISETTE
Didn't they call you...?

FRANCALOU
                 "A rhyming ignoramus."
What they and you don't know—is that I'm famous!
Now keep this mum. No idle scuttlebutt.

LISETTE
Monsieur, these two lips are epoxied shut.

FRANCALOU
Justice! Oh, my revenge has been so sweet!
Each week, *Parnassus* runs a lyric tweet
From a strange poetess in distant Brittany.
She's caused a firestorm with her far-out poetry.
A "genius," all our biggest brains concur.
Well, how's this for a laugh? Lisette, *I'm her*.

LISETTE
This woman?

FRANCALOU
              With a pen-name that's ideal.
I write as "Meriadec de Peauduncqville"!
And it's all garbage! Tripe! Is it not sad
Some Breton cretin could become a fad?
My greatest fan's *Damis*, a poet-fool
Who every issue bathes himself in drool.
And *this* week, oh, Lisette, you're going to crow,
Damis asks for my hand in marriage.

LISETTE
No!

FRANCALOU
(reads from Parnassus)
"Mad Shepherdess, you have ewes, I have rams,
Should we not couple flocks—and epigrams?
Wed me and lo! how high my heart has leapt!"
So what do you think, Lisette? Should I accept?

LISETTE
That's up to you. Or, *ewes*. But while we're blathering
The party's started and your guests are gathering.

FRANCALOU
Yes, yes, and I've a million things to do.

(MONDOR ENTERS.)

MONDOR
Excuse me, sir, is your name Francalou?

FRANCALOU
Just ask Lisette, she'll help you. Toodle-oo!

(FRANCALOU EXITS.)

MONDOR
"Lisette," is it? And you're his aide-de-camp?

LISETTE
You are...?

MONDOR
Mondor! Valet and gifted scamp!
Among my talents being a knack for kissing.

LISETTE
And you're here why?

MONDOR
My master has gone missing.
He should be here, according to my dope.

LISETTE
Your boss's name?

MONDOR
Damis. You know him?

LISETTE
                                        Nope.
But wait. *"Damis"*...that somehow rings a bell...

MONDOR
And then there's always me.

LISETTE
   Nice try.

MONDOR
                                        Ah, well.
(LISETTE starts out. HE heads her off.)
But hey, before we wave and say ciaobella,
Consider this: am I a lucky fella?
To find myself here in this ritzy house
With you, a maid who's made to be my spouse?

LISETTE
A maid who's made for richer men than you. [*Starts out again.*]

MONDOR
This *is* the home of Monsieur Francalou...?

LISETTE
It is.

MONDOR
   He's got an only child?

LISETTE
   That's right.

MONDOR
She just got home from college?

LISETTE
                                    Late last night.

MONDOR
You're putting on some kinda play, or show?

LISETTE
A set, a moon, some painted trees. Hel-LO!

MONDOR
There's fireworks? Dinner? Dancing? All that jazz?
Plus bachelors, to add to the pizzazz?

LISETTE
A hundred suitors, each one hot to be here.

MONDOR
This is the place! My master's *got* to be here!

LISETTE
Okay. His looks? His hair? His build? His cloak?

MONDOR
Oh, you can't paint Damis in just one stroke.
Depending on his mood or what he's thinkin'
His looks'll change without him even blinkin'.
I swear! He's thin one minute, now he's squat,
He's blue-eyed, now he's brown-eyed, now he's not.
He works all day but never does a thing.
He'll pace, he'll moan, stand on one leg, he'll sing.
Most of the day he spends inside his mind—
His head stuck firmly up his own behind.

LISETTE
So he's a poet.

MONDOR
Right! You know these nerds!
Two empty pockets and some ten-franc words!

LISETTE
We have a poet-guest.

MONDOR
It's him! Or he.

LISETTE
The problem is, his name is not Damis.

MONDOR
Well, lead me to him. Then we two can play.

LISETTE
He's coming now—so you boys play away.

(LISETTE EXITS DAMIS ENTERS, writing in a NOTEBOOK.)

MONDOR
Monsieur...

DAMIS
Mad Shepherdess, can it be you?
O, bliss! It's you, who like celestial dew

Silver each daisy through your argent art!
As it is you who own my ardent heart!

MONDOR
Yeah, look...

DAMIS
Ye GODS, must we two live in twain?
Who are one heart, one soul, a single bwain? Brain?
Come tend my flocks with me forevermore!
Marry me!

MONDOR
Sir...

DAMIS
What is it now, Mondor?
How long have you been there? Aren't you embarrassed?

MONDOR
Look, I been chasing you all over Paris!
Nobody knows you here, what is this game?

DAMIS
Well, did you ask for me *by my own name*?

MONDOR
How else? Aren't you my boss, Monsieur Damis?

DAMIS
Shut up! Or you'll alert some buzzing bee.
Within these walls I've got a *nom de plume*.

MONDOR
A different name? It's oddball, I assume.

DAMIS
"Cosmo de Cosmos"!

MONDOR
Perfect! Oh, that's *ace!*
Cosmos! A synonym for *empty space*.

DAMIS
That name's a passport pungent as chartreuse.

MONDOR
Yeah, getting back to *earth?* I've got bad news...
[*Produces some BILLS.*]

DAMIS
It won me entry to this fecund house
Whose owner treats me like some second spouse.

MONDOR
Monsieur...

DAMIS
Why not? The way I dazzle him!
At meals, extempore, I frazzle him,
Shoot coruscating phrases toward the skies
So luminous he has to shield his eyes!

MONDOR
...I've got...

DAMIS
Poor fool, he thinks he too can write.
But God, his stuff's so limp, so lame, so trite.

MONDOR
...BAD NEWS.

DAMIS
Oh, will you cease your litany?
We're leaving.

MONDOR
Leaving? *This*?

DAMIS
For Brittany.

MONDOR
Brittany? That's nowheresville, it's outer sticks!
The chicks there carry Brittany spears! They're hicks!

DAMIS
It's where I'll meet my predetermined dove.
You see, my trusty servant, I'm in love.

MONDOR
Who, you?

DAMIS
Yes, me.

MONDOR
With who?

DAMIS
With *whom*.

MONDOR
Who's she?

DAMIS
My natural partner! A celestial bard
Whose poems have rocked the Paris avant-garde!

MONDOR
And this broad, *bard*, has a name? A name that's real?

DAMIS
Her name is Meriadec de Peauduncqville!
That's where she lives.

MONDOR
In Peauduncq...?

DAMIS
Peauduncqville.

MONDOR
When did this happen? Why'd I never glean her?

DAMIS
How could you know of her? I've never seen her.

MONDOR
WHAT?!

DAMIS
No one has—except through reading glasses
By gazing on her poems here in *Parnassus*. [*Shows MAGAZINE.*]
Works of sheer genius from a coarse Bretonne!
Can't you see her, in cap and rough cretonne,
Scribbling a poem while milking some sad goat?
Producing masterworks beside a stoat?
Hermited all alone up there...aloof...

MONDOR
Master, you are a master.

DAMIS
Rhymester?

MONDOR
Goof.
You see these bills? You're broke, with zip to borrow!

DAMIS
Mondor, I'm going to pay all those *tomorrow!*

MONDOR
Oh. Great. I mean, if what you say is true...

DAMIS
So what's the damage? To the final sou.
My tailor?

MONDOR
Fifty.

DAMIS
Barber?

MONDOR
Hundred twenty.

DAMIS
Landlord?

MONDOR
Two C-notes.

DAMIS
Grocer?

MONDOR
Oh, sir, plenty.
Plus all my wages.

DAMIS
Dating from?

MONDOR
The Middle Ages.

DAMIS
I have the money.

MONDOR
In your hand? Who says?

DAMIS
(produces a THEATRE BILL)
This flyer from the Comédie Française.

MONDOR
"The Talking Flute." Monsieur, what is this crap?

DAMIS
A comedy that's bound to cause a flap.
Debuting tonight, composed by whom but me.

MONDOR
It says *"By Bouillabaisse."*

DAMIS
My stage name. See?
I'm all the rage before the curtain falls,
You get your wages at the curtain calls.

MONDOR
I'm gone. [*Starts out, DAMIS pulls him back.*]

DAMIS
Mondor, this vehicle's pure pork!
It'll tour everywhere! Marseilles, New York.
Then, riding on my name...

MONDOR
Which name?

DAMIS
My name,
I marry Meriadec at Notre Dame.

MONDOR
Dom.

DAMIS
Dame. We breed some kids with acme wits
Who still with acne start producing hits!
Our first a new Molière, a comic master,
Our second a Racine who does disaster,
A third who in the opera writes a smash,
Our novelist daughter's raking in the cash,
And you'd leave me when we're this, no, *this* close?
With points not on the net but on the gross?

MONDOR
You haven't even *met* this dame! You're crazy!

DAMIS
I grant you, some of the details are hazy.

MONDOR
Yeah, what if she's a dog? She send a photo?

DAMIS
Great poetesses don't look like Quasimodo.
Pack up. [*Starts out, MONDOR pulls him back.*]

MONDOR
But I just met this maid, real kitteny...

DAMIS
Good. You can write, inviting her to Brittany. [*Starts out.*]

MONDOR
But...but... She's *here!*

DAMIS
Who's here?

MONDOR
Your Meria-broad.

DAMIS
You mean under this roof?

MONDOR
I swear to God! [*Winks to audience.*]

DAMIS
She's in this house? Where is she?

MONDOR
In...cognito.

DAMIS
My God, I sense the stirrings of libido!

MONDOR
Already? That's what I would call rapport!

DAMIS
I am poet to the bone, Mondor!
My stock in trade is actualizing dreams.
Poets love love! We're sated by what seems!
Then, unlike chatterers who speak in herds,
We seek the best of all possible...words.
I'm going to find her! Press her to my side!

(*DAMIS EXITS.*)

MONDOR
(*calls after him*)
But sir, there's *more* bad news! [*To us:*] Okay, I lied.

She isn't really here, his phantom bride.
But hey, all's fair in love and comedy.
(LISETTE ENTERS.)

LISETTE

Are you still here?

MONDOR

Divine Melpomene!

LISETTE

(from twenty feet away)
Slap!

MONDOR

Ow! You coulda settled for a shrug.

(DORANTE ENTERS.)

DORANTE

Lisette?

LISETTE

Monsieur Dorante?

DORANTE

Give us a hug!

MONDOR

Have I a rival, madam? Who's this bug?
All right, then, fine. I'll go, if that will please you!

(MONDOR EXITS.)

LISETTE

Sir, how did you get in? What if he sees you?

DORANTE

Who, Francalou? He's never seen my face.
So, wow! He keeps a forest in his place...?

LISETTE

Francalou is your father's bitterest foe.

DORANTE

That ancient libel suit of theirs, I know.
But what's to me their years of legal slaughter?
And aren't you throwing a party for his daughter?
The fair Lucille, our city's brightest match,
A plum whom some fine bachelor should catch?

LISETTE
Oh, sir. Not *her*. You're mad! It's bonafide!

DORANTE
Where is she? Lead me to my future bride!

LISETTE
Lucille?

DORANTE
I idolize the girl, Lisette.

LISETTE
One small detail? *You two have never met*.
You'd settle for a sight-unseen romance?

DORANTE
Lisette, are you forgetting? This is France!
I hear she's handsome. And she's well-to-do.

LISETTE
She's worth a million francs.

DORANTE
 Well, I'm worth two.

LISETTE
Her Dad has asked a hundred men here, son!

DORANTE
Then count me in. I'll make a hundred one.

LISETTE
But if...

DORANTE
 Enough what-ifs! Aren't I a steal?

LISETTE
Monsieur Dorante, this is the limp Lucille!
A prize? Oh, yeah. These hundred guys are proof.
But sir, she's pathologically *aloof*.
She's distant, she's inert, she's nonchalant.
She sure would never flirt with some Dorante.
I'd be amazed if she were ever wived,
Locked in her room *reading* since she arrived.
See, she's a metromaniac. That's her curse.

DORANTE
Crazy for subways?

LISETTE
No, crazy for verse.
And inflammation of the mental bursa
Where verse becomes your vice, and vice-a-versa.

DORANTE
Poetry, huh.

LISETTE
      Especially poems with sheep.
A shepherd with a harp? She thinks that's deep.
She's scribbling poems up there all night and day.
And you would take Lucille to wife? Oy vey!

DORANTE
It's not a natural match, when you consider it.

LISETTE
She's an anthology and you're illiterate!
But here comes Venus, rising from the ink.
Shoo!

(DORANTE hides in "the woods" as LUCILLE ENTERS. She wears a sky-blue dress and twirls a lock of her hair.)

LUCILLE
    Morning, Lizzie.

LISETTE
      Afternoon, I think.

LUCILLE
Whatever...Listen, what's this crowd about?

LISETTE
Thinking you something to be proud about,
Your father's throwing you a great big party.

LUCILLE
Oh. Cool...

LISETTE
    A hundred men, each hale and hearty.
These males don't make you slightly lose your poise?

LUCILLE
Boys are all right, I guess—if you like noise.
(Wandering in the "trees," oblivious of them. DORANTE hides.)
In this loud world one wants a quiet glade,

A sylvan forest where there's dappled shade,
A rock or two, a moon that's always bright...
Is this a forest?

LISETTE
For our play tonight,
This glade's the inside of a co-ed's brain
Who too much poetry has driven insane.

LUCILLE
Wow. I could swear I know a girl like her!
No, really. Can't you see this character?
A heroine who's mad for the Ideal,
Who scorns the sordid, sweaty, petty Real,
Where all is buyable and biddable.
She wants The Undoable, Undiddable,
A world of people eloquent and deep
Where shiny men tend perfect little sheep.
She's probably a rich girl, slightly sad,
Who's had it all and, driven slightly mad,
Wanders a mansion looking rather scruff,
Petting a small stuffed toy, her weasel, Fluff.

(She produces, briefly, a small STUFFED TOY.)

LISETTE
Looks like our play is true to life enough.
Nice chance for you to meet the bachelor classes.

LUCILLE
I'd rather read this issue of *Parnassus*. [*Shows the MAGAZINE.*]
Commune with *Him*.

LISETTE
A guy? Who is this "he"?

LUCILLE
My shepherd minstrel?

LISETTE
Yeah.

LUCILLE
His name's *Damis*.
God keep his flocks and bless his warbling notes.
I see him now, scribbling amidst his goats.

LISETTE
Wait. Someone said he's *here*! I swear to God!

LUCILLE
My hero? Wielder of Apollo's rod?

LISETTE
Yeah, him! A real Olympian torpedo!

LUCILLE
Where is he? Tell me, Liz!

LISETTE
He's in...cognito.
So circulate!

LUCILLE
I'll meet him?

LISETTE
You can try.
Or if not him, why not some other guy?
Like one who doesn't want to push a plow.

LUCILLE
My hair's a mess. Mwah! Thank you, Lizzie. Ciao!

(LUCILLE EXITS. DORANTE ENTERS from "the wood.")

LISETTE
See what I mean? Monsieur? Monsieur...you heard?

DORANTE
I saw a vision! Didn't hear a word.

LISETTE
What's this? What are you doing on your knees?

DORANTE
It's love! Oh, help me win her, Lizzie, please!

LISETTE
You want to guide *her* toward a marriage bed?
You'd have to pry her first from her own *head!*

DORANTE
I'll do it! Anything! Just name the task!
Does she want wine? I'll find the finest cask!
Tulips, like her two lips? I'll grow a tree!

LISETTE
A tree won't work.

DORANTE
What would work?

LISETTE
                    Poetry.
So write some!
           DORANTE
           Me?

LISETTE
           The perfect calling card!
An Ode To Livestock? Baby, she'll fall hard.
Cough up a canto, or a triple distich.

DORANTE
I don't know what those are. I'm not artistic!

LISETTE
A double dactyl? Something to enchant…

DORANTE
I'd talk in rhyming couplets, but I can't!
She doesn't just lack some necessary enzymes?

LISETTE
What Lucy lacks are necessary end-rhymes.
Without some verses you will never get her
And she will never wear your letter sweater
Her old man, too. He's got the poetry tic—
So praise his work and you could get in thick.

DORANTE
He hates my Dad! Their libel suit's at bar!

LISETTE
You simpleton. Don't tell him who you *are*.
Suck up to him, make him a happy host.
But find some poem for her, or you are *toast*.
(LISETTE EXITS.)

DORANTE
Oh, sure. Just find a poem. Should be simple…

(DAMIS ENTERS.)

DAMIS
*"Descend, O Muse! Unbind thy winding wimple!
Show us thy face in rosy beauty cupp't…!"*

DORANTE
Damis! It's me!

DAMIS
No, no. Don't interrupt.
Never before have I been so afire!
I am a rhyming, chiming, sliming (well, not sliming) choir! [*Writes.*]

DORANTE
I'll tell you this: you're not a clairvoyant.

DAMIS
Monsieur, will you please cease your...Christ! *Dorante?!*
(*They embrace.*)
It's been ten years! How are you? Where've you been?

DORANTE
I thought you went to law school! Didn't get in?

DAMIS
Oh, I got in, then fled those dusty hallways.
How's your old man?

DORANTE
Still blustering, like always.

DAMIS
Your father treated me like your lost brother.

DORANTE
I think he loves you more than my own mother.

DAMIS
But why're you here? Don't tell me! Some romance.

DORANTE
Damis, this one's The One. Don't look askance.
A girl *celestial*, not some dumb coquette.

DAMIS
Her name?

DORANTE
I'd rather not divulge that yet.
Not till I've won my father to my side.
He's got a legal gripe against my bride.

DAMIS
That's all that stands between you? Strife back home?

DORANTE
There's worse. My future wife's a metronome.
Maniac, I mean. About which I know nada.

And now I need a poem as my armada.

DAMIS
Here's luck then, poetry's my new métier!
What would you like? A sonnet? Rondelay?
Haiku? Too arty. Limerick? Too cheap.

DORANTE
I'll tell you what I need. Something with sheep.

DAMIS
Friend, I'm so intimate with sheep it's astral!
I ought to *bleat* my ballads, I'm so pastoral.
(Opens his NOTEBOOK.)
A georgic or an eclogue?

DORANTE
    Take your pick.

DAMIS
Here's one half-written that might do the trick.
"*Dithyramb To A Lamb.*"

DORANTE
    Great!

DAMIS
              Sweet but weighty.
I only need to plug in your fair lady.
So who's this maid? Enumerate her charms,
I'll hang a twangling lyre inside her arms.

DORANTE
You know I've never been too cool with words.

DAMIS
My friend, she's waiting for her wooly herds!
Just free-associate. Pour out some stuff.

DORANTE
She's beautiful...

DAMIS
       Stop there! I have enough!
(Scribbles in NOTEBOOK.)
Yes...! Good...! Fantastic...!
(Rips out the POEM and holds it out.)
            It's a little rough.

DORANTE
Thank you! Gosh. Sorry to deplete your stock.

DAMIS

(taps his NOTEBOOK)
This quiver's full of arrows. Chock-a-block!
And may I say, continuing the argot,
That my own shafts have found a worthy target...?

DORANTE

You're hinting something.

DAMIS

Am I? Take a whirl.

DORANTE

Don't tell me...!

DAMIS

Yes, I've also found a girl.
"*Celestial*," too, if we're being adjectival.

DORANTE

Wow, that's terrific! (Wait! Have I a rival?)
Who is she?

DAMIS

You won't name your lover true,
So why should I? Oh, all right, here's a clue:
She's here right now beneath this very roof.

DORANTE

Yeah? What's she like?

DAMIS

You might call her...aloof.
Her distance, though, is part of her appeal.

DORANTE

(Damnation! His girl's got to be Lucille!)
Does she like poems?

DAMIS

She writes them night and day.
She has the time, up there, all locked away.
I picture her right now beside her cow...

DORANTE

Her *cow?*

DAMIS

She loves me.

DORANTE
And you know this how?

DAMIS
The site where we two meet: *Parnassus*. [*Shows MAGAZINE.*]

DORANTE
Damn!

DAMIS
I'm sorry...?

DORANTE
Boy, you are a lucky man!
You know, our host here has a well-read child.

DAMIS
Does he?

DORANTE
(He's toying, now, to get me riled.)

DAMIS
If you want more, I'm Cupid at your service.

DORANTE
(Let's see if budding rivals make him nervous.
Yes...! Now I think of it, she said "Damis"!)

DAMIS
What is all this? "To be or not to be"?

DORANTE
Sorry. So tell me, do you know our host?

DAMIS
He shadows me like some adoring ghost.

DORANTE
Why don't you introduce me, just for kicks?

DAMIS
What, Francalou and you? You'd never mix!
The man's a dilettante! A would-be poet!
A dimestore-rhymester "artist," quote unquo-et.
Oh, he's a lovely man, don't get me wrong.
Generous and open, sunshine all day long.
But then in middle age he gets this itch
And now he writes the world's most hopeless kitsch!

Oh, sure, he'll say he wrote it "for a laugh"—
Then make you sit through every lumbering gaffe.
Tonight we're putting on his so-called "play"…?
But wait. I see him coming. Run away!

(FRANCALOU ENTERS with LISETTE.)

FRANCALOU
You turn your back and everything goes bust!
My play, my whole production—in the dust!

DAMIS
Oh no.

FRANCALOU
    Without the kindness to alert me
Three actors pick this moment to desert me!
He playing the servant fell and cut his head;
Our lover caught the pox; our uncle's dead.

DAMIS
The nerve.

FRANCALOU
    Just kicks the bucket, matter-of-factly!

DAMIS
He couldn't wait?

FRANCALOU
    My sentiments exactly.
Have you a grumpy uncle I could use?

DAMIS
I have a grumpy uncle in Toulouse…

FRANCALOU
I bring together family, friends and beaus,
I write a play for Lucy—and we close!
Of course I only wrote it for a laugh.
Still, there are passages of golden chaff.
Like this, for instance…[*Prepares to recite.*]

DAMIS
NO!

FRANCALOU
    The first act climax.

DORANTE
I'd love to hear.

DAMIS
I'll wait for it in iMax.

FRANCALOU
The show is off, why shouldn't I recite?

DAMIS
Because I've solved your nasty casting plight!
A servant you can pluck from those who hover.
Any old grouch could be the uncle's cover.

FRANCALOU
You're playing the nephew. *You* can't play Dorante.

DORANTE
"*Dorante*"?

FRANCALOU
The missing character I want.
The role calls for a handsome, sporty sort.
A hunk in love. Your classic swain, in short.

DAMIS
Then, sir, you have right here the swain you want.
Please meet my dear old friend—

DORANTE
Eraste.

DAMIS
"*Eraste*"?

DORANTE
I'm yours, sir, if you think I've got the stuff.

FRANCALOU
If you're a friend of Cosmo's, that's enough.

DORANTE
Who's Cosmo?

FRANCALOU
Who is Cosmo, says your buddy.

DAMIS
He's acting! See? How's that for a quick study?

FRANCALOU
(arm around Damis's shoulder)
I'd marry this man, sir—were he a girl.

When he starts rhapsodizing? Mother-of-pearl!

DORANTE
But what of *your* work, sir? Oh, geez! Oh, *man!*

FRANCALOU
You like my work?

DORANTE
I'm just your biggest fan.
Why else would I be here if not for you?
Your, your, your...adverbs, and your...commas ...? *Whoo!*

FRANCALOU
It just so happens I've a brand-*new* play...
[*Produces MANUSCRIPT.*]

DORANTE
Oh, may we hear it?

DAMIS
Maybe Saturday?

FRANCALOU
I only wrote it for a laugh, of course.
It's on the death of Alexander's horse.
"*Bucephalus: A Dirge In Seven Acts.*"

DORANTE
Genius!

FRANCALOU
Some of the rhymes are not un-lax.

DORANTE
The rhymes? I thought you said it was a play.

FRANCALOU
Well, aren't all plays composed in verse today?

DORANTE
Just kidding! Now, about this open part...?

FRANCALOU
Can you portray a swain who's lost his heart?
Was your soul ever slain by love's disdain?
One must first live to feel, and feel to feign!

DORANTE
I'm sorry, what was that again? More slowly?

FRANCALOU
You have to've lived a part to act it wholly.

DORANTE
Then search no further, sir. I *am* this role!
For she who is my life, my love, my soul
(Into Damis's face:)
LOVES SOMEONE ELSE! I swear, disdain's my curse!
My girl, who *is* a poem, is averse!

FRANCALOU
I like you.

DORANTE
    Thank you.

FRANCALOU
            And you've won the part!
(To LISETTE:)
One costume, madam! Something trim and smart
For—sorry, you're...?

DORANTE
    Eraste.

LISETTE
          Sir, how d'you do.

DORANTE
(slipping her the POEM Damis wrote)
(And if you'd slip this poem to You-Know-Who...)

(MONDOR ENTERS.)

MONDOR
Another inch, sir, and I'll cut your gullet!
You'll never win my lady-love, you mullet!

FRANCALOU
Now this is drama of the brightest pan!
But wait! Could you impersonate a man?

MONDOR
A man?

FRANCALOU
    A servant, in a modest part?

MONDOR
Depends what kind of servant.

FRANCALOU
          Honest. Smart.

MONDOR
Monsieur, you have described my inner twin!
But *act*...?

FRANCALOU
      I'd pay you half a crown.

MONDOR
               I'm in!

FRANCALOU
A servant's rig for this enthusiast.
Locate our uncle and our show is cast!

LISETTE
One lackey outfit and one love-sick pup.
(Quietly, to DORANTE:)
(You soften Francalou, I'll follow up.)
(LISETTE EXITS.)

DORANTE
But, sir, you've some new masterwork to share?

FRANCALOU
You really want to hear it?

DAMIS
    No.

DORANTE
          Yes. Where?
Where should we go to bask in your, um...

FRANCALOU
              Strophes?

DORANTE
Exactly.

FRANCALOU
    Cosmo?

DAMIS
      Sir, poetic trophies
Like yours deserve a really small recital.
Let me be satisfied with that bold title,
"*Bucephalus*"! Which none dare call cliché.

FRANCALOU
(to DORANTE)
It seems it's you and me, then.

DORANTE
Lead the way!

(FRANCALOU EXITS WITH DORANTE.)

MONDOR
I said there's more bad news? It's Judgment Day.
(FRANCALOU RE-ENTERS.)

FRANCALOU
You're absolutely sure…?

DAMIS
I wish I could!
Your new work no doubt redefines what's "good,"
But, umm, some friends have sought my legal wisdom
Since I've connections in our legal system.

FRANCALOU
I only thought…it's new…you'd want to hear…

DAMIS
But is it true, sir? Meriadec is here?

FRANCALOU
Where did you hear that?

MONDOR
Oh, that's just a rumor.

FRANCALOU
(confidentially)
In fact—it's fact!

DAMIS & MONDOR
She's here?

FRANCALOU
Though, given her humor,
And out of tact, of course she's *incognito*—
Lest someone recognize our famed mosquito.

DAMIS
Mosquito? She's a giant, by your leave!
You know her? Oh, sir, may I touch your sleeve?

FRANCALOU
You mean you *like* the work of Meriadec...?
Don't find it muddled, self-indulgent dreck?

DAMIS
Muddled? Of course it's muddled! But *refulgent!*
Oh, God, would I were half as self-indulgent!
The way she'll chronicle her every pimple?
That's poetry's future! Spewing, pure and simple!

FRANCALOU
You sound like this Damis, priest of her credo.

DAMIS
He is nearby.

FRANCALOU
Damis's here?

DAMIS & MONDOR
Incognito.

FRANCALOU
Monsieur de Cosmos, I go pink with shame,
That he, a poet so dim, so dull, so lame,
Would share my house with you, who glow so brightly.

DAMIS
To tell the truth, I know him more than slightly.
We two have been inseparable since birth.

FRANCALOU
Damis? That scribbling dribbler? Of no worth
Except perhaps to lick your wingèd shoe?
If anyone's refulgent, sir, it's *you.*
He's second drawer! No, third! A whining jerk!

DAMIS
I find a few good lines amongst his work.

FRANCALOU
And you think Meriadec's has got a kernel?

DAMIS
It's fertile as the spring, and as eternal!
Beside her, Sappho and Propertius cloy!

FRANCALOU
Watch out, or you might turn her head. *Dear boy!*
[*Embraces DAMIS.*]

DAMIS
Please, may I meet her, sir? I thrill! I thrum!

FRANCALOU
I'll think on it. But listen—keep this mum.

(FRANCALOU EXITS.)

DAMIS
She's here...! She's actually in this house! I'm numb!

MONDOR
Well, now hear this and you'll be numb-er, chum.

DAMIS
First, though, I need to step in for Dorante.
I'll write his father, old Monsieur Geronte! [*Starts writing.*]

MONDOR
Monsieur Damis—DISASTER FROM AFAR!

DAMIS
(*writing*)
"Your son's in love but there's some legal bar..."

MONDOR
You're listening?

DAMIS
No.

MONDOR
                         Hang up your wingèd shoes.
Judge *Baliveau*'s arrived here from Toulouse.
Your grumpy Uncle Baliveau?

DAMIS
            Your point?

MONDOR
He's come to Paris, pal! He cased your joint!
The guy who these ten years paid your tuition?
(My God, this is a lot of exposition!)
You think he found those law books he endowed?
A law degree or *license*, Mister Cloud?
The only license you got is poetic
And Baliveau hates anything ass-thetic.

DAMIS
(*rips LETTER out of NOTEBOOK*)
Mondor, this letter goes with all due grease
To one Monsieur Geronte, rue St. Sulpice.

A missive that will fix Dorante for good.

MONDOR
"Fix him"?

DAMIS
For good.

MONDOR
Well, primo. Understood.
But what about rich uncle? Your response?
Besides this empty show of nonchalance?

DAMIS
Have you forgotten? Where've you been? *Beirut*?

MONDOR
Forgotten what?

DAMIS
My play! *The Talking Flute!*
You think when uncle sees I've got a hit
He'll mind his loot, or what I've done with it?
He'll only heap my head, and yours, with more!
Tonight our fate will change at eight, Mondor!
Just take that letter for me, off you go,
And have no fear of Justice Baliveau.
He'll never find me anyway! We're safe!

(DAMIS EXITS one way with MONDOR as FRANCALOU ENTERS the other way with BALIVEAU.)

FRANCALOU
Baliveau, you arrive here like some waif.

BALIVEAU
I'm on a mission, you might say. I chafe,
While you're the same old temper: *tally-ho*!

FRANCALOU
It comes of seeing you here, Baliveau.
Give us a hug and *then* you can be vexed.

BALIVEAU
Is that a *forest* there? Good Lord, what next?

FRANCALOU
It's for my play tonight—a one-night run.
You're going to come, and love it, and have *fun*!

BALIVEAU
I wish I could work up the proper glee.
My mission here 's my nephew, one Damis.

FRANCALOU
The poet?

BALIVEAU
Don't tell me you know the knave.

FRANCALOU
Not face to face.

BALIVEAU
He'll put me in my grave.
Ten years he's been here—studying Law, I thought—
I come and learn he's *in* debt *and* untaught,
A vagabond to whom a home's abhorrent.
That's why I'm here! I want to get a warrant,
I want him locked up as an arrant thief.
You're well connected. Will you aid my brief?

FRANCALOU
A warrant for a poet? I'd find that hard.
Even Damis, who's not my favorite bard...
But you're my friend, so—yes! He'll be bastille'd!

BALIVEAU
We'll have to find him first. He's gone afield.
For all I know he's clubbing on the Lido.

FRANCALOU
But he's right *here*!

BALIVEAU
My nephew?

FRANCALOU
Incognito.
By great good luck we've one de Cosmos here.
He knows your nephew, *and* (be of good cheer)
Has legal friends who'll sign the proper paper!
It's fixed! I'll put de Cosmos on this caper—
Though I've a tit-for-tat.

BALIVEAU
It's done. Just say.

FRANCALOU
Take on the grumpy uncle in my play.

BALIVEAU
You're joking.

FRANCALOU
Not at all!

BALIVEAU
I, act onstage?

FRANCALOU
A justice from Toulouse who's just your age?
You only have to stand there to be he!
And howl a bit. [*HE HOWLS, demonstrating.*]

BALIVEAU
I have my dignity.

FRANCALOU
Who knows you here? Besides, you *are* this fellow!
For shield, we'll call you *Signor Pirandello*.

BALIVEAU
I'd be ungrateful not to play along.
But in return you'll help me right my wrong?

FRANCALOU
Damis is toast!

(LISETTE ENTERS.)

LISETTE
Monsieur...Sorry, you're busy.

FRANCALOU
Lisette, no, here's our howling uncle!
(BALIVEAU tries to HOWL.)

LISETTE
Is he?

(BALIVEAU howls.)

FRANCALOU
(gives BALIVEAU a SCRIPT)
Just learn your lines by eight. No rush, no pressure!

BALIVEAU
I'll try. Your elfin wood should give me leisure
To practice howling to my heart's content.

FRANCALOU
Yes, good! Let fly! I want to hear you vent!

(BALIVEAU EXITS into "the wood.")

LISETTE
They're costumed, sir, the lackey and the gent.

BALIVEAU
(in "the wood")
Aaaaaaaaaahhhhhh!

LISETTE
A tart addition to our juicy gig.
Now I should get into my Lucy rig
To play your daughter.

FRANCALOU
                    Things are coalescing.
Now gods of drama, give us all your blessing!

(DORANTE ENTERS unnoticed, and slips behind a "tree." He is now dressed in a "lover" costume.)

DORANTE
(I'll listen in, see how my suit's progressing.)

BALIVEAU
Ahhhhhhh!

(BALIVEAU howls, startling DORANTE.)

FRANCALOU
Oh, God, I love my daughter so, Lisette.
If she could find a mate I'd pirouette.
You're not acquainted with some handy beau?

LISETTE
Why not de Cosmos?

DORANTE
(WHAT?!)

LISETTE
(explaining, as FRANCALOU hears that)
                    Your madman.

FRANCALOU
                                    Oh.

(During the following, we're aware of DORANTE in silent, writhing agony,

listening in from the "wood.")

LISETTE
You like de Cosmos and his buoyant style.

FRANCALOU
I would joy to march that couple up the aisle.
I can't imagine any better match!

LISETTE
He's isn't rich...

FRANCALOU
     Who cares? I've got the scratch!
I'll be his in-law patron, make him natty.
What sweeter pastime than play sugar daddy?
I'll buy him robes to put a pocket in!

LISETTE
Sir, if you like this plan then lock it in—
Before Miss Lucy falls for some fine churl
Who as too often happens *has* a girl.
This what's-his-name you just put in your cast...?

FRANCALOU
Dorante?

LISETTE
  You *know* that he's Dorante...?

FRANCALOU
         Eraste?

LISETTE
Eraste! A wealthy guy, attractive, steady.
But I have heard that he's in love already.

FRANCALOU
He mentioned some young miss, and how he feels.

LISETTE
Should Lucy fall for *him*, head over heels...

FRANCALOU
She'd find his heart was pledged—

LISETTE
     —and hers would break.

FRANCALOU
I must prevent that, for my Lucy's sake.

LISETTE

I urge you, disallow him. I *insist*.

FRANCALOU

Well thought, Lisette. It's done. His name's dismissed.
I'll go tell her right now he's off the list!

(FRANCALOU EXITS. DORANTE steps forward.)

LISETTE

Speak of the devil.

DORANTE

            Devil, dear, yourself.
What are you *thinking*, evil demon *ELF?*
Who *are* you? Lobbyist for my competition,
Monsieur de Cosmos? Aiding his position
While flushing me straight down the lover's loo?

LISETTE

What are you, nuts? I did all that for *you*!

DORANTE

Who, me? Who you just helped disqualify?
And you stand there and look me in the eye?

LISETTE

If you want Lucy, sir, you have to trust me.

DORANTE

Oh, sure! When I just overheard you bust me?

LISETTE

My masterstroke.

DORANTE

            To diss me? It's absurd!

LISETTE

I've culled you from this hundred-headed herd!
She'll *race* for you once you're out of the running—
And *shun her Daddy's choice!* Is that not cunning?

DORANTE

Just tell Lucille I love her. Bang, I'm made!

LISETTE

I don't know why I bother lending aid
To men so stupid they need help to fart.
Monsieur, this isn't craft I'm doing, it's *ART*.

DORANTE
Yes, where's that poem gone since I wangled it?

LISETTE
The thing worked like a charm. I dangled it—
And Lucy grabbed it from my hand by force.
Needless to say, I didn't reveal the source.

DORANTE
She doesn't know the poem's from *me*? Why not?!

LISETTE
Suspense, monsieur! The heart and soul of plot!
She's coming.

DORANTE
What'll I say?

LISETTE
      Say nothing. *Stumm*.
You bow, then go away and leave me room.

(LUCILLE ENTERS with the poem DORANTE gave LISETTE.)

LUCILLE
Lizzie, this poem's, like, exquisite. Sublime...!

(DORANTE bows to LUCILLE, moves to exit, comes back, gestures, about to speak, then EXITS as LISETTE motions him off.)

LISETTE
Now *there's* a cavalier who's in his prime.

LUCILLE
Not very verbal. What is he, a mime?

LISETTE
My amorous pick, if *I* were forced to vote.

LUCILLE
He seemed okay, as far as I could note...
And anyway my amorous ballot's cast.
Daddy forbade me someone named Eraste.

LISETTE
No!

LUCILLE
 Yeah.

LISETTE
The handsome swain who's in his play?

LUCILLE
I've never seen the guy, I couldn't say.
Anyway, Daddy made him sound so bad
I'm half-inclined to wed the lethal cad.

LISETTE
("bursts into tears")
Forgive me, Miss! I didn't mean it! Honest!

LUCILLE
Forgive you, why?

LISETTE
For praising that Adonis! [*i.e., DORANTE.*]
I thought he had the right ingredients!
I never meant to foster disobedience.
Forget you ever saw him. Subject closed.

LUCILLE
That was Eraste?

LISETTE
The dude your Dad deposed.

LUCILLE
As I remember now, he's kinda cute...

LISETTE
You guessed he wrote that poem. You're so *astute*.

LUCILLE
That guy composed my dazzling dithyramb?
Be still my heart and fluttering diaphragm!
What's weird is that he writes just like Damis.

LISETTE
All right, Miss. I can tell you now. He's *he*.

LUCILLE
Who he?

LISETTE
The fellow in the cast, who passed?

LUCILLE
That's guy's Damis?! You mean...?

LISETTE
          Damis's *Eraste*.

LUCILLE
He penned these tropes, these metaphors, these puns?
And then he has those legs, those thighs, those buns?
O fallen star from constellation Ursa!
They're one and the same?

LISETTE
          And vice-a-versa.

LUCILLE
I'm dizzy, Liz. And Daddy, please stand clear!

LISETTE
(I think Dorante can pick things up from here.)
But listen, he might stroll by any sec,
So show some girlitude. All tits on deck!

LUCILLE
I look a mess...!

LISETTE
          Calm down. This won't go south.
You've got a weapon handy. Do *The Mouth*.

LUCILLE
The Mouth?

LISETTE
(puffs her lips as models do)
          The Mouth. It shows you're really lusting.
Lean in and pucker up.

LUCILLE
          Liz, that's disgusting.

LISETTE
Miss Lucy, he's a man! Forget the term!
It's stupid stuff like that that makes 'em squirm.
Try it.
(LUCILLE does THE MOUTH.)
That's great. Don't worry, I can kibbitz.
He's coming! Better plump all your exhibits.

(LUCILLE EXITS, MONDOR ENTERS from another way.)

MONDOR
All right, where is he? Lead me to the swine!

LISETTE
You have to leave.

MONDOR
You're not Dorante's! You're mine!

LISETTE
You have to leave!

MONDOR
(produces PISTOLS)
You see these guns?

LISETTE
They're fake.

MONDOR
Well, I'll still wave 'em!

LISETTE
Go, for heaven's sake!

MONDOR
Who needs them anyhow? We're stuck like glue!
My boss gets Lucy—I inherit you!

LISETTE
Your master isn't in the running.

MONDOR
No?
Your boss has not decided he's her beau?
The future pusher of her baby's pram?

LISETTE
I thought your master's named...

MONDOR
Damis.

LISETTE
Oh, *damn!*
So he's de Cosmos?

MONDOR
They're one and the same.

LISETTE
Well, thanks for really screwing up my game!

MONDOR
You want to slip your man in, please don't bother.
See, my boss wrote Geronte, Dorante's old father.
To step on him, he said. Dorante gets nixed,
My master wins, your boy gets 86'd,
You and I are one. How does that re-tune you?

LISETTE
If I had time I'd bare my butt and moon you.
Now go!

(MONDOR EXITS. LISETTE puts the PISTOLS aside. DORANTE ENTERS and goes to LUCILLE.)

DORANTE
(bows)
        I am Dorante.

LUCILLE
        You mean Eraste?

[*She does The Mouth.*]

DORANTE
I...What? Oh, yes, "Eraste"! You see, I'm cast
As one "Dorante" and had forgot myself.

LUCILLE
Oh, sir, you can put pretence on the shelf. [*Does The Mouth.*]
I know your true identity. [*Mouth.*] I'm wise. [*Mouth.*]

DORANTE
I'm sorry...?

LUCILLE
        Who you are? [*Mouth.*] Minus disguise? [*Mouth.*]

DORANTE
I'm still at sea.

LUCILLE
        So fine. We'll leave it moot. [*Mouth.*]
Your need for anonymity's acute.

DORANTE
Because of that old pending libel suit?

LUCILLE
Monsieur, we seem to be two passing ships.
(Does The Mouth more aggressively.)

DORANTE
Do you have some affliction of the lips?

LUCILLE
I'm *lusting*.

DORANTE
For?

LUCILLE
A certain poet!

DORANTE
Oh?

LUCILLE
You do know who composed this bright morceau.
[*Shows POEM.*]

DORANTE
I'll kill him!

LUCILLE
Who?

DORANTE
The source of that debris.

LUCILLE
Monsieur, I mean the man I love. *Damis*...?

DORANTE
I'll massacre the dog!

LUCILLE
The what?

DORANTE
Him!

LUCILLE
Who?
Monsieur, my pointed reference was to *you*!
The author of my dithyrambic lamb?

DORANTE
I will not lie to you, nor fiddle, nor sham.
I did not write that poem.

LUCILLE
Oh, don't be coy.

DORANTE
I read the sports page!

LUCILLE
Don't be such a boy.

And Meriadec?

DORANTE
What's that?

LUCILLE
Your love's bestower?

Will you just throw her over?

DORANTE
I don't know her!

LUCILLE
Nobody does.

DORANTE
They say that love's insane.
This conversation's knotting up my brain!
I don't write poems, I flunked French twice, I'm stupid!
But I've been visited by Mr. Cupid
And thanks to naked baby this is true:
I *love* you. *I* love *you*. You. Me. I. You.
That's it! That's all I got! I'm done, I'm mute!

LUCILLE
I hate to say this but you're very cute.
So if you want me I'll be by some tree...

(LUCILLE does The Mouth over her shoulder and goes off into "the wood." LISETTE comes forward and accosts DORANTE.)

LISETTE
So who's unhappy now?

DORANTE
I'll tell you: *me*.
She loves that poem's author!

LISETTE
Yes! You're he!

DORANTE
Except I'm not!

LISETTE
She's got the fatal yen!
You should be blissful!

DORANTE
But how can I when
She'll find out I'm a fiction, I'm a fake?

LISETTE
When *isn't* love, thank God, one big mistake?

DORANTE
I did, right in the middle, get the yips.
You know she does this weird thing with her lips?

LISETTE
Desire.

DORANTE
Thanks to a gift I don't possess.
So now I'm rival to...myself, I guess!
Plus Cosmo/slash/Damis, lord of misrule—
Who I'm convinced is playing me for a fool.
Maybe you're playing me, too, to make me writhe.

LISETTE
Monsieur Dorante, you're lucky I'm so blithe.
I have been slaving as *your confidante*,
Not as a spy for some an*ti*-Dorante,
And, you may notice, doing all this for *free!*

LUCILLE
(in "the wood")
Eraste...?

DORANTE
She's calling someone. Oh, it's me.
I'm going to have my eye on you, so watch it.

LISETTE
I help devise this plan and then you'd botch it?

DORANTE
Maybe you date him, work in symphony.

LISETTE
This date, monsieur, will live in infamy!
And so of course you realize: this means *war!*

DORANTE
We'll see which suitor's side you're working for.
All right, it's war! To death! At any cost!

(DORANTE joins LUCILLE in "the wood.")

LISETTE
I have to change...

(MONDOR ENTERS, now in a flashy servant's livery.)

MONDOR
How's this?

LISETTE
(from twenty feet away)

      Slap!

MONDOR

      OW!

LISETTE

      Get lost!

(LISETTE EXITS one way.)

MONDOR
I know you're only putting on this frost!

(DAMIS ENTERS another way.)

DAMIS
So did you take my note to St. Sulpice?

MONDOR
I might have. Or might not.

DAMIS
    What's this? Caprice?
Since when does "servant" mean the disobeying one?

MONDOR
In this [*i.e., his costume*] I'm not a servant, I'm just playing one.
I'm not even here! I only *seem* to be.

DAMIS
Would I could only *seem* to be Damis
Since being him only brings me indigestion.
Damis or not Damis.

DAMIS & MONDOR
That is the question.

DAMIS
(sits on a "rock." It's foam, and deflates beneath him.)
I searched for Meriadec. Does she exist?

MONDOR
Maybe this broad's like you: a kind of *mist*.

DAMIS
Would we two even be simpatico?
Were she like Francalou...upbeat, aglow...
If she had his élan, his verve, his vim.

MONDOR
Forget this Meriadec. Just marry *him!*

DAMIS
Mondor, I'll do it?

MONDOR
Marry him?

DAMIS
Forget her.
I'm sorry I ever met, well, never met her.
My Shepherdess, 'twas lovely but farewell!

MONDOR
Too bad, just when you two were doing so swell.
Hey, why not find a person of her sex
And substitute her face for Meriadec's?

DAMIS
Yes...! Find some random proxy to adore...!
I sometimes marvel at your sense, Mondor.
Just pick a stand-in! Excellent! But who?

MONDOR
Have you checked out Miss Lucy Francalou?
Pink dress, gold hair?

DAMIS
Exploit my host? No thanks.

MONDOR
She is his heir, sir, and you got no francs.
Plus did you know she's nutso for fine verse?
She reads it, writes it—*and* comes with a purse.
Plus *plus*: her father, on crusade for her,

Is telling everyone you're made for her!

DAMIS
All right, where is she?

MONDOR
You wait here, I'll check.
(MONDOR EXITS one way. FRANCALOU ENTERS another.)

FRANCALOU
My friend, I've just communed with Meriadec.

DAMIS
Where is she?!

FRANCALOU
She's so close you two could peck.
But by the by, have you yet met my child?

DAMIS
I haven't had the pleasure...(Wait. That's wild.
Lucille writes poetry. Meriadec as well...)
You're close to Meriadec?

FRANCALOU
As nut to shell.

DAMIS
(I think he's throwing out a tentacle.)

FRANCALOU
So close we're practically identical.

DAMIS
(That's it! Lucille is Meriadec for sure!)

FRANCALOU
I'll try to find her, and...[*Shakes hands.*] Good luck, monsieur!

(FRANCALOU EXITS.)

DAMIS
That's why Mondor was pushing me. He *knew!*
But hid it from me, as did Francalou.
Meriadec's Lucy, not off in some hut!

(LISETTE ENTERS, dressed as Lucille for the play.)

LISETTE/LUCILLE
(I ought to pass in this...)

DAMIS
Stay, goddess!

LISETTE/LUCILLE
What?

DAMIS
Mad Shepherdess!

LISETTE/LUCILLE
I'm sorry...?

DAMIS
Is it you?
O, bliss! It's you, who like celestial dew
Silver each daisy through your argent art!
As it is you who own my ardent heart!

LISETTE/LUCILLE
Well, 'bye...

DAMIS
Ye GODS, must we two live in twain?
Who are one heart, one soul, a single bwain?

LISETTE/LUCILLE
Brain?

DAMIS
Brain.
To think I thought I loved you up to now!
To think I thought you owned a cow!

LISETTE/LUCILLE
A cow?
Yeah, look, I gotta sprint...

DAMIS
Oh, drop this role.
I know who you are in your deepest soul.
Your secret's out, thanks to your father's spiel.

LISETTE/LUCILLE
My father...?

DAMIS
Yes.

LISETTE/LUCILLE
(He thinks that I'm Lucille!)

DAMIS

Another hint. Does "Peauduncqville" ring bells?
Those rabid rhymes, those violent villanelles?
Since I first read your work I've been a wreck.

LISETTE

I see...(He also thinks I'm *Meriadec!*)

DAMIS

May Pegasus the Wingèd never fly,
May all the streams of Hippocrene run dry,
If I don't pledge my soul to you—forever.

LISETTE/LUCILLE

(aping Lucille)
Yeah, well...That's cool...Why not, I mean...Whatever.
(FRANCALOU ENTERS.)

FRANCALOU

Lucille...

LISETTE/LUCILLE

(turns away)
        Yeah, Dad?

FRANCALOU

        You two have met, then. Good.

DAMIS

I love your Lucy, sir!

FRANCALOU

And so you should!

DAMIS

You didn't tell me of her secret, though.

FRANCALOU

The real Lucille beneath the surface? No.
And may you two find bliss unto the last!
Now, I've just penned a poem that has surpassed...

LISETTE/LUCILLE

You know who'd like to hear that, Dad? Eraste.

FRANCALOU

You're absolutely right. He'll go berserk.

(FRANCALOU EXITS.)

LISETTE
(That'll pay back Dorante for being a jerk.)

DAMIS
Lucy, we are a knot no blade can sever.

LISETTE/LUCILLE
Yeah, hey...Why not, I mean...That's cool...Whatever...

(THEY EXIT. As they do, DAMIS drops his NOTEBOOK. MONDOR ENTERS.)

MONDOR
You dropped your notebook, sir! [*To US:*] Boy, am I clever?
Look at him! Tight already with our heiress,
Like he's the greatest gigolo in Paris!
Maybe this poetry really works on chicks.
Let's see here, maybe I'll pick up some tricks...

(He studies the NOTEBOOK as DORANTE and LUCILLE ENTER from "the wood.")

LUCILLE
O, sweet Damis! I can't believe it's true!

MONDOR
(reads from NOTEBOOK)
Mad Shepherdess!

LUCILLE
I'm sorry...?

MONDOR
                    Is it you?
O, bliss! It's you, who like celestial dew
Silver each daisy through your argent art!
As it is you who own my ardent heart!

LUCILLE
Sir, you're a poet?

MONDOR
Not yet a paying one.

LUCILLE
You're not a servant?

MONDOR
No, just playing one.

DORANTE

Lucille...

MONDOR

Ye GODS, must we two live in twain?
Who are one heart, one soul, a single bwain?

LUCILLE

Brain?

What glorious words! Like sun from warming south!

MONDOR

(I think she likes me.)
(Yeah, she's doing *The Mouth!*)
But wait a sec, now wait a sec. Who's he?
Didn't I just see you float off with Damis?

LUCILLE

He *is* Damis.

MONDOR

Who, *he*?

LUCILLE

(to DORANTE)

Aren't you?

DORANTE

Who, me?

MONDOR

This jock, this creep? Damis? Don't make me laugh.
He wouldn't know a sheep from a giraffe.

LUCILLE

(to DORANTE)
Show him! Well? Rhapsodize! Play your pan-pipes!

MONDOR

I wouldn't use this piker's poems for hand-wipes.

LUCILLE

Go on!

DORANTE

Behold, forsooth! A leaping bock!

MONDOR

Don't strain yourself. No, really. Take a rock—
While I shoot coruscating phrases toward the skies

So luminous, you'll have to shield your eyes!

LUCILLE
Be still, my heart! I know that style and tone!
Such eloquence could be Damis's alone!
(Notices the NOTEBOOK and looks inside.)
Look at these odes! I recognize the script...
And look, here's where my lilting lamb was ripped!

DORANTE
I have an explanation.

LUCILLE
Well, unroll it.

DORANTE
That poem, the one I sent to you...?

MONDOR
He stole it.

DORANTE
Shall I run for a sword? Feed you its blade?

MONDOR
Go run and finish fiddling with her maid.

LUCILLE
My *maid*?!

DORANTE
Lisette?

LUCILLE
Lisette.

MONDOR
(This oughta show her.)

LUCILLE
Next explanation, please.

DORANTE
Okay, I know her.

LUCILLE
(from several feet away)
Slap!

DORANTE
OW!

LUCILLE
(to MONDOR)
So you're Damis.

MONDOR
Here in the flesh.

LUCILLE
I love you!

MONDOR
Well then, hey, what say we mesh?

(LUCILLE kisses him hard.)

DORANTE
I know what's going on here. I'm not blind!

LUCILLE
I thought I loved you. Oh, well. Never mind.
(To MONDOR:)
You want me? I'll be splayed beneath a tree.

(LUCILLE goes off into the "wood," doing The Mouth over her shoulder.)

DORANTE
I know who masterminded this. *DAMIS…!?*

(DORANTE starts to run off, but FRANCALOU ENTERS.)

FRANCALOU
Ah, there you are!

DORANTE
Who, me?

FRANCALOU
Where've you been hiding?
I hear you want to hear what I've been writing.

DORANTE
Says who?

FRANCALOU
You don't?

DORANTE
You see...I have to go...

FRANCALOU
It isn't long. Three thousand lines or so.
I wrote it for a laugh.

DORANTE
No, please, sir...NO...!

(FRANCALOU leads DORANTE off.)

MONDOR
(to US)
Now here's a comfy place to take a pause...

(DAMIS ENTERS from the "wood.")

DAMIS
Mondor—Mondor, I am in Cupid's jaws.

MONDOR
Well, luckily for you the kid is toothless.

DAMIS
So this is love! Ecstatic! Vatic! Ruthless!
I've never known its like, my stout auxiliar.

BALIVEAU
(from "the wood")
Aaaaaaaah!

MONDOR
Jesus!

DAMIS
Wait. That voice sounded familiar.

MONDOR
Monsieur, I'm holding here for wild applause.

LISETTE
Yoo-hoo!
(DAMIS goes into the wood)

MONDOR
So like I say, we'll take a pause...

DORANTE
(entering)
I'll kill you! Though I can't recall the cause...

MONDOR
What, understand this *plot?* Sir, life's too brief.

DORANTE
So I don't have to think? That's a relief.
Wait—yes, I have to think! And win Lucille!
So bring it on! Whatever the ordeal!

FRANCALOU
(entering, reading)
"Thus Alexander conquered all Punjabi..."

(DORANTE runs out, followed by FRANCALOU.)

MONDOR
Now for that pause. Feel free to crowd the lobby
And puzzle out our plot with alcohol.
So who am I again...?

LUCILLE
(cooing, from the "wood")
                    Damis...!

MONDOR
                    I'm coming, doll!

(MONDOR lifts to his mouth a pair of imaginary pan-pipes and we hear him playing as he EXITS into "the wood," dancing like Pan.)

CURTAIN

END OF ACT ONE

ACT TWO

(The same, a while later. MONDOR ENTERS.)

MONDOR
Welcome back, all, from coffee and the pot!
All gadgets off? Good! Let's review our plot.
This guy looks worried. No, there'll be no quiz.
Let's just tote up where everybody is.
First, splayed upon our forest's bosky floor,
Lucille is picnicking with me, Mondor—
Though she thinks I'm Damis, her rhyming hero.
The odds I'm gonna clear that up? Um—zero.

LUCILLE
(from the "wood")
More caviar, dar'ing?

MONDOR
Just a pinch, my finch.

LUCILLE
A sip of brandy...?

MONDOR
I could stand an inch.

(They do The Mouth to each other and LUCILLE EXITS into the "wood.")

MONDOR (CONT'D)
Judge Baliveau, a foe with razor tines,
Is in a thicket memorizing lines...

BALIVEAU
"Aaaaaaahhhhhhh!"

MONDOR
...howling from time to time without much talent.
Dorante, our play's exasperated gallant,
Paces the house...
(DORANTE ENTERS, pacing.)
...growling...
(DORANTE growls in frustration.)
...then takes a post...
(DORANTE stands still.)
Then sighs a bit...
(DORANTE sighs miserably.)
Then tries to flee his host.
(FRANCALOU ENTERS, with MANUSCRIPT.)

FRANCALOU
"And then Bucephalus, like mighty bronze..."
Where are you going? "...*amazed the Amazons*..."

(DORANTE EXITS, fleeing, with FRANCALOU following.)

MONDOR
Damis, now one of history's great Don Juans,
Basks in possession of his longed-for pet.

(DAMIS STROLLS THROUGH with LISETTE on his arm.)

DAMIS
You're mine, Lucille!

(DAMIS and LISETTE EXIT.)

MONDOR
    Too bad "Lucille's" Lisette.
Nor let's forget, among our many plot points,
The Talking Flute, [*shows FLYER*] one of our coming hot points.
Tonight it lights the Comédie's marquee.
Damis thinks it'll make him rich. We'll see.
But hark! I hear more plot, thanks to this fellow...

BALIVEAU
(entering from the garden)
"Aaaaaaahhhhhhhh!"

(FRANCALOU ENTERS as MONDOR EXITS back into the "wood.")

FRANCALOU
Are you word-perfect, Signor Pirandello?

BALIVEAU
If nothing else today, I've learned to bellow.
And though I did resist I have to say
That I've been truly tickled by your play.

FRANCALOU
It's brilliant?

BALIVEAU
    No! But could be, with a nudge.
And I could swear I know this prickly judge! [*I.e., in the script.*]
In him I see my every flaw, my faults—
He had my stomach doing somersaults—
Yet moved me, as did all your panorama.

FRANCALOU
And there you name the heart and soul of drama:

Empathy, simple empathy for all,
Prickly or unprickly, august or small!
These shades are us! They speak, they act, they fade.
But with some added sauce...

FRANCALOU & BALIVEAU
The sexy maid!

BALIVEAU
Your poet-nephew harrowed me with pity.
I saw Damis—adrift in this cruel city...
Alone and starving, coughing in some bed...
And as I read, Well, *damn* the Law, I said!
Jail my own flesh and blood? It's a disgrace!
When next I meet Damis we shall embrace!

FRANCALOU
Good man! And wait till you rehearse with Cosmos!
When he gets here, you and this judge will osmose!

BALIVEAU
Your Cosmo plays my nephew in the scene?

FRANCALOU
With him for target how your edge will keen!
For life has this in common with performance:
A partner shapes our laughs and shares our torments.
(Glancing into the wings.)
But here comes Cosmo now, let's set the stage.
You're pacing at the top. You're in a rage.

BALIVEAU
"Ahhhh"

FRANCALOU
Good, ambush him the moment he appears.
You can't be too extreme.

BALIVEAU
I'll singe his ears!

FRANCALOU
Warm up your instrument. BAA BAA, BO BO.

BALIVEAU
BAA BAA, BO BO.

FRANCALOU
He's coming. Places! *Go!*

(FRANCALOU *hides behind a "tree" to observe.* DAMIS *ENTERS, carrying his script.*)

BALIVEAU
"*Ahhhhhhh! So it's you, then, is it?*"

(DAMIS, *hearing his uncle's voice, turns away so* BALIVEAU *can't see his face.* BALIVEAU *keeps his eyes on his script.*)

DAMIS
Waaaah! Uncle! You?

BALIVEAU
"*Yes, it is I, you! Scoundrel come to spew!*
My poison! Boy! So this is how. You use me?"
BAA BAA BO BO, BAA BAA BO BO.

(FRANCALOU *slips away with a thumbs-up.*)

DAMIS
Excuse me?

BALIVEAU
"*I find you here pursuing a poet's fame,*
Not even using your own..." What's it...

DAMIS
Name?

BALIVEAU
"*...own name?*"
So you don't want to face me?

DAMIS
I'm ashamed.

BALIVEAU
Yes, good! Put on a show of being blamed.

DAMIS
Under the circumstances, sir, I'm reeling.

BALIVEAU
You *should* be, given all you must be feeling!
Surprise. Disgrace at having lost my trust.

DAMIS
Yet hope for mercy, knowing that you're just.
Please, Uncle, I...

BALIVEAU
"Enough! Ungrateful cur!
I've no doubt there's some girl?"

DAMIS
I love her, sir.

BALIVEAU
"Silence! You've wooed the wench! Wepent, repent, in woe!"

DAMIS
(That sounds familiar...) [*Checks his script.*]

DAMIS & BALIVEAU
"Heed my charge—or go!"

BALIVEAU
Wait, that was *my* line. Why're you so amused?

DAMIS
At finding life and theatre so confused...
(*HE turns around.*)
Uncle.

BALIVEAU
Damis! Dear boy! [*Embraces him.*] Is this amazing?

DAMIS
"Amazing," uncle, would be paraphrasing.
And an affectionate embrace? What's this?

BALIVEAU
I've had a total metamorphosis!

DAMIS
So I don't irritate, don't rankle you...?

BALIVEAU
No! Thanks to this mad farce of Francalou.
But why are you here, and what's this *nom de guerre*?

DAMIS
I could ask you the same, please be aware.

BALIVEAU
Now listen...

DAMIS
None of that. You've metamorphed.

BALIVEAU

You're right. My former prickliness being dwarfed,
I here abjure all rage, decry all spats!

DAMIS

We're actors, too, who're nature's democrats.

BALIVEAU

Well, now you're overdoing it a fraction...

DAMIS

Theatre is democracy in action!
It's people gathering, just as in our wood,
To put their minds toward making something *good*.
Each person valuable, each adding gifts.
Imagine, uncle, all the wars, the rifts
We'd heal if life were theatre all the time!
We'd be in costume somewhere! Speaking rhyme!

BALIVEAU

A strong defense, my equal under make-up.
You have a sense for law. [*Getting angry:*]
Why not *wake up*...? So you're amused again?

DAMIS

                        Because it's droll
The way you bleed right back into your role.

BALIVEAU

Oh, do I.

DAMIS

       You're transformed...

BALIVEAU

                        Damn transformation!
And damn your high-hat insubordination!
Will you give up this Poetry? Well, boy, speak!

DAMIS

We're on page 66. "*To quote the Greek...*"

BALIVEAU

To quote the Greek, you're an ungrateful cur!
So run to ruin! The devil be your spur!
Go crawl with poetry to some lightless crypt!

DAMIS

Well, now we've *really* left behind the script...

BALIVEAU
You were the only good my brother left me.
And see the way you've robbed me, have bereft me
Not just of gold but of a would-be son.
For poems?

DAMIS
          For what great poets have always won:
Glory. You think war's harder, swords more real?
To wield a pen each day takes arms of steel!
For poets take the field against the best—
Sophocles, Shakespeare, Plautus, all the rest
Who quoted by us now make us seem sages!
I want to write the thoughts of future ages.
So yes, I'll study law. The laws of art!
And pass the hardest Bar: the human heart!

BALIVEAU
Take half my fortune now. Take all, I plead!

DAMIS
But there's no call, sir! *This* precludes the need! [*Shows FLYER.*]

BALIVEAU
"*The Talking Flute*"?

DAMIS
       "*The Talking Flute.*"

BALIVEAU
                             What's that?

DAMIS
My handiwork. In gold—a million flat!

BALIVEAU
It says one "Bouillabaisse" composed this piece.

DAMIS
Me! Future owner of the Golden Fleece!

BALIVEAU
Well, isn't this wonderful, tip-top, first-rate!
(*Aside to us:*)
(You see how well I've learned to simulate?
In truth, I'll see to it that this play fails—
And see him off to test our Paris jails!)
(*To DAMIS:*)
But if this flops? That happens, don't forget.

DAMIS
I'm so sure, Uncle, that I'll make a bet.
If my play's not an undiluted smash
I'll give up poetry and trade panache
For Law—no, *tax* law, peak of legal boredom.
I'll pledge my days to greed and legal whoredom.

BALIVEAU
You're on! [*They shake on it.*] But where's this girl?

DAMIS
                                                      My heart's ideal?

You'd really like to meet her, sir?—*Lucille!*
She's my host's heir, and spun from eiderdown!

(*LISETTE ENTERS, still dressed as Lucille.*)

LISETTE/LUCILLE
Uh-huh?

DAMIS
Lucille, my uncle's come to town.

LISETTE/LUCILLE
Hi.

BALIVEAU
    Meeting you, my dear, my prayers are paid!
(Does he suppose I'm blind? This girl's the *maid!*)

DAMIS
Secretly, sir, she's Meriadec!

BALIVEAU
                She's who?
I thought she was Lucille!

DAMIS
                She's Lucy, too.
She's no mere human, she's a whole new phylum!

BALIVEAU
To house you two, one needs a whole asylum!

(*DORANTE sneaks into the "wood" again to eavesdrop.*)

LISETTE/LUCILLE
I love Damis, sir. He's, like, so unique.
Just rub his head and you can make him speak.

DAMIS
(as LISETTE/LUCILLE rubs his head)
"By the shores of Gitchee Goomee,
By the shining Big Sea Water..." Keep going!

DORANTE
(She never rubbed *my* head and got me flowing!)

(DORANTE EXITS unnoticed.)

DAMIS
Did you see that, sir? She's a poetry *lever*.

LISETTE/LUCILLE
A pleasure meeting you, Monsieur Whatever.

(LISETTE EXITS.)

DAMIS
Doesn't Lucille just *glow*?

BALIVEAU
She's silver-plated.
But let's not tell our host yet we're related.

DAMIS
Gladly—if you won't tell about my show.
I want to bask in secret in the glow
Of sparkling notices and rave reviews!

BALIVEAU
Your future, nephew, is a lighted fuse.

(FRANCALOU ENTERS.)

FRANCALOU
How goes it here?

BALIVEAU
Oh, very well indeed.
(Privately to FRANCALOU, as THEY START OUT:)
I want that warrant, friend—at double speed!
You said you had some guest with legal traction?

[FRANCALOU is about to say "De Cosmos"...]

BALIVEAU
I don't care who it is. I just want *action!*

(FRANCALOU and BALIVEAU EXIT.)

DAMIS
And all these years my uncle seemed so tart.
Turns out the man's a pussycat at heart!
And what a scene, when we two first collided!
The way truth and illusion coincided.
I'll put it in my notebook...Wait. It's gone.
Dorante asked...Well! How's *that* for goings-on?
Who'd ever think my friend was such a louse
He'd steal my poems for his prospective spouse!

(DORANTE ENTERS.)

DORANTE
Monsieur, I must request you leave this house
Or meet me with a weapon in your hand.

DAMIS
It hardly suits a thief to sound so grand.

DORANTE
I'm a thief?

DAMIS
      Hand it over.

DORANTE
          What?

DAMIS
              My book.

DORANTE
I haven't seen it.

DAMIS
Kleptomaniac!

DORANTE
            Crook!

DAMIS
Oh, *I'm* a crook?

DORANTE
      With more than rhymes to steal—
So hand her over.

DAMIS
      Hand her who?

DORANTE
Lucille!

DAMIS
It's true that we're in love. What's that to you?

DORANTE
To me? The man she pledged her future to?

DAMIS
My Meriadec?

DORANTE
What is a MERIADEC?!

DAMIS
So you don't know.

DORANTE
Know what?

DAMIS
You'd better check.

DORANTE
Look, I am sick and tired of being your dupe—
Yours and our host's and all your comic troupe
Who've hatched this plot to make of me your butt.

DAMIS
I didn't know you knew Lucille!

DORANTE
You *what?*
Look. We had a friendship. Now you'd see it bleed?

DAMIS
She loves my poetry. You can hardly *read*.

DORANTE
Oh, really? I?

DAMIS
Name any writer. One.

DORANTE
Well, William Shake...spool, shaft, stein...can be fun.

DAMIS
I think the facts speak for themselves, my friend.

DORANTE
What *are* the facts?

DAMIS
I'm hers, you're not, The End.
And here she comes to clarify who's who.

(LUCILLE ENTERS with MONDOR, who carries Damis's NOTEBOOK.)

DAMIS
We've spoken, sweetie. Tell him.

LUCILLE
Who are you?

DAMIS
She's joking.—Don't you want to rub my head?

LUCILLE
Rub this. [*From a distance:*] *Slap!*

DAMIS
OW!

MONDOR
'Scuse me. Rub mine instead.

(LUCILLE rubs Mondor's head and he pants like a dog.)

DAMIS
He has my notebook! Give that back, you clown!
[*Takes NOTEBOOK.*]

MONDOR
(takes NOTEBOOK back)
This? Where I've copied my sestinas down?

DAMIS
(takes NOTEBOOK back)
Since when does "servant" mean "betraying one"?

LUCILLE
(takes NOTEBOOK)
He's not a servant! He's just playing one.
You can't judge Bouillabaisse like some low brute.

DAMIS
Bouillabaise?

MONDOR
Author of...[*He shows the FLYER.*]

DAMIS
The Talking Flute?!
You, you, you worm...You are *vermiculate*!

LUCILLE
And you, monsieur, are inarticulate.
He vanquished me as Caesar conquered Gaul!
Now Bouillabaisse, shall have my heart—and *all*.

MONDOR
C'mon, Poopsie. Let's go finish that champagne.

(LUCILLE and MONDOR EXIT.)

DORANTE
You staged all this! It's part of your campaign!

DAMIS
Staged that? For *what*?

DORANTE
For...reasons...clear as crystals.
But what's this here? A pair of dueling pistols?
Pick one and die or else forever rue it!

DAMIS
I've never faced real death before. I'll do it!

DORANTE
And what've we here? A grove designed for duels!

DAMIS
How do we do it? Do you know the rules?

DORANTE
Three steps and fire is how the precept runs.
Is this thing loaded...?

DAMIS
I'm inept with guns.

DORANTE
Never mind! So! Prepare to enter history.

(They stand back-to-back.)

DAMIS
Thus goes Damis to face the final mystery!
To cross the transcendental Hellespont!

DORANTE
Mother, remember me! I was...

DAMIS
    Dorante.

DORANTE
        ...Dorante!
One, two, three!
(They march three steps, turn and fire. We hear a pathetic "pop!")
    DAMN it! That's right! Go on, smirk!
We'll try again—this time with guns that work!

(FRANCALOU ENTERS, with MANUSCRIPT.)

FRANCALOU
Ah, there you are!

DORANTE
    Oh, no...

FRANCALOU
    A chilly greeting.

DORANTE
I bet Lisette urged us to have this meeting...?
(To DAMIS:)
You know? *Lisette*? Your second in this game?

DAMIS
Lisette? I know no person by that name.

DORANTE
You fake! You fraud! You ranting, canting liar!

FRANCALOU
Well! Backstage drama? Trouble in the choir?

DAMIS
There's been some inexplicable snafu.

DORANTE
Like this conspiracy—*which you foreknew*?
Is that what you would call some odd, crossed *WIRE*?!?!

FRANCALOU
Give your Dorante a touch of this same fire.

DORANTE
I *AM* Dorante!

FRANCALOU
You're cast, it's understood.

DORANTE
I mean for real!

FRANCALOU
A method actor. Good!
It seems you're everything de Cosmos says.

DORANTE
You know Lucille's in love with Bouillabaisse?

FRANCALOU
The soup?

DORANTE
The nut! Who's probably his shill! [*i.e., Damis's.*]

FRANCALOU
I know no one named Bouillabaisse.

DORANTE
You will!
The fact is, sir, I love your daughter so.

FRANCALOU
Does she love you?

DORANTE
She did an hour ago—
Till Judas here slipped in and took my place.

FRANCALOU
And then...?

DAMIS
She rubbed my head and slapped my face,
At which my servant stole our Aphrodite.

FRANCALOU
I've never known Lucille to be so flighty.
But good! It means she's showing signs of life!

DORANTE
She's rubbing servants who should be my wife!

FRANCALOU
(reads from his ms.)
"*Act Six, Scene Ten. We hear a Persian fife...*"

DORANTE
Monsieur, this is no time for dramaturgy!
What I need is a ring, and her, and clergy!

DAMIS
You really love her, then? Full out, grand slam?

DORANTE
I *told* you when I begged you for a lamb!

DAMIS
I swear I didn't know.

DORANTE
That is so *lame*.

DAMIS
You never said Lucille was your girl's name.

DORANTE
Oh. *Oh*. That's your excuse? Some pale cliché?

DAMIS
We're like some mini-plot from this man's play!

FRANCALOU
Yes Cosmo, how's your "uncle" in that scene?

DAMIS
So real and so convincing I feel green.
I wonder that you managed to engage him.

FRANCALOU
A dilettantish nephew has enraged him—
Your pal Damis.

DORANTE
His "*PAL*" Damis?! That's *HIM*!!!

FRANCALOU
Monsieur, I know that you're upset, you're grim,
But I've got matters of my own to tend.

(To DAMIS:)
He wondered if you had some legal friend...

DAMIS
Who'd get his nephew dangling from a noose?

FRANCALOU
Oh, I think jail-time's quite enough abuse.
We wouldn't want to loose the law's full torrent!

DAMIS
Let me inquire about the proper warrant
(Though a *smash play* may save our dilettante).
Your servant, sir. And your true friend, Dorante.

(DAMIS EXITS.)

FRANCALOU
A spirit adversity could never daunt!
That's odd. He called you...

DORANTE
Sir, I *am* Dorante.
Not in your play. I mean Dorante in truth.

FRANCALOU
Son of Geronte?!

DORANTE
Yes. Blame it on my youth
And on my admiration for your daughter...

FRANCALOU
No, I will blame that pettifogging plotter—
Your father, whose black blots will never dry!
Who on his knees could not indemnify
The time I've lost to legal to-and-fro.
I could have been a poet years ago!

DORANTE
So youth must pay for age's sometime folly?

FRANCALOU
That was quite eloquent.

DORANTE
Not bad, huh? Golly!

FRANCALOU
Well, damn all eloquence. I've no remorse!
Leave my house!—Well, after the show, of course.

DORANTE
I'm sorry, sir, but I am done with posing.
(*DORANTE throws off a piece of his lover costume and EXITS as LISETTE ENTERS, still dressed as Lucille.*)

FRANCALOU
Another actor lost!

LISETTE/LUCILLE
Who cares? We're closing.

FRANCALOU
Closing? Before we opened? It's absurd!

LISETTE/LUCILLE
Go chase your guests if you won't take my word.
Some play debuts at the Française tonight [*shows FLYER*]
And, getting wind of it, they all took flight.

(*DAMIS ENTERS.*)

DAMIS
It's true? They've all run off to my, to this, premiere?

LISETTE/LUCILLE
Some kind of masterpiece, from what I hear.

FRANCALOU
Well, then, we'll have to see this thing first-hand—
Since if it's good, no doubt it will get panned.
"*By Bouillabaisse...*" That somehow rings a bell...

DAMIS
He isn't who you think he is.

FRANCALOU
Well, hell,
Who is? Let's catch this while it's still on view.

DAMIS
I'll wait, with better hopes for it than you.
Besides, I want a moment with your daughter.

FRANCALOU
Lucille? Good, good. Then I'll attend the slaughter,
The *play*, with Pirandello on my arm—
See if this romp contains sufficient charm
To clear his mind of woes his kin beget.

LISETTE/LUCILLE
Have fun, then, "*Daddy.*"

FRANCALOU
Yes, good night, Lisette.

(FRANCALOU EXITS.)

DAMIS
Lucille...Did he call you "Lisette"?

LISETTE/LUCILLE
Pet name.

DAMIS
Lisette or Meriadec, it's all the same.
For now I see, no matter how I feel,
That you were born to make another kneel,
That I'm not steel, but a genteel shlemiel,
That I must check, for good, my heartfelt zeal,
That I can't seek to suck on love's pastille.
In short, we're wrong no matter how I want.

LISETTE/LUCILLE
Who's right for me, then? Bouillabaisse?

DAMIS
Dorante.

(DORANTE ENTERS unnoticed and listens in. LISETTE has her back to him.)

LISETTE/LUCILLE
(strokes Damis's cheek)
Sweet man.

DAMIS
He's watching. Wishing for a kiss.

LISETTE/LUCILLE
Let's seal our separation, then—with this.

(She kisses DAMIS. We hear TINKLING STARS. DAMIS EXITS in a daze. LISETTE remains with her back to DORANTE until noted.)

DORANTE
Madame, don't let me interrupt your bliss.

LISETTE/LUCILLE
Dorante...

DORANTE
No, no, don't speak. All right, then, speak.
Explain how we could wander cheek to cheek

In this same wood not half a day ago—
How you could say "I love you," cheeks aglow,
How everything we had could so diminish.

(LUCILLE ENTERS and listens, standing right behind DORANTE, unnoticed.)

LISETTE/LUCILLE
Dorante...

DORANTE
Don't speak. Or speak. No, let me finish.
I only want to say—you are divine!
(LISETTE is trying to stifle a laugh as he gets more dramatic.)
You're trembling! But for whom? Who cares? You're mine!
You've been mine since before the birth of Jove!
Eons before we kissed within this grove.
You hate me?

LISETTE/LUCILLE
No.

DORANTE
You mean that kiss was real?!

You love me?

LISETTE/LUCILLE
Yes.

DORANTE
I *knew*! [*Kisses LISETTE.*]

LUCILLE
Dorante.

DORANTE
Lucille...

(Realizes:)
Lucille? Lucille! Lisette? Lisette!

LUCILLE
Lucille.

DORANTE
Lucille, I swear, this isn't what you think!

LISETTE/LUCILLE
Oh, sir, you're such a card. Wink, wink.

DORANTE
"*Wink, wink*"?!
Lisette—I mean, Lucille, I thought her you!

LUCILLE
She's dressing as me now. That's something new.
I think I spy a kink, for pink, so be my guest.

DORANTE
Lisette, will you please lay her fears to rest?

LISETTE/LUCILLE
Who, me?

DORANTE
How you're just costumed for a part?

LISETTE/LUCILLE
What part?

DORANTE
How I MISTOOK you, for a start?

LISETTE/LUCILLE
So you don't love me? That was all delusion? [*"Weeps."*]

DORANTE
(to LUCILLE)
She's joking! *Please!* Imagine my confusion!
Who *wouldn't* think her you in silhouette?

(MONDOR ENTERS, drunk and disheveled, carrying a BOTTLE.)

MONDOR
How's everybody doin'?—Hello, Lisette.
Oh, man, oh, man, am I a happy squirt?
You don't believe me, just check out my shirt.
Filet mignon, profiterole, some lipstick...
In the machine of life, I'm Cupid's dipstick!

(MONDOR dozes off standing up, leaning against LUCILLE.)

DORANTE
Don't tell me you're with this.

LUCILLE
I know he's stained.

DORANTE
You can't be serious.

LUCILLE
I know you're pained.
Granted, he seems uncouth, to some degree.

DORANTE
He's Bozo!

LUCILLE
Yes. But *underneath*—Damis.

DORANTE
He's *not* Damis! And she, I thought, was you!

LISETTE
Miss Lucy, everything he says is true.
What can I do to show there's no foul play?

LUCILLE
Would you mind hosing down my fiancé?
And rendering him a bit less comatose?

LISETTE
He's kinda cute, if you look really close.

DORANTE
Well, thanks a lot, Lisette, for all your aid.

LISETTE
I'll just say this, monsieur: you're justly paid.
Mistrusting me, who's labored for your side?
I wouldn't tell you this but for this bride—
De Cosmos wrote a letter to your Dad.

DORANTE
Oh, God. Oh, no.

LISETTE
If you think *this* is bad...

DORANTE
If he hears that I'm here, I'll get the hook.

MONDOR
(waking up)
Is there more caviar?

LISETTE
Let's take a look.

(LISETTE and MONDOR EXIT.)

DORANTE
You heard her. *Well*, Lucille? I'm innocent!

LUCILLE
Oh, God, I wish I still were indolent.
But when Lisette brought me this lilting stanza [*produces POEM*]
I came to life…Life! That extravaganza
Where wife's not just a word nor love mere ink,
Where two lips warmly touch and, touching, drink.
With this I learned existence does exist,
From you I learned it's here, it's flesh, it's grist,
That skies are truly blue, birds really sing…
Except *you never WROTE the goddamn thing!*

DORANTE
I needed bait to win you, that came free!

LUCILLE
Who wrote it for you? Bouillabaisse?

DORANTE
           Damis.

LUCILLE
Now wait a sec. Who's he…?

DORANTE
           De Cosmos.

LUCILLE
           Oh.
So now I have to marry *him*? Oh, no!

(BALIVEAU ENTERS and listens from the "wood," unnoticed.)

DORANTE
You're going to marry *me*! Except you can't.

LUCILLE
Not even if I want? Who's this "Dorante"?

DORANTE
Dorante. That's me.

LUCILLE
    Oh, God.

DORANTE
           I'm incognodo.

LUCILLE
Nito.

DORANTE
You see? I told you I'm a dodo!

LUCILLE
Who cares? I love you! Now—why can't we wed?

DORANTE
Some legal case. Our Dads would have our head!

LUCILLE
And that's your ace? For that you'd give up hpe?
Well then to hell with parents! Let's elope.

DORANTE
We can't just...

LUCILLE
What's the problem, man? Be bold!

DORANTE
Your father...

LUCILLE
Oh, where are the knights of old?
I'll talk to Daddy. Legal case—avaunt!

(LUCILLE EXITS.)

DORANTE
But Lucy—hey, remember? Nonchalant?

(BALIVEAU steps forward.)

BALIVEAU
Monsieur, you are the son of old Geronte?

DORANTE
I am. Or was. I think. My brain's a turd.

BALIVEAU
It just so happens that I overheard.
Sir, I can help you in your amorous plight.
I know your fathers are estranged by spite
Yet I've the means to mend their ancient grudge.

DORANTE
But how? This law suit...

BALIVEAU
Young man, I'm a *judge*.
Abracadabra, I take on the case—
And each side wins with neither losing face.

DORANTE
I can't believe...! You'd really do all that?!

BALIVEAU
With pleasure—though there is a tit for tat. [*Shows FLYER.*]

DORANTE
Bouillabaisse!

BALIVEAU
Your foe, judging by your frown.
Well, I would like to see this play go *down*,
I want it booed until the last act ends.

DORANTE
It's done, monsieur. I can alert some friends.
We'll see to it the players are never heard.

BALIVEAU
A failure's guaranteed?

DORANTE
You have my word.

(*DORANTE EXITS.*)

BALIVEAU
(*to us*)
Alas, Damis's first play will be his last.

(*BALIVEAU EXITS as DAMIS ENTERS. During this speech, the scene changes to evening around him. SERVANTS light lamps where noted.*)

DAMIS
They should be starting soon. [*Checks watch.*]
This could be fast...
Maybe I'll sit. [*Sits.*] Or not. [*Stands up.*] Four minutes past.
The house is packed now, stacked up to the rings,
I see it all as though I'm in the wings—
Eye to the peephole. Yes, the dames and dandies
Have got their Playbills, bought their drinks and candies.
Upstairs, a mass of maids and one lone page.
Now one by one the lamps are lit onstage—
And at a stroke I doubt my every word.
My cast seems talent-free, my play absurd.
Here comes our lead. Applaud and look relaxed.

Oh, God, our ingénue—who should be axed...
Darling! Yes, break a leg! Mwah! Hold for laughter!
We changed that line, remember! See you after!
That actress is a penance for my sins.
Abruptly—curtain up! The play begins.
The crowd's gone quiet. What is this, mass hypnosis?
Oh, great. A cougher. Mass tuberculosis!
Was that a chuckle—somewhere at the back...?
Our ingenue's of course a *painted plaque*.
Speed up, speed up! Well, good. A solid laugh.
What are you...? *Speak!* Don't moo like some lost calf!
She flubbed her line. Show's over! That'll spoil it!
I'm in the men's room puking at a toilet.
Why didn't I trust my Uncle Baliveau?
He's wise, he's decent, generous, he should know...
Was that a laugh out there? Was that a *roar?*
Back to the peephole, watching someone—snore.
Some blimp who's barred my way to being famous.
The word is BUT, not AND, you ignoramus!
That was a hearty laugh. I may's well stay.
You know it's really not too bad, this play?
Thank God we hired that ingénue. She's brilliant!
I love these actors! Funny, smart, resilient.
But wait. Is that the final scene they're in...?
My guts have turned to sponge, my legs are tin.
Another laugh...another...now a burst!
The crowd's so wild you'd think they'd been rehearsed,
My lines are landing now like shining spears,
A line, a laugh, the final speech, and...cheers!
Shouts, rocking the Française! The crowd's ecstatic!
Someone is kissing me! Is this dramatic?
"Author" they're shouting. Is my collar straight?
I stride onstage and bow—Damis The Great!

(FRANCALOU and BALIVEAU ENTER.)

FRANCALOU

You missed it!

DAMIS

And your verdict Were you wowed?

FRANCALOU

You never saw a more illustrious crowd.
The King with Lady X., his current prop.

DAMIS

I mean, how went the *play*?

FRANCALOU

The play? A flop.

DAMIS
When you say "flop"...

BALIVEAU
Let's say no one was cooing.
You couldn't hear the lines through all the booing.

DAMIS
So—a catastrophe.

BALIVEAU
Par excellence.

DAMIS
But did it merit that malign response?

FRANCALOU
Well, I saw gleams of genius here and there,
Heard passages of wit and heart so rare
That words and thoughts conjoined like lovers kissing.

BALIVEAU
One hopes the author didn't hear the hissing.

DAMIS
Yet should he take to heart such passing shocks?
A pilot learns his trade amongst the rocks,
Not in the easy calm of balmy seas.
A tempest teaches better than a breeze.

FRANCALOU
Excelsior! Bravó, lad! That's the stuff!

DAMIS
Why should this playwright stop and cry "enough"
If this disaster makes his writing sager?

BALIVEAU
(pointedly, to DAMIS)
Unless this playwright's made a certain *wager*...?

FRANCALOU
(giving DAMIS a SEALED NOTE)
Oh, by the way, this letter came, express.

DAMIS
A note for me...? [*Reads it.*] Yes! Now things coalesce!

(DAMIS EXITS.)

FRANCALOU
Is he a wonder? I am such a fan.

BALIVEAU
You share his hobby.

FRANCALOU
No, I love the *man*!
His heart, his words! That pilot and those rocks?
Did you not hear? The pulse, the paradox?
If *he* wrote plays, all Paris would exult!
And I'd dare you to jeer at the result.

BALIVEAU
Get me my warrant. Then you'll see me thrilled.

FRANCALOU
I think your wish may just have been fulfilled.

BALIVEAU
How so?

FRANCALOU
I think he had it in his hand.

BALIVEAU
Who did?

FRANCALOU
De Cosmos.

BALIVEAU
I don't understand...

FRANCALOU
I told him of your nephew. He stepped in—
With such dispatch you'd think you two were kin.

BALIVEAU
God damn it all to hell!

FRANCALOU
What's all this pique?

BALIVEAU
Your protégé's the nephew whom I seek!

FRANCALOU
De Cosmos is Damis?

BALIVEAU

That's what I mean!

FRANCALOU

Good Lord! Then why this bitterness, this spleen?
He's upright, spirited, committed, true...

BALIVEAU

What you mean is that he's a fool like you!

FRANCALOU

You'd doom that gorgeous butterfly to Law?
How petty, how pathetic, how bourgeois!

BALIVEAU

I'll sue you, too! I'll put you in the pillory!
But what's this here? [*Finds PISTOLS.*] Some small artillery.
Take one. And he who's wrong is he who drops!

FRANCALOU

Baliveau...

BALIVEAU

Take it, blast you!

FRANCALOU

Those are props.

BALIVEAU

Then have him! I abandon him to you!

FRANCALOU

My friend, this is no way to say adieu.
So how's this for a plan to cure your angst?
He'll have my Lucy—and a million francs?
He mentioned that they'd had a passing fling.
The prelude to church chimes, that passing *ping*?
It's up to her, of course, or else it's deadlock.
But I've no doubt our clans were meant for wedlock.

BALIVEAU

A million francs...? And you thought that I was miffed!
I always knew he had a mighty gift.

FRANCALOU

I thought you'd see the light. My Baliveau!
(*The two embrace. Calls:*)
Monsieur Damis!

BALIVEAU
Who's he?

FRANCALOU
Your nephew.

BALIVEAU
Oh.

(DAMIS ENTERS.)

BALIVEAU
Ah, there you are! Congratulations, lad!

(BALIVEAU embraces him and dances about.)

DAMIS
I see since our last meeting you've gone mad.

BALIVEAU
Insane with glee, since how's this for a scheme?
You'll be his son-in-law! Is that a dream?

DAMIS
Lucille's a miracle. A jeweled cup.

BALIVEAU
See there? A perfect match!

DAMIS
We just broke up.

BALIVEAU
Broke UP?! Well, is there hope you'll...?

DAMIS
Not a speck.
I've lost Lucille, and with her...Meriadec.

FRANCALOU
Meriadec?

DAMIS
Meriadec. Who's Lucy 2.
(FRANCALOU lets out a hoot.)
Why are you laughing, sir?

FRANCALOU
Oh, not at you
But at the genius of our jokester gods

Whose plots defy all dramaturgic odds.
Lucy and Meriadec! You thought her she?

DAMIS
You mean she's not? So Meriadec's still free?

BALIVEAU
What in God's name are you two ON about?!

DAMIS
Here comes Lucille right now, to quash all doubt.

(LISETTE ENTERS, dressed as herself again.)

DAMIS
Lucille...But why're you dressed as a soubrette?

LISETTE
A what?

DAMIS
A maid.

LISETTE
I'm sorry, have we met?

FRANCALOU
Cosmo, may I present our maid, Lisette.

BALIVEAU
Who this girl is, is unassailable!
The point is, *Lucy's* still available!

DAMIS
What about Meriadec?

BALIVEAU
Will you forget her?

DAMIS
How can I uncle, when I've never met her?

BALIVEAU
You've met Lucille, though?

DAMIS
Frankly, I don't know.
I do know here's Lucille's most recent beau.

(MONDOR ENTERS, out of the fancy livery, hung over.)

MONDOR
Nobody talk. My brain is oozing booze.

BALIVEAU
This lout?!

MONDOR
The grumpy uncle from Toulouse!

FRANCALOU
Fess up! Who are you in this maddening maze?

MONDOR
To tell the truth, it's all a kind of haze.
My costume's off, so I'm myself, I seem...
Oh, I have had the most amazing dream!
Words cannot hear! Eyes cannot see! And so on.
I was in love, by what I have to go on.
This cuckoo girl in a luxurious house.
The joint looked just like this...

BALIVEAU
(takes him by the collar)
                              Excuse me—*louse*.

MONDOR
Monsieur, you have my absolute attention.

BALIVEAU
Are you Lucille's, too or is that invention?

MONDOR
It's kind of hard to tell with all the wine

LISETTE
Forget the wine, forget Lucille, you're mine.

MONDOR
I knew you looked familiar!
(Bends LISETTE over in a big kiss.)
                              Yeah, it's her!

BALIVEAU
Will you stop that?

MONDOR
            What's it to you, monsieur?
We're poor folk but we're horny. Find your own!

FRANCALOU
Here comes the real Lucille.

LISETTE
        Or Lucy's clone.

(LUCILLE ENTERS.)

FRANCALOU
Sweetheart—you *are* my daughter, I assume—
Behold the man I'd like to be your groom.
A blazing nova yet to glow at peak.

LUCILLE
Excuse me, father, but if I might speak?

LUCILLE
You see, there's one small problem, and here's why:
I am in *luvvvvv*. Oh, God, I want the guy!
I see that dimple where his lower lips joins?
I get this smoldering deep down in my *loins*,
I want us groin-to-groin from dawn to dusk,
I want to smell his stink, I crave his musk.
I want him now and I want him *forever*.

FRANCALOU
Well, quite a change from Mademoiselle Whatever!
He's literary, too—your fragrant friend?

LUCILLE
I doubt he's read a sentence end to end.
But who would judge a man by any book
Who broadcasts poetry with his every look?

FRANCALOU
Then there's no problem! Or am I deluded?
But wait, is this the fellow I excluded?
I had good evidence...

LUCILLE
        You've lost your plea.
You thought he had a girlfriend? She was me!

FRANCALOU
Then I exclude him now because his father
Has caused me years of dreary legal bother.

BALIVEAU
May we return to our end of the plot?
Will your Lucille betroth Damis or not?

DAMIS
I am Damis.

ALL
We know!

BALIVEAU
A genius, lass,
If in his previous life a rampant ass.

(DORANTE ENTERS.)

DORANTE
All right, so have I won? I'm hers to choose?

BALIVEAU
Excuse me, but I'm leaving for Toulouse.

DORANTE
Now just a minute here. We had a pact!
You'd back me if I got this play attacked.
(Shows FLYER, and points to MONDOR.)
A play by *him*, no less! Who's gotten his due!

MONDOR
Not quite. You missed an episode or two.
(Moves Dorante's pointing finger to indicate DAMIS.)

DORANTE
You wrote this play?

DAMIS
I was the perpetrator.

DORANTE
Well, this whole mix-up has your imprimatur.
Revenge, for tangling Lucy in your net!

DAMIS
In this case I think Lucy was Lisette.

FRANCALOU
Enough! I don't care who, what, where or why!
Lucy will never, not while I stand by,
Marry the son of my old nemesis!
I swear it!

DAMIS
Sir, you might just glance at this. [*Gives LETTER.*]
It's from his father and may change your mind.

FRANCALOU
I've sworn an oath no letter can unbind—
(Glances at LETTER. Thunderstruck:)
Good *God!* Why, it's a full and fond retraction!
Professing love—regretting all detraction—
Signed here "Geronte" with his familiar cramp.
Though tears have softened it. See there, it's *damp!*
(Joining the hands of DORANTE and LUCILLE.)
I now pronounce you man and wife. We're done.

DORANTE
But sir, your oath...

FRANCALOU
You're married lad. Have fun.

ALL
HOORAY!

DORANTE
Wait, wait! Before we two can blend
I have to beg forgiveness from my friend.
I scotched his play, misread him to a fault...

DAMIS
Oh, let's not spoil this feast with excess salt.
My matrimoniac friend, you have my *thanks*.
For what a day! From facing death by blanks
To falling deep in love and getting slapped—
I'm still not sure by whom, but that seems apt—
These hours were packed with life, real life, galore.
So thank you, sir—you two—Lisette—Mondor,
For such demented, transcendental woe.
Plus extra-special thanks to Baliveau!

LISETTE & LUCILLE & DORANTE
Who's Baliveau?

DAMIS
Kid bro' to my begetter.

LISETTE
Well, if you're Baliveau I have a letter...
[Gives BALIVEAU a LETTER.]

BALIVEAU
This? This is from my ex-wife in Peru!

MONDOR
(I see our exposition isn't through.)

BALIVEAU
*"Have spent so many nights here missing you.
And just discovered veins of silver ore.
Would we could locate our lost son Mondor."*

MONDOR & DAMIS & LISETTE
MONDOR!

DORANTE
Now wait! Who's he?

MONDOR
Mondor? That's *me!*

[*Grabs LETTER.*]

BALIVEAU
(*embracing MONDOR*)
M'ijo!

MONDOR
Mi padre!

LISETTE
How'd that letter *reach* you?!

MONDOR
Who cares? We own a mine in Machu Picchu!

LUCILLE
But poor Damis is left with none to dote on.

DAMIS
For that you'd have to find my lost Bretonne,
Mysterious Meriadec de Peauduncqville!
God knows if my mad muse was ever real.
Her memory will always harry me.

FRANCALOU
Then there's just one solution. [*Kneels.*] *Marry me!*

DAMIS
You're *she?*

FRANCALOU
As surely as you are Damis.

DAMIS
Yes, but. Yes, but. Yes, but…

FRANCALOU
But?

DAMIS
Oh, all right.

FRANCALOU
Who would have dreamed this was my wedding night?

BALIVEAU
If this is drama, I am truly smote!
In fact, I'd like to read a play I wrote...

MONDOR
Let's save that, Dad—till dinner's in our hand.

DORANTE
There's one plot point I still don't understand...
[THEY ALL shout him down.]

FRANCALOU
My friends, we've food and drink to sate five score.
Let's feast until it's gone, then feast some more!
And there's a sylvan grove in this salon
Where those in love may wander till it's dawn.
Do as you please! Enjoy! That's all I ask!
(To audience)
And with that blessing I may now—unmask.
You see, this day once happened. It's all true—
Except for this: I wasn't Francalou.
Oh, he was there, his house, a painted tree.
He was my host, and my name was...Damis.
These hours of lunacy sparked my career,
Started me writing plays like this one here,
And taught me life's a multi-stranded plot
So intricate who knows who tied each knot!
Too mad, you say? Too many a twisted switch?
It's how my plays are made—and why I'm rich.
I wish you all such madness, as your friend,
And may your exposition never, ever end!

CURTAIN

END OF PLAY